AF332968

My Road to Emeritus

My Road to Emeritus

Elmer Ellis

The State Historical Society of Missouri
Columbia

∞™ This paper meets the minimum requirements of the
American National Standard for Permanence of Paper for
Printed Library Materials, Z39.48, 1984.

ISBN 0-9622891-1-6

Contents

Foreword

This volume is the autobiography of one of the nation's preeminent educators—Elmer Ellis, a name synonymous with the University of Missouri and higher education for more than three decades. Upon reading Dr. Ellis's *My Road to Emeritus,* one is struck by the thoughtfulness and the honesty of the writer who, as one colleague aptly stated, "has been at the center of things." Through his written recollections, Dr. Ellis presents an important manuscript that should be welcomed by friends and supporters of the University of Missouri system, and consulted by elected officials, higher education administrators, newspaper commentators and anyone interested or intrigued by the history of higher education in Missouri. Readers will also find his recounting of his early years highly informative and delightfully presented.

After becoming "President Emeritus," Dr. Ellis briefly describes his activities. He writes: "The group that kept my services the longest was the State Historical Society of Missouri. . . ." That statement belies the actual fact, as Dr. Ellis continues to provide important and appreciated advice and service to the Society's administration and its missions.

Dr. Ellis, today, remains a valued member of the Society's Executive Committee. He has been a trustee of the Society for more than thirty years and served as a member of its Finance Committee as early as 1955. He became president of the Society for a three-year term at the 1974 annual meeting. Four years later, at the annual meeting, Dr. Ellis was presented the Society's Distinguished Service Award, and since 1973 has been one of the Society's permanent trustees. Therefore, it is appropriate and gratifying that the State Historical Society, an organization to which he has devoted countless hours, can express its appreciation through publishing this printing of his autobiography.

Two friends of Dr. Ellis's, professors emeritus Louis G. Geiger and Lewis E. Atherton, have generously given of their time to review the manuscript. The always gracious Mrs. Ruth Ellis, as those who know her would expect, provided important and useful insights. Dr. R. Douglas Hurt, associate director, and the executive director of the Society have also examined the manuscript. The flavor of the author's original writing has been retained. Very few sentences were recast. Only punctuation, capitalization, proper names and titles and misidentifications were standardized or corrected.

The University of Missouri Press oversaw the preparation of the volume. Beverly Jarrett, Sue Denny and Jane Lago of the Press, in particular, lent their assistance. To help defray the printing costs Chancellor Haskell Monroe, and the University of Missouri–Columbia, provided part of the funding. In this sesquicentennial year of the University of Missouri, the Chancellor of the Columbia campus may have said it best: "If anyone associated with the University deserves to have their memoirs printed, it surely is Elmer Ellis."

In the preface Dr. Ellis tells the readers why he began this project. His original intention in 1988 was to have only a few copies privately printed for his friends. After reading the volume it will be easily understood why *My Road To Emeritus* deserved to be made available to a wider audience.

The State Historical Society of Missouri
James W. Goodrich, Executive Director

Preface

This book was not started as an autobiography. When John Weaver succeeded me as President of the University of Missouri in 1966, he asked me if I would write a sketch of my administration and its problems for his use. I told him I would but I was rather heavily involved in the consulting work that I had agreed to do and could not produce very soon.

Nevertheless I started this while Weaver was with us, but I was not much over half through what I had agreed to do when he left for the University of Wisconsin. I continued the sketch until I had completed it. It was written from memory, occasionally checking a name for accuracy. This gradually grew, however (as I quit consulting with my trip to India in 1970), and I was not entirely sure what I should do with this manuscript which had been prepared at Weaver's request. Without any real planning I began to add to it—adding first the closest experience to that at Missouri that I had and going back to my high school days. I stopped there for a time thinking that was as far as I would go. In the meantime I continued to work on improving certain parts of the manuscript.

The manuscript continued to be primarily autobiographical, since it was my experience with various types of education that I worked with. I finally decided that I might as well add the early years of my life as well as those after high school, and I wrote the early chapters. Again I wrote almost entirely from memory. Consequently, I have produced an autobiography through my presidency at the University of Missouri. It is still of interest chiefly to people who are interested in the University of Missouri.

Acknowledgments

I have been assisted in writing this by my secretary Darlene Schroeder who has prepared the manuscript and copy for the book. My friends, Emeritus Professor of History at the University of Missouri–Columbia, Lewis E. Atherton, and Emeritus Professor of History at Iowa State University, Louis Geiger, kindly read the manuscript and made many useful suggestions. My wife Ruth Clapper Ellis has, as in all my publications, served as a writing assistant who has been most useful.

My Road to Emeritus

Chapter 1

Background

All my grandparents had similar backgrounds. My father's parents were born in Maine and New Hampshire and my mother's in Vermont and western New York State. They joined the westward movement around 1860. As far as my Grandfather Ellis, who came from Maine, was concerned, it was probably partly due to the movement of the lumber industry to a more productive area, but in all cases they were also tied in with farming. They all reached southeastern Minnesota before 1860 and were there, as far as I am aware, until about 1880 when the two families of my grandparents moved into the Valley City area of North Dakota. They both moved from southeastern Minnesota to Barnes County, North Dakota, by using their horses and carrying considerable farming equipment. It is a family story that my mother's father, Ira Butterfield, fattened his oxen and sold them for beef and used that money to buy horses because he wanted faster transportation to move west.

Another family story is that Grandfather Levi Ellis was riding horseback for an exploratory trip to the Red River Valley in 1876 at the very time of the notorious James Brothers' Northfield fiasco. It was so timely in fact that he was arrested in St. Paul on suspicion of being a member of the gang. In any case both families became farmers presumably on land put on the market by the Northern Pacific Railroad. Grandfather Ellis went into a type of bonanza farming, as it was called, raising large amounts of wheat on this beautiful, flat, treeless land. The size of his operation was large enough, as the family story had it, to require a cook car all the year around when his operation was at its height, but the combination of grasshoppers and drouth ended that venture. Most, if not all, on the Ellis side moved back into Minnesota to nearby Detroit Lakes and resumed farming and lumbering.

Prior to their leaving the Valley City area, my parents, Thomas Ellis and Lillie Butterfield, had been married. Father and his older brother, Everett, who was also married, acquired farms in that area, Father's being near the town of Audubon. After a period of rather desperate efforts to pay off a mortgage that covered their land and having built a house with lumber earned by working in a lumber mill in the winters, they got the western fever, stimulated locally by the building of the Soo Railroad southeast and northwest across North Dakota. A large group of neighbors went to the then terminus of the railroad line in the McHenry County area and filed on land with the U. S. Government. After filing, Father worked again in the lumber mill near Audubon to earn lumber for a home on the claim. He spent most of the winter accumulating livestock and seed grain and lumber, and then went by railroad from Audubon to what became the town of Anamoose. As I remember the family stories, it sounded almost as though our community of family and friends had moved from Minnesota and Barnes County to western North Dakota as a group. Our family had four children, Charles, Earl, Martha, and Wilfred (Bill). Mother took them to visit her mother who still lived in Valley City, Grandfather Butterfield having died in the meantime. She and the four children stayed with her mother until our father had a barn erected, and some land under cultivation to meet the terms of the Homestead Law, and then Mother and the children joined him. They lived in the barn he had built until he was able to add a house before the winter came. It took five years to build up the claim and meet the requirement of the law. It was during those years that my sister Grace and I were born.

In the meantime, a great many members of the Ellis family had moved into the same area, including Grandfather and Grandmother Ellis who moved onto a small place of about forty acres very near the town of Anamoose. One of the family stories is that they had to promise Granddad they would bring out a large amount of lumber for him to have on his "retirement" place. And years later when I took care of the farm for a few weeks following his death I was using those Minnesota poles as gates to the pasture, and living in a house that had been made from that lumber that had come from the Detroit Lakes area.

Largely I suspect because of mother's insistence, since she was really worried about my father's health and the education of the children, they exchanged the claim for a grocery store in the town of Anamoose. We moved into town and occupied a quite large house on the edge of a large slough called a lake which took off from our backyard and extended about a mile farther south passing Granddad's forty acres on the way. I could not have been over a year old myself when we moved to town and have few memories of it; my memories are those of older members of the Ellis family. I do remember that slough and remember walking around it with some of my older brothers and sisters and cousins. I also remember there were muskrats in it which Earl tried to trap, and also many ducks in the fall and spring when their seasonal migrations took place. Our house had a big yard and the family kept a milk cow and raised chickens, ducks and geese.

While the population around Anamoose had a great many of the old neighbors from both Detroit Lakes and Valley City, the bulk of the population that came in was heavily German—not the German Russian who came a little later but the Germans who had come directly from Germany, or, as my Uncle George and his family did, indirectly by way of Canada. George Abelein married my father's sister, Minnie, and operated elevators in Anamoose and nearby towns for the grain companies that owned them. They had a fine large house closer to the middle of town than ours. It became a place that I knew almost as well as our own house. I also knew Grandfather's place very well, but these were about the only memories I have going back that far, except of people. Many of our friends and relatives were still on farms around Anamoose, and I recall vaguely a Sunday when a church picnic was somewhere in the area of our former farm. My father, in taking the family with a team and buggy to the picnic, drove by the farm to show everyone what had happened to the place since we had left. That is the only memory I have of the farm.

Before we left the farm, my parents had been involved in starting a Congregational church in Anamoose for the Yankees who were settling in the area. My father was the treasurer of the church and he and Mother were very active in it. I have no knowledge of my father's store. His older brother, Everett, who had taught in the local school, went into county politics and ran for Clerk of Court to which he was elected. This required a move of his family to the county seat at Towner, which was on the main line of the Great Northern Railroad between Minneapolis and the Pacific coast.

Through some transactions after Uncle Everett had settled in Towner, he and my father and their younger brother, James, bought a hardware store there and renamed it the Ellis Brothers Hardware. In the process Father sold his grocery store in Anamoose and we moved to Towner. I recall only a group of visits to relatives who were still on the farms around Anamoose before we left. When we left, our furniture was loaded on two hayracks and brothers Charles and Earl each drove one to Towner. Mother and the smaller children were taken over by our Uncle Jim in a buggy drawn by a team of horses. I recall that on the trip I sat on a box that contained the family clock and whenever the buggy hit a sharp bump the clock would strike. I remember also that we overtook Earl with his hayrack load and stopped and ate lunch with him. This was 1906 and, if it was after July 27, I was five years old. Our house in Towner was different from that in Anamoose. We were directly across the street from the courthouse, which was under construction, and only a block from the new school which was a quite impressive looking building in its newness. Beginning that fall the older children were all in school which had been an important motive of Mother's and Dad's in moving off the farm.

In fact, Granddad Ellis had built a house in Valley City when they lived near there for the convenience of that generation of children attending school. It is very difficult in my memory to separate the things that happened the first year in Towner from those that happened later.

One thing I do remember about the building of the courthouse, however, was that all of the boys at least my age and considerably older came into possession of the little square marbles that were used in building the courthouse floors and they were a medium of exchange among the boys, although I know of no use we ever made of them. The big difference in our family after the move was that Earl remained in Anamoose with Grandfather and Grandmother Ellis. They had insisted that they deserved one of the children and they were very fond of Earl. I have no doubt Earl felt crowded in our large family and was glad to be the only child of his grandparents. The family life in Towner was much like it had been in Anamoose except that we were all getting older, and younger ones were being added almost every two years. I became thoroughly familiar with the school which seemed to me a wonderful building. The four older children who were home were heavily involved in school and that stirred up my interest. One of my memories is of a wooden box about two feet square that had belonged to Earl and Charles which they had brought from Audubon full of their books. Martha, Bill and Grace were also acquiring literature of that kind. Mother, who had been a schoolteacher before she was married, never ceased to practice her old trade on her children. The reading I remember best from the early days was the magazine *The American Boy* which came in Charles' name. But my mother also had *The Youth's Companion* which was her favorite, and she did her best to make it ours, as she read aloud to us from it at times when the household work permitted. These magazines were accompanied by the books *Horatio Alger, Edward S. Ellis, G. A. Henty,* and a miscellaneous collection of more mature literature. The one I recall best was the *Boys of Seventy-Six* by C. C. Coffin which was a juvenile account of the war for independence. It remained my favorite for several years. Again we had a barn with a milk cow and a flock of chickens, and after the first year, a big garden which my father took care of when he was home.

Family of Thomas Clarkson and Lillie Butterfield Ellis

Charles Thomas	May 23, 1892
Earl	January 31, 1894
Martha Valentine	February 14, 1896
Wilfred Murry (Bill)	October 11, 1897

Grace	September 29, 1899
Elmer	July 27, 1901
Evelyn Dorothy	August 8, 1904
Donald Butterfield	May 20, 1906
Bryan Dale (died at 2 years)	November 24, 1908
Robert Ira	May 2, 1911
Marietta	August 3, 1913
Susan Jane	December 27, 1917

Chapter 2

Towner to Maxbass

The closeness of our home to the school at Towner was a most important factor in my childhood. The neighboring children all played in the schoolyard during the summer and also at other times during the regular year when school was not in session. There was no city water system when the school was built, but it had been built to take advantage of the system when available as it soon was. Before I began as a pupil, the toilets of the school consisted of temporary structures behind the school building, but by the time I entered school they had been replaced by standard sanitary facilities within the building. It had a large playroom that doubled as a basketball court for both high school boys and girls and was probably the most inadequate feature of the building as the ceiling was too low to have a standard court. In the years after I finished school, however, an addition was built that provided for a respectable high school court.

An active five-year old, however, found it quite disappointing to see children no larger than he going to classes a year before he would be welcomed. The primary teacher, Kate Mitchell, the oldest teacher in the school system, regularly had one concession she made to children like myself. On Friday afternoon after recess she turned her primary class into a speaking performance and invited those of us who were not old enough to attend regularly to come to that session. The last session of the year, she also invited the visitors to speak pieces in which I participated with considerable enthusiasm with a humorous piece my father had taught me. The school was a consolidated school which took in the families in the rural area around the town, who were served by home-made buses and who brought their lunches with them. Some of the country children who came were older than the normal six years for a first grader as they had been in situations where there was no school available. It was not uncommon to have two children from the same family in the first grade. They seemed, however, to spread out more as they attended school. My second grade teacher was a much younger woman named Phoebe Jones, whose sister Ruth taught the third grade. They lived in an apartment downtown in one of the better buildings which included in its first story a bank, a jewelry store, and the post office. While I was in the second grade, I acquired a job from the Jones sisters for Saturday morning. I would go down around 9 o'clock, carry their trash out to a burner behind the building and burn it, a job for which they compensated me with a nickel and usually a store cookie or two. I got a surprise though at the end of that year because I was not promoted to the third grade. I reasoned this was because of my poor spelling which was the only subject where I seemed to have any difficulty where grades were concerned.

Several years later when I was in high school my mother heard me explain to someone that I stayed two years in the second grade because of my poor spelling and she corrected me. She said, "Phoebe kept you in the second grade because she was in love with you. She didn't want to pass you on to Ruth's class for your third year." This was an easy explanation but I think my mother was humiliated because I was the only one of her children who failed to pass a grade. The next year when I was promoted to the third grade and we were to be in a new school in a different town, she made a case for my being entered in the fourth grade, which was arranged, and in spite of the fact I was out of school until Christmas I found no problems with the fourth grade.

One thing that should be added for a complete history was my Sunday School. At Anamoose my parents had participated in establishing a Congregational Church. When we moved to Towner there were four denominations, the oldest church being the Presbyterian, which the original settlers including many Scots in that area had established. The next was the Episcopal which was to some extent British because among the early settlers had been a number of Canadians. The newer Catholic and Norwegian Lutheran groups had not yet built churches although they were conducting services in various ways. We and other members of the family that were there went to the Presbyterian Church and I attended its Sunday School. I had a teacher who was retired from school teaching named Jean McNaughton Stephens. She was a native of Edinburgh who, after teaching in local schools, had married a Civil War veteran and they were living largely on his pension. She was an interesting person and I profited considerably from her Scottish background during my youth. As I got older I acquired a fine teacher in J. H. Colton who was the superintendent of schools and taught in the high school. He was an exceptionally fine teacher in every sense of the word.

One of the more important things that happened during my childhood at Towner was leaving it for a long year. My father and his brothers dissolved their partnership and sold their hardware store in Towner. Uncle Jim, whose wife Lulu had died, took his family and moved to Saskatchewan where he began farming. Uncle Everett first moved to a small town named Wildrose near the western edge of the state and after a trial at banking, disposed of his interest in that and went to Moose Lake in northern Minnesota where he also went back to the land. After a brief period my father acquired some other mercantile interest on the branch line of the Great Northern from Towner 40 miles up to a town named Maxbass, named as the Great Northern had a habit of doing for someone in the organization. North Dakota was blessed with two towns, Max and Maxbass, named for the same official. Most other railroads were less parochial and used their town names to attract immigrant settlers. McHenry County had a Bergen, a Karlsrue, and a Kief. Father bought a general store in Maxbass. He managed the store for some time before the family moved to Maxbass. About the same time he acquired a hardware store at Newburg which his brother Eugene managed. My first visit to Maxbass was in that period. Father had told my mother I could take the branch train on Saturday afternoon and come up and spend Sunday with him. He was living at the little hotel, and this was a new experience for me. I got on the train and the conductor asked me my name and he said, "Your father told me you were coming."

We set up a sort of conversation that lasted the entire trip. About seven miles from Towner, the train slowed down and the whistle blew repeatedly and I asked, "Mr. Grainey, what's that?"

"Oh, it's cows on the track!" Shortly before we got to Maxbass the train slowed down and the whistle began blowing again.

I asked, "Is that more cows on the track?"

"No, same ones," Grainey answered, which got a good laugh from the passengers.

When we moved to Maxbass, we did not sell our house in Towner but rented it to the Catholic Church to use for the priest in their new church which was across the street and at the other end of the block. Father had arranged for a very large and handsome house in Maxbass, unquestionably the best house in town, and except for the lack of running water probably the best house we ever lived in as it was all new. But we could not get into that until near Christmastime so we were in a temporary house that was inadequate. Maxbass was a town of about 300 people. It was built around a square in the center of which was a building that housed the bank and the post office. There were three general stores, of which Dad's was the smallest, and two hardware stores. Our house was just a block from the school again and we arrived just in time to get started in school. As far as our home was concerned it differed little from our Towner one as we had a milk cow and chickens to help with our family diet. My mother made arrangements for me to enter the fourth grade which I did. It was a bad year for me as the worst illness I was to have in my life took place about a month after our arrival. The town had no water supply except from wells and some of them were polluted with typhoid fever. In our family, our oldest sister Martha was the first to become ill. She soon recovered but I was the next victim. The other children all escaped. I am not sure of all the medical treatment that was involved. The town had a father and son doctor combination as the only medical help. Both of them were English-trained and had come to Maxbass by way of Canada. I have no reason to think they were not as competent as those at Towner. I was put on the typical starvation diet that was the treatment for typhoid but I did not improve. Some heart complications developed and my parents brought in a heart specialist from the larger town of Minot some fifty miles away. I remember the occasion very well because he immediately had my mother prepare an eggnog which tasted mighty good to a boy who had been on a beef-tea diet. Anyway, I began to improve slowly but did not get back to school until after Christmas.

In the meantime, our father's parents from Anamoose had joined the family, which was one reason that my father had taken that large house. Most of my memories of my grandmother are of her trying to entertain me when I was bedfast. She tried to teach me to knit and crochet and to help her with the fancy stitching on the crazy quilt she was making. I stitched some on it but my mother told me later Grandmother ripped it all out and redid it herself. The only memento I had from this was a pair of bedroom slippers, the tops of which I had crocheted and then with Grandmother's help sewed them to prepared soles. I would lie in my bed and hear the schoolbell ring and wish that I were there.

Before Christmas we were all set up in the new big house, and I was soon in school in the fourth grade and finding a great deal to do. I do not remember the church situation in Maxbass too well. The church we attended was a Congregational church. I remember my Sunday School teacher, a young farmer named George Campbell. I thought he was a good teacher. He was unmarried at that time and "batching" as we said on the farm. After Sunday School one day in the spring he took me out and showed me the farm. He was proud of it and I thought it was a fine place. The main thing I remember about Sunday School was that we had a baseball team in the summer. We were not too careful about taking in a few ringers who might not have been able to qualify theologically but were good baseball players. We were small children—fourth and fifth graders—and the only game I remember playing was one that someone arranged for us with a team from a town named Russell. The size of our team can probably be judged by the fact that we made arrangements with the garageman to drive the nine of us there. We got in one Model T with the top down and all went to Russell in that vehicle, along with our equipment and driver.

Among other memories of Maxbass was that of the local police officer, a man named Nichols who owned the large livery barn. Like most of the buildings in Maxbass it was quite new. His boy, a little older than I, was a leader to some extent among the younger boys. He took some of us up the stairs to an attic-like room over the main office of the livery barn and introduced us to the game of draw poker using shingle nails in place of money.

Also, the next summer I managed to earn some money by helping at a butchershop which was in the same block with Dad's store. They slaughtered livestock at a place a mile or so from town three or four times a week. The man in charge of the slaughtering wanted some help. I helped with skinning the beef carcasses. He never did let me touch the sheep, a reason I never understood until later when I found out how persistent the oil on wool is in contaminating the taste of the meat if it is allowed to come in contact with it.

September of the next year found us back in Towner as my father had disposed of his store as a bad venture. This was not the end of our connection with Maxbass, however, as Dad was soon back there in the employ of a wholesale house trying to rescue one of the hardware stores from bankruptcy. He kept occupied that way for several years and so we often saw people from Maxbass over those years when they came to Towner as they had to if they traveled by railroad.

Chapter 3

Back to Towner

One thing that living in Maxbass had taught me was how much the river at Towner meant to boys in the community. There was no river at Maxbass and consequently no swimming and little skating although there was considerable skiing. About one mile from Towner was a river which flowed down from Canada, turned around gradually and went back into Canada, following the geological Lake Souris. In North Dakota it was called the Mouse River, but in Canada it was known as the Souris River, a name which the federal government later forced upon the North Dakota people. The big thing it supplied to youngsters was a place to swim, or maybe I should say, many places to swim. In the winding river going by the town there were many sites within a mile or two which could be used for that purpose. Primarily we had one we called the Shallows which was used only by very small boys and the Deep which was used by all boys and men and usually had a rough diving board. Close by the Deep was a hobo jungle where in the late summer of the year the itinerant harvesters and threshers frequently camped out. It was fairly standard during the hot weather of summer that boys went down every day to swim in the Deep and it supplied us with very fine recreation.

Another thing the river supplied was a place to camp. And there were several favorite camping places much used for that purpose. I could not have been much over 10 when the father of one of my playmates, Donald Fouts, organized a squad of the Boy Pioneers which later merged into the Boy Scouts. This was the beginning of considerable scouting activity of which camping was the favorite. Most of our camping was an overnight activity. On one occasion when we were more mature I remember a 10-day camp at what was called the Old Fishing Grounds about eight miles from town that we managed by ourselves, being supplied with walltents and cooking our meals over a campfire. The most diligent of our various scoutmasters was J. H. Colton, who was Superintendent of Schools. The County Superintendent of Schools, A. C. Berg, also served from time to time and joined us while we were on one trip to Buffalo Lodge Lake some 25 miles away where we had a change from camping by the river. That camp lasted a week or slightly more.

In addition the river supplied some fine skating in the fall after the river first froze and before it got covered with snow. When we did not have a skating rink downtown, which was unusual, our own enterprise kept a stretch of river ice clear of snow for a time into the cold weather. Fishing by means of spearing through the ice was another occupation of the men and boys and a very interesting one. Generally we made our own minnows out of soft wood and tobacco can tin, weighted them with melted lead and dangled them on a string through a hole in the ice to attract the fish, and when one came, we speared it with a 5-tine spear. Fishing in the summer with hooks and lines was not a common occupation. Some farmers and ranchers along the river set up nets and gathered fish that way for food.

With this background was also a system of home chores for each child in the family. One tragedy that happened before James Ellis and his family left for Saskatchewan was the death of his wife Lulu. She died of an illness after childbirth and left an infant girl who my mother proceeded to care for along with her own baby, Donald. This required an expansion of chores, too, as the supply of milk was not adequate for the older children and two infants. Consequently, we acquired a second milk cow. Fortunately for me, Baby Lulu had been passed on to some other relatives and the two milk cows were not on my schedule of chores when I arrived at the age that I took care of the milking. In some ways the harder job was hauling water. Until the city water system was completed, all houses along our street had their own wells, ours included. Unfortunately, our water was heavily impregnated with iron salts and humans had great difficulty drinking it. Fortunately, the cow and the chickens did drink it. But down the street a block away one of our more distinguished neighbors, Judge Horace Bagley, had fine water, and we and other neighbors made use of it. Before going to school in the morning I would go to the Bagley well, fill an 8-gallon cream can with water, and take it back to our house. I used a well-made iron cart with large wheels that was designed to haul a barrel of water and the large wheels made for quite easy pushing. One can of water each day would normally take care of the cooking and the household drinking. If not, a second was always possible after school. Saturday was a different story because that was washday in the Ellis family and it was bath night as well. It would take 8 to 10 cans of water to keep the household supplied. I had no trouble with this particular job as I turned my sled into a vehicle for deep snow, still preferring the large wheeled cart for light snow. One winter, however, was an exception. We lived across the street from the courthouse and back of the courthouse was the jail. Back of our house and barn was an old building which was for rent and much of the time unoccupied. The renter this particular year was a prisoner incarcerated in the jail for what people elsewhere would have called bootlegging, but in North Dakota it was known as blindpigging. Why, I do not know, but that was the name. North Dakota had entered the Union in 1889 with prohibition in its constitution and so there was no legal sale of liquor in the state. However, any citizen could order liquor from Minnesota and the train could bring it to him. The old house in this way turned out to be a refuge for the family of a prisoner named English, which consisted of his wife and two small children. The house did not have a well, but when my mother found Mrs. English's situation, she assured her immediately that Elmer would get her water for her. Well, Elmer did what his mother told him, but I must admit during the winter when he was facing a good northwest wind pushing his cart with its precious water—only a little over two blocks—his mind was on that husband in that nice warm jail playing cards with the other blindpiggers as Elmer tried to protect his face against a frost-bitten nose or ear. When spring came, English was released and he took his wife and two children somewhere else, much to my delight.

Back at Towner from Maxbass it was school time again and I was in the fifth grade with a lot of children I knew. My only recollection of anything out of the ordinary in those years was the fact that when we reached the eighth grade we had our first man teacher. All of our teachers after Kate Mitchell in the primary grades had been young women usually teaching three or four years before marriage, which I think was the common history of all of them. Our man teacher in the eighth grade was probably a good change for us educationally but it was not a very pleasant experience for many of the students. The gentleman was from Pennsylvania and completely inexperienced in any other region. I am not sure what could have induced Ezra B. Smith to take this venture into North Dakota for a year's teaching, but I am sure he learned a great deal. He was not a poor teacher in a real sense, but his great hobby was grammar and the diagramming of sentences in order to illustrate grammatical structure. My memory of that year was that our blackboards were always filled with diagrams and usually there were one or more persons at the board diagramming sentences. I have to confess I did not get along well with Smith. I have to presume that I got along too easily with my other teachers and found him an unpleasant change. One little incident will illustrate the kind of thing that developed frequently in his class. I have already commented on the North Dakota expression of the blindpig. An illegal liquor store was a blindpig and a man who ran it was a blindpigger. This happened in one of our civics classes where we all had a copy of the long state constitution which had a great deal of statutory type law involved in it at that time. This was our textbook. The lesson for the day was a long section on "maintaining a public nuisance" which was described in some detail. It so happened that the evening before I had been reading the local paper which reported that a neighbor a few blocks away had been arrested for maintaining a public nuisance. Not knowing exactly what it was, I asked my father, "What's happened to Frank Hyatt?" My father answered, "Oh, he has been pigging again and they arrested him."

The class assembled the next day for civics and the first question Mr. Smith asked was, "What is maintaining a public nuisance?"

All of the class looked blank except for me and he grudgingly turned to me and said, "Tell us, Elmer, what is a public nuisance?"

I answered, "It's keeping a blind pig."

His mouth opened for a moment and then he said, "I don't think that keeping a blind pig is any more of a public nuisance than keeping any other kind of a pig." It came to me as it often did in these cases that he was the only one in the room who did not understand what my answer meant. I was tempted to tell him but I was afraid to and I let it go.

He related this experience to a number of fellow teachers during the noon hour, and one of them repeated it to my sister Martha who carried it home. I was told that I should have explained it to Mr. Smith, but they didn't know Mr. Smith quite as well as I did.

Sunday School and church were very important affairs in our lives as children and during this period I had the good teaching from Colton and enjoyed it very much. The church had really been started by Scottish trained Canadians. The preacher who was there when we first came was named McClain and was born in Scotland, and his successor whose name I do not recall was a very young man from Ulster, Ireland. Before our family moved to Maxbass it was decided that the children who had not been baptized—Grace, Elmer and Evelyn in that order in age—should receive that blessing. It was an unusual affair because Minister McClain and his wife came to the house one evening and baptized those of us who had not been baptized, and to our surprise that included our father who was not sure he had been baptized as he had no memory of it. Anyway I recall very distinctly that when the baptism was over and the McClains were visiting with my parents, my mother happened to come out to the kitchen where some of the children were and found me standing on a chair holding the baptismal water and Evelyn holding the family cat for me to baptize—an activity Mother ended in a hurry. It probably indicated what little baptism meant to many of the children who went through the ceremony. At least it did for us.

The early population at Towner had included a substantial number of Scottish people. Our Superintendent of Schools when I started school was also named McClain and the town distinguished between them by calling them Preacher McClain and Professor McClain. The Scots' influence as a group though while continuous lessened relatively, for the new people coming in later were not Scottish. They were the older settlers and their families.

Chapter 4

Earning Money

Life in Towner after the return from Maxbass began to include more and more paid employment. The most available employment for men and boys was farm employment especially during the summer and fall haying and threshing season. Towner was the center of a good deal of cattle raising, and haying was a large occupation of those farmers who had natural meadows. The best of these of course were along the river and were often under water early in the spring.

My first experience haying was soon after we came back from Maxbass. I took a job on the Henry Erickson ranch which was located in the sandhill country directly south of town. I doubt that my father would have let me go had he been home. The people at the Erickson store hired me and I am sure the foreman would not have selected me had he been doing the hiring. Technically I was employed as a stacker driver which was commonly a job for boys. However, as in most cases where that happened I wound up on a mowing machine cutting the native grass for curing and stacking into hay. I was fond of horses and enjoyed working with them. However, on this occasion I found that I was not tall enough to throw the harness on the team assigned to me. One of the older boys did it for me. I also had trouble on the mowing machine itself, as my legs were not long enough to reach the footrests and I had to hold on to the iron seat by twisting my feet under its support. I got along with the help of my friend in harnessing and unharnessing my team for two or three days before I became sick eating choke cherries that grew profusely in the sandhills near the ranch buildings. Like many youngsters I ate them too green and the ranch foreman's wife took me into the house and kept me in bed most of one day. That evening one of the men was going to town and I went home by the same means that I had come out on the previous Sunday, and that was my first venture in farm work.

A few years later I had a job with a pair of brothers who owned horses and haying machinery and "put up" hay for various ranchers. This was along the river and again, while I was primarily driving a mowing machine, I occasionally was assigned to a sulky rake to get the hay in windrows. Then the bullrake could pick it up and take it to the stacker.

After finishing the seventh grade in 1915 I held down a job that paid a man's wages.

Granddad Ellis died during that summer. Help was needed at his little farm at Anamoose to take care of the chores while Father's youngest brother, Eugene, who had been taking care of it, joined a threshing crew as separator man. I was picked as the available grandson and went from my haying job to a chore job, helping Aunt Mary and two small children on Granddad's farm. After Grandfather's death, Grandmother had gone to live with her daughter Minnie Abelein, who had become postmistress in Anamoose. My work consisted of milking two cows, feeding three calves, and looking after the crops Granddad had left. The main task was harvesting about three acres of navy beans, which was a regular crop with him but an unusual one for most farmers. First I had to pull the beans and stack them around a contrivance that Granddad had developed to a stack about six feet high, and then top them out with grass so the rain would not damage them. Then at a later period, I threshed them. I had fields of corn and potatoes that I worked with also, cutting and shocking the corn and digging the potatoes. I had no horses and when I had to haul some potatoes to town, which happened a couple of times a week, I walked into Abeleins and got Cousin Amy's pony and cart and drove it out. I hauled my potatoes, and left the pony and cart at the Abeleins and walked back to the farm, a distance of about one mile.

It was an interesting period in my boyhood because I was living in the house that Granddad had built. There was also a fine springhouse which served as a refrigerator, where the milk and butter were kept.

School started before Eugene's threshing was over so I was missing school at home. But I refused the offer to attend the school at Anamoose and continued the farmwork until he came home. Mary bought me some new clothes to wear home as I was going on the train. I took the night train from Anamoose to Minot and the morning Great Northern to Towner. I was glad to get home but I left the old farm with some regret. I had slept in the attic, Earl's old quarters, which was assigned to me with a good bed and a kerosene lamp and where I had found piles of old magazines. I was particularly interested in the cartoons of the Russo-Japanese War, and had clipped them and had made a scrapbook of the series. Chiefly, they were from the *Review of Reviews* and the cartoons were reprints from newspapers. That was the main possession I took home.

Another type of work available for boys who wanted to earn money, but not so commonly done, was delivering groceries. There were two principal general stores in Towner that I suppose satisfied ninety percent of the town and country grocery business. One of them, the smaller of the two, was called the Towner Supply Company and was owned by some men in Minneapolis-St. Paul who were in the wholesale business. They sent in a manager. The first one I knew was named Momgren. I worked a short time for him but later worked for Charles Feldman for several years. He was followed by Captain Giesler. Delivery was limited to the city and was, during the school period, an after-school job, and a full-time Saturday job. You did everything else around the store that needed doing. One of the first things I was taught was how to test cream, as most of the farmers who traded there brought in an eight or ten gallon can of cream each week which the store bought for a creamery in Minnesota. That consisted of learning to operate a Babcock tester to find the percentage of butterfat the cream contained, calculating the value of the cream, and writing a check to the farmer for the amount. It was a particularly busy operation on Saturday which was the farmers' favorite shopping day. One did not work at this job long before he was waiting on trade behind the counter in his spare time, helping to sweep out the store after it closed, and restocking the shelves with goods. I think I worked every year in the Towner Supply Company when I was in high school, except two summers which I spent on a farm Father had purchased near Granville. I went up as soon as school was out and helped Uncle Eugene with the work of the farm, cultivating corn, haying, and harvesting grain. Father's farm was only a quarter section of land but had the necessary buildings, and Gene farmed adjoining land on shares. I had an arrangement with my father that I was to help Gene for the summer, but in the fall I was to have a team and a hayrack for hauling grain bundles to work on a threshing crew. I would have the money I made with the team, which would be my pay for the summer. I was paid the standard wage for threshing in the fall which was the best paying job in farm work. The going wage was three dollars a day for a man and two dollars a day for the team. The five dollars a day looked like pretty rich wages for a high school boy. The trouble was you could not thresh in wet weather. A great deal of your time was spent in waiting for the grain to dry so it could be threshed and there was no pay for waiting although you were fed. As I did not like sleeping in the haymows which was standard for threshing crews that went from farm to farm, I slept under my wagon on the ground except in the rainy weather when I had to have a better roof over my head. My team of course was tied to the wagon and I was responsible for feeding them oats and hay. Meals were supplied at the cook car manned by a couple of farm women and the food was plentiful and good. The first year of my threshing was the hardest as we worked from sun-up until dark. Each of us who drove bundle teams had lanterns to harness and feed our team by and to unharness after we finished our work. That was the only year, however, that was so strenuous. The next time I threshed we were on something like a nine-hour day with no other changes in our routine.

The summer of 1918 was an exception for me, which was partly due to the war. One of my freshman high school teachers, Christopher Smith, had not returned during my sophomore year, but had gone to Wyoming to manage an irrigated farm for his father. He had written to an older classmate, John Johnson, offering him a job for the summer. He said that plenty of jobs were available, and urged him to bring me with him. Because of the excitement of the war and the recruitment of military personnel which went on at a rapid pace in late 1917 and 1918, I had talked to the recruiting agent of the North Dakota National Guard, which later became part of the Rainbow Division, about joining, under encouragement from some older boys from Maxbass. When he asked me about my age, he said I would have to get my father's written permission, which I tried to do but was unsuccessful. My father pointed out that my brothers Bill and Earl were in service, which was quite enough for the family at least until I became 18 years old. I became 17 in July and at that time had reached my full growth. I decided then to go to Wyoming with John, and we made our arrangements for that trip, traveling daycoach on the railroad to Torrington, Wyoming. Smith joined us that night in town, and immediately after breakfast we left in a lumber wagon for his farm which was about 25 miles south in the direction of Cheyenne.

My first job was working on an irrigation ditch digging crew driving a four horse Fresno, which I had never seen before. Later on I switched to a ranch where there was a job haying. Our haying crew on the ranch consisted of a foreman, his wife as cook, his younger brother and me. I did not like the arrangements there and toward the end of July, I had a letter from Charles Feldman urging me to come home and help out at the store and offering what seemed to me attractive pay. I was happy to quit my ranch job. I was soon on my way home having the experience, however, of not realizing that railroad fares had increased during the summer and the money I had was not adequate to get me home. Eventually I arrived home, worked the rest of the summer in the store, and continued during the school year.

Chapter 5

High School

High school was quite a change from grade school in that you had fewer subjects, and instruction was on a more mature basis. I remember some good teachers, such as Harriet Edgerly, a mathematics teacher who also was principal for the high school my first two years. I enjoyed working with her. Another very good principal was a young Army captain named Jack Urness who came the second half of my junior year. I was not lucky enough to have any courses with him, but I was a member of the debate team which he coached. I carried a usual high school course, taking four units each year, and really not overburdening myself as I could have carried five just as well. But I was busy with work and also very heavily involved with basketball. We also played baseball in the spring but the season was too short to compare with basketball.

Our playing gymnasium was not at all adequate, and the members of the school board were not interested in improving it. Consequently, we players ran basketball ourselves. We succeeded in renting first an empty store downtown which had a concrete floor, and later we moved to the Women's Relief Corps Hall for which the rent also had to be found. There we had the best court of my high school years, but still far from regulation in size. Its low ceiling and nine foot baskets were a great handicap to our team when we played on regulation floors. We did not play games with other teams during 1918 because of the war and the influenza epidemic, although we kept playing at home with considerable regularity. The next year which was my junior year our team played a lot of games with other high schools in the area, going to the district tournament at Minot and being eliminated in the early part of the tournament. During that year we had a good coach, P. K. Cesander, who was our superintendent of schools and a graduate of St. Olaf College. We learned a good deal about basketball from him. Unfortunately, he moved to a new job the next year and his replacement knew less about basketball than the janitor. We started then without a coach and eventually as I was captain of the team, it made me also the coach. I had some correspondence with Cesander, getting welcome advice. Four of us on the team were seniors and the other three, as you were limited to seven including your substitutes, were younger. One of them was a regular guard. He was a Polish boy named

Petroski who was not large but had made himself an excellent player. We won our first two games at the district tournament and in the finals came up against Minot, the largest high school in our district and usually the winner of the tournament. We won that game by a one-point margin and went to the state tournament at Fargo, where, after defeating Devils Lake, we met Fargo which was the largest high school in the state and had a team that outsized us considerably. To add to our difficulties in that game, Frank Erickson, our largest and strongest player, went out with five fouls early in the second half. We had to substitute very young material to finish the game, and we lost. I have to admit as I look back at it, basketball as my greatest interest in high school, and I might say my greatest pleasure.

Our high school senior class which consisted of 12 members was not a distinguished class at all in our small high school's history. I received some kind of certificate which stated that I had led this class in grades. That induced Fargo College to send me a scholarship which would pay my tuition as long as I maintained a high average. I know my brother Charles received a similar certificate when he graduated. Charles and Bill both attended Fargo College which influenced me to go there my freshman year. I admit too that basketball was part of the picture as both brothers had been on the team for the college.

As I look back at the experience, undoubtedly the most important thing that happened to me in high school was the meeting of a young lady when I started my sophomore year. The junior class had a new girl attending who was living with the Bagley family a block down the street. She was Ruth Clapper from Grilley Township School, forty miles northwest of Towner. She had taken the two years of high school offered there and had moved along very fast since she left Towner where she had been in the second grade for a few months at the same time I was. I knew her older brother Cecil but hardly knew her at that early period.

Our high school classes at Towner were small and they were thrown together for a great many activities rather than trying to do them strictly as a class. In the second year of her attendance, which was Ruth's senior and my junior year, the junior and senior classes went together to put on the senior play. In fact, the senior class "borrowed" boys from the junior class in order to properly stage the play that had been chosen. That took us into joint activities although that was certainly not very necessary as we were living only a block apart. Early in the second year we had begun to go together in the way young people did in small towns at that time. We were in classes together and one I remember particularly was a psychology class which was in her last semester.

Besides that we were associated on the debate squad that year. After she graduated Ruth took over a rural school near her home, a one-teacher school, and taught that for the year. That year I finished high school and both of us went to college the following year. Ruth's Aunt Ara Robison invited her to come to Columbia, Missouri, and attend college. Arriving too late to enter the University of Missouri with the regular freshman class, she enrolled in Stephens College.

By the time my senior year was over, we were informally engaged, but no date had been set as neither of us saw a livelihood ahead at that time that we wanted to accept.

Chapter 6

Fargo College

I finished high school in the spring of 1920 and went to the farm at Granville. I stayed with Gene and Mary and helped Gene with the farm work as I had before. When threshing began I took Dad's team and went with a crew that was working north of Granville and worked most of the season.

In the meantime I had been debating with myself and my parents and some of my friends about where I would go to college. It never occurred to me that I would not go. During the summer I wrote to Fargo College and asked if there were any part-time jobs available that I could secure to help pay my way. Going to college seemed to be a tradition already in our family as the older boys had all gone, even Earl who had never finished high school, a condition that I suppose reflected back on the fact that he was living with our grandparents and did not have the same motivation that my parents gave the rest of us. But obviously my father's income was not anything that could give us much help. While he did help Charles and Earl some, I do not recall he helped Bill unless it was with a loan or something of that sort. Earl had gone to the agricultural college at Fargo in a program where he did not need to be a high school graduate. It was a practical farm husbandry course that ran three months in the winter for three successive years. I am not sure how much Earl got out of it except a job on the college's experimental farm near Williston at the end.

While I was threshing I received a letter from Fargo College telling me about a job near the college with a family named Steele, which furnished one's room for doing household chores. It had been held by various students before and seemed like a passable job. I accepted it.

I arrived a week late at the college having asked for a late arrival to take advantage of good threshing weather, and I went directly to the Steeles' home where I introduced myself. Mrs. Steele seemed very glad to see me. Later her husband, a retired regular Army major and a very pleasant person, arrived. They showed me my room which turned out to be in the basement but decent and well-furnished. In fact, it was quite a change from sleeping under my wagon as I had been doing.

I registered the next day and it turned out the man I had corresponded with had been Dean Guy Vowels, a Rhodes Scholar and an Oxford graduate. He had been a friend of brother Charles and was a delightful person. He put me in his French class, and being late, I found the pronunciation most difficult. By the end of the week, I took my problem to him and told him I did not think I could catch up and asked to be put in a course in economics that some of the other boys had told me about, which he readily did. Had the language been German or Norwegian, I would have been all right but only Advanced German was offered that year. The dean had suggested that I eat in the girls' dormitory. The dining room was in the basement of the administration building and quite a number of the boys from outside of Fargo took their meals there. I followed his advice and it got me immediately acquainted with several boys and later several girls. The closest friend I made was Otis Lee, a boy from Dickinson, whose parents had been born in England and who now owned a laundry in Dickinson. Otis was probably the best student in the college, certainly the best freshman. If he had a competitor, it was Sam Richmond, a Fargo boy whose father had the title Master of the Synagogue.

My memory is not very clear on exactly which semester certain courses were taken that did not run through the year. The Freshman English and I believe the Modern European History were year courses. In addition the first semester I had a course in college algebra with an interesting teacher named Shibli, a Syrian who had been brought to the United States by Congregational missionaries. He was a very small dark man and meticulous in his class management. As we had enough room we were all seated a seat apart. Algebra was one of the few courses in high school in which I had not done well in sharp contrast to geometry in which I had led my class. But with Shibli I had no trouble. He was an excellent teacher and a most enthusiastic one. I recall one day his working out a complicated problem on the blackboard and then covering another blackboard with a method of proof, the details of which I have forgotten. But when he came to the end and showed it all proved out correctly, he just glowed, stood back, admired it, and said, "Isn't that beautiful? Isn't that art?" and to him it was. It would be difficult not to appreciate a teacher with that kind of enthusiasm.

I have a vivid memory of meeting Shibli on the evening of the presidential election of 1920. We happened to meet in the crowd that was watching the election returns being projected on a screen in front of the newspaper office of *The Fargo Forum.* We visited and stood together while the returns came in. He was deeply disappointed in the Harding landslide, as I was, both of us I suspect thinking in terms of the League of Nations which probably meant a great deal more to him than it did to me.

Another course that I enjoyed was a course in the New Testament, taught by the husband of the woman who taught my Freshman English. He had a theological degree and was doing some preaching in the Fargo area. But as I had a long and varied Sunday School experience, I had little trouble in doing well in the course and enjoying it too. I learned much about biblical literature that I had not learned in either my Presbyterian, Congregational, or even my Lutheran background when our County Superintendent of Schools A. C. Berg had organized a special class for high school boys who had quit going to Sunday School. Using a Norwegian Lutheran text in English, he had given us quite a course in biblical history.

Another course that I recall was a two-hour course in Shakespeare's tragedies taught by a woman teacher named Frank Lamb. Otis was in this class with me and we had a great deal of pleasure with the Shakespeare material that she presented. Her presentation was largely her notes, we discovered, from a graduate course on the subject she had had at the University of Minnesota. I think our favorite of all was *King Lear*, which strangely enough I have never seen performed. Of course we had some sport between ourselves about the various literary forms in which she classified the Shakespeare and we applied them to the 15-cent movies we went to frequently on Saturday nights.

I was really looking for another job to supplement my small savings but the boys I got to know, particularly Otis and Sam, insisted I come out for football. As a very small boy, I had seen a football game in which my older brother Charles played. That was my experience with football. About the third day they had talked to Coach Watkins, who urged them to bring me around which they did.

I knew a great deal about Coach Fenwick Watkins as both of my older brothers played under him and Charles particularly was fond of him. One of the things I knew was that he was a black man and the first black man any of us had ever known. He had come from the University of Vermont and originally had taught mathematics in the college as well as coached. But by now he had gone into the real estate business and did nothing at the college but coach in season. He was a light-colored Negro, married to an attractive white woman. I was a guest in their house twice during the year. I suspect that neither he nor possibly his ancestors had ever lived in the American South, and he was very sensitive on color line questions as I had occasion to learn. He was universally liked by his players who referred to him among themselves as "Watty."

I protested to the coach that I was a baseball and a basketball player and had never played football. In fact, he told me he had seen me play basketball in the state tournament the year before when we had beaten Devils Lake but had been eliminated by Fargo. I was easily talked into it, and after throwing the ball around and getting into a poor uniform from the well-picked-over supply, he put me on the squad trying to play end opposite Sam Richmond on the other end. It was a different style of play, and he gave that up after a while and began to work me in the center where he had an extremely weak spot defensively, although the senior lad was a good passer to the various members of the backfield. He did well on offense, but was useless on defense. Coming off the threshing crew, I was in pretty good condition, but I found the dormitory food was not as substantial as I was used to getting in the cook car, and I found myself hungry most of the football season. I usually ate two breakfasts on Monday when we had no classes. I went to the dining hall and was ready to go to work when the Steeles sat down to breakfast. Mrs. Steele always asked me to breakfast on Monday—my rug cleaning day.

In the meantime I was doing well with my courses. My special favorite was Modern European History which I was taking with a fine gentleman named Correll. We were using the Carlton Hayes text, the first volume of which was then new. The economics was also interesting, the teacher being a Canadian who apparently had some lung affliction. He was not an expert teacher like C. M. Correll. I had an English course, taught by a very pleasant woman, and a course in Chemistry where the instructor and I did not get along very well. In fact, I disliked the laboratory work because the problems he assigned could be worked out in a few minutes on paper and I never saw the purpose of trying to prove my mathematics by test tubes.

I must confess as I look back on that year I got my greatest pleasure from athletics. Through Otis I enjoyed a great deal of music as he was an excellent violinist, was taking lessons and put in at least a solid hour of practice every day. The football season of course was in many ways most interesting because it was new. Two days after I joined the squad we played our first game against Concordia College and won 7-0. I did not play. The next game was the worst game of the year as far as the team was concerned, as we played the University of North Dakota which had a team that had had experience and was considerably larger man for man than our college team was. They ran over us badly and they were running through the center of the line so readily that Watkins inserted me in at the beginning of the second quarter. I must admit I made a lot of mistakes, but they did not go through the center of the line after I went in and I stayed the entire game, coming out battered and bruised especially about my head. Thereafter I started every game, once or twice at end, but most often at center. The football season ended fairly early for us in North Dakota with the final game against our traditional enemy, the State

Agricultural College on the other side of town. We lost the game 7-0 but presented a far better game than any we had played that year.

The end of that season was the beginning of basketball and here the coach knew I was a good prospect. He again paired Sam Richmond and me off as forwards which was the proper place for both of us but he often varied his lineup. We had a much better basketball than football team.

The only difficulty really with my participating in athletics was I was not earning money. In fact, I had no regular part-time job except at the Steeles. When I went home for Christmas, my difficulty increased because the First National Bank at Towner closed during the holidays and my small checking account was gone. That was not a disaster but my father's account was there too, and I lost my personal banker. I did not have railroad fare back to Fargo among other problems, but Dad took a war bond out of his file somewhere and gave it to me. It was one of the minimum ones that had been sold to mature at $25. I took this to a bank which gave me as I recall around $18.50 for it and with that I returned to Fargo to make out the best I could. I began working for the college. One job I did for some time was to help the engineer in the heating plant by cleaning out the ashpits daily, filling the empty sweeping compound cans and carrying them up to the ground level where the truck collected them. It took time, but it was not a disagreeable job. I do not remember anything about compensation, but I moved from that to other jobs such as the storm window removal in the spring as well as some yardwork up and down our street. This got me through the winter and spring after a fashion. I was sending my laundry home to my mother and when it returned it usually included a package of my favorite cookies. With this I got by, still eating at the dormitory. The only effect it had on me was to make me very tired of being without money, and that is partly responsible for the decision I made not to return.

My father had lost his county judge position and was out of that job after the first of January, but immediately moved over to the Towner Supply Company where I had worked when I was in high school. Mother was concerned about his bad hernia condition and no doubt he was also although he never mentioned it to me. Anyway it had been decided he would have an operation that summer, and my sister Martha, who had graduated from Michael Reese Hospital in Chicago, would come home and take care of him during and after the operation. The family physician, Dr. Craise, would do the operating. I was clearly conscious too that the family was short of money with Dad's salary gone, so I wrote that I would take over his store job for the summer and did.

One memory of that summer stays with me as an illustration of living in a small, closely-knit town as contrasted with larger places. The incident occurred in this way. I came home from the store as usual between 6:30 and 7 p.m., as it took that long for us to clean up the place after we closed technically at 6. The family had eaten supper but Mother had mine on the stove and a place set for me. I was not more than halfway into my meal when Mother came in and said, "As soon as you are through, I want you to get on your good clothes and take Alcinda for a walk." Alcinda McDonald was a neighbor across the side street from us whose older sister Jean had been in my class at school. Alcinda was a year or two younger. She was a close friend of Ruth's during their two years of high school together. I had seen Alcinda a few times in Fargo in the winter where she went to the Sacred Heart Academy, the only private high school, I believe, in the state and of course conducted by the Catholic Church. The times I had met her were at the Presbyterian Church and I had walked back to Sacred Heart with her which was at the opposite end of town from where I lived.

I protested to my mother that I was tired and that we had had a hard day at the store. I wanted to read the paper and go to bed. But she insisted that Alcinda was very lonesome and very unhappy. She had had an unhappy childhood, I well knew, as her father was an unsympathetic sort, and the girls' mother had died when they were quite small, and the stepmother had no kindness whatever for Alcinda. The senior McDonalds were on a summer trip to the west coast and Alcinda was taking care of the house. But they sent her to a boarding high school largely to get her out of the way during the greater part of the year. As usual my mother prevailed, and I got cleaned up, dressed up, and went out the front gate and south on the sidewalk across the street. Alcinda was sitting on the porch. Being no one's fool, when I turned in there, she said, "Your mother sent you." Of course I lied like a gentleman. Eventually Alcinda and I started down the sidewalk going north which would take us through the business district to the railway tracks and on to the city water tower where the sidewalk ended, the usual evening walk for young couples. On the way back, we stopped in at one of the drugstores and had ice cream which was part of the routine. I felt I had done my duty when I left her at her door and had the satisfaction of feeling she felt a good deal better than she had before our walk.

I did not give any further thought to it until the next day when an older friend of mine, Joe Flanagan, who had been a great football player in his college days and had played minor league baseball when he was young enough to pitch, confronted me. He was the heart and soul of our town baseball team, and I had played with him enough to have learned a great deal from him. To my surprise, Joe came into the store and back into the warehouse where I was testing a farmer's cream. He burst in upon me alone and said, "Elmer, you were out walking with Alcinda last night."

I said, "Yes, I was."

"Well," he said, "you belong to Ruth."

I alibied, "But my mother made me."

To which he replied, "Elmer, you have to remember younger boys look up to you. You were captain of the basketball team and the baseball team, and you have to keep in mind that you are an example for them." (I might add that Joe was the father of several children).

I told him, "I appreciate that and I try to behave myself."

He conceded, "Well, you do, but walking out with another girl does not help."

Chapter 7

I Become a Teacher

I had been thinking about what I would do next year to make and save some money and had decided the best I could do was teach school. I talked it over with A. C. Berg, County Superintendent of Schools. He was all for it and suggested a way whereby passing a series of ten examinations I could qualify for a principalship of a consolidated school. The State Department of Education's series of the examinations had been set up in Minot and a few other cities so I took leave from the store and went up to Minot for a week. Half the examinations were on content—history, mathematics, and so forth, and half were classified as pedagogical subjects—psychology, education, and technique of teaching and the like. I had had a course in psychology in high school, but that was the only one of the pedagogical subjects I had studied. The content courses I assumed I could handle without any preparation which proved true. The examinations were given two each day, the content test in the morning and the pedagogical one in the afternoon.

I had borrowed textbooks on the pedagogical subjects from Berg and I had them with me. I put in each evening reading the book on the next day's examination and I found they were within reasonable terms of my knowledge. The content courses were not difficult. The examinations were sent to the State Department of Education, and eventually I received a notice that I had passed them.

Berg had been inquiring into small town and open country consolidated schools and had found a vacancy in Bottineau County about eight miles from Antler and also eight miles from the Manitoba-North Dakota boundary.

Although Dad's operation had not been completely successful, he had agreed to administer one of the largest estates in the county, that of the owner of a very large store in Velva. While this helped him financially, it required that he move the family to Velva. Looking toward my year I had been discussing with him what I might do because I would need a car. I suggested since his new job furnished him a car, he might sell me his old Chevrolet which was a relic, in fact, a Chevrolet made before General Motors took over the company and started to produce them. I have forgotten how we worked it out. I had paid the grocery bills at the store out of my checks during the summer. We agreed on somewhere between $200 and $300 for the car.

During this time he had been busy moving the family to Velva. When I went to apply in person to this school, I went by way of Velva, picked up the car and from there went toward the school. After spending the night at the Clappers where I visited Ruth I was again on my way. When I went through Glenburn I stopped and bought a stiff collar. I had ceased to wear them but I put it on now as I thought it would make me look older. The road was not good although it was the best one north of Minot. I learned later it was the road by which the booze runners went to Canada for their supplies of liquor and came by the school every night.

I arrived at Sherman School early in the afternoon and looked up the secretary of the board, Mr. Price, who lived within a mile of the school. He called the president of the board and, as I recall, one other member, and we all met at the school where they showed me what the job would be. It was a three-teacher school, the first three grades under a primary teacher, the middle three under an intermediate teacher, and the seventh grade and the first year of high school under the "principal." There was no eighth grade that year as a result of careful planning. The other part of my job had the less-distinguished title of "janitor" but they had a steam heating plant that looked very good to me. They also took me over to the teacherage, which consisted of two one-room schools moved together in the shape of an L, and the teachers had the privilege of living there. The beauty of the job was that it paid $175 a month which seemed to me that with the teacherage to live in, I could save some money—not properly evaluating how much it would cost to run that old car through the year. The school building had a good basement with a big playroom but the school rooms consisted only of two large rooms, the middle and upper grade sections divided by a cloth curtain.

I had a few surprises after I took over my job because I found the $175 was not in cash but in warrants which were discounted at the bank by 15 percent as they had to wait for the money. The other surprise was there apparently was no provision made or expected for a housekeeper. Presumably the two other teachers and I would do our own housekeeping.

I liked the members of the board that I met very well. The township which was the school district was divided about equally between Hoosiers and Norwegians. There were a few others of course. I remember I had two Irish families, one of whom had abandoned the church as self-proclaimed "free thinkers" and chose to consider me the single other intellectual in the district. The president of the board and his wife, who were Swedish, were really most helpful. Their three children were the brightest kids I had in my own grades, and I developed considerable fondness for the entire family. The Norwegians were an odd sect of Lutherans who called themselves Lutheran Brethren, and as they were a very evangelical confessional type of church, I decided not to attend. The Hoosiers were Methodists but had no church, and occasionally held a service in someone's home or in an old one-room school.

I was offered the position and I accepted. I thought I was luckier than I probably was, although it all turned out well. Upon talking to the board I found that the intermediate teacher would be inexperienced and a graduate of Minot Normal, and the primary teacher was a graduate of Valley City Normal and had taught four or five years. I had no way of getting acquainted with them until the day before school started when we all met at the teacherage.

Monday morning school opened and my memory consisted chiefly of a mother who brought two boys less than a year apart in age to enter the first grade. She came in to tell me she did not think the older boy would stay and she would wait. I told her I thought she should go on home. I told her we would see that he stayed, and it would make it more difficult if she were there. Nevertheless she insisted on it. I had no sooner called my classes to order than the primary teacher called me and told me the youngster in question had left the school and was running across the field. I was surprised he had not stolen his mother's horse and buggy. I started over the fields after him. I felt it was a little beneath my dignity to run, and as I walked faster than he could run I overtook him about a quarter of a mile from the school. Fortunately or unfortunately, Mr. Price, the school board secretary, worked the next farm, and he saw me. All winter I heard stories about that particular incident. Anyway I reached the lad. He fought, kicked, and screamed while I held him by the collar and dragged him back to school, kicking all the way. We had a pretty large audience by the time we got back to school. Consequently, I took him into the basement where I laid him across a spare desk and paddled him firmly. I admit I did not do this on the pedagogical ground. I was just angry.

When I finished he blubbered a bit but went up and sat in his seat, and we had no more trouble with him the rest of the year. In fact, it was probably a good way to begin although farm children were never much of a discipline problem in my day. I at least had established my reputation in the school and community as one who would maintain some kind of order. In the meantime, I lectured the mother about getting home as soon as she could and leaving the children to us.

I am amused at myself looking back on this particular incident. I did not think of it at the time, but it impresses me now that this was the last action I would have chosen to begin a teaching career. But it was done, and I had to live with it.

I was pleased with my two classes. I had some very attractive children, and they seemed to know how to study and expected to work. Textbooks had been bought by the teachers of the year before and, in my classes at least, were good selections. I had a tentative schedule worked out, and it proved to be adequate for our needs as the state course of study would not allow a lot of choices for the seventh grade. The high school classes had to be fitted in. One of my pupils, Ernest, the younger Nelson boy, proved to have a slight stammer. His mother talked to me about it and made some suggestions that she had learned from her own experience with him. I approached that problem rather slowly and for the first several weeks never called upon him to say anything that called for more than a one word response which he usually managed without any trouble. I was more pleased with my work with him than anyone else, as by the middle of the year he was able to stand in front of the other students and their parents and recite without a quaver from the poetry he had learned in his English class.

Our main problem was domestic and the two women teachers had to work out some arrangements about meals. We had already arranged for one of the families to send milk and eggs on a regular schedule for our use but the problem of going into Antler for other groceries was not easy, especially when my car ceased being dependable. Our first real problem climaxed at the end of the first week. The primary teacher, the one with experience, could not stand the prospect of spending a winter out there on the lonely prairie a mile from the nearest neighbor. The first Friday night after school was dismissed and the children had all gone home, I was doing some janitorial work around the school building when the intermediate teacher came over to tell me that the primary teacher had packed her suitcase and was walking down the road toward town. I got into the car and drove after her and talked her into coming back to the teacherage for the night. I agreed that I would take her to town in time to catch the train in the morning. I immediately called my board president and told him what had happened. He had had experience and was not too disturbed. He said, "I will call the Minot Normal School." He was sure that a teacher would be found, and he was right. On Sunday night we had a teacher who, while she lived in the eastern part of the state, had close relatives living in Sherwood, one of the towns nearby, and they brought her to the teacherage on Sunday afternoon.

The next surprise after losing the primary teacher was the sudden appearance in Antler of an elderly woman who had been sent by my mother to keep house for us. I did not know the woman although I knew her family well. I suspect my fellow teachers got some amusement from the fact my mother had sent her without asking me if we wanted her. Anyway we installed her in the teacherage and she proceeded to cook our meals and keep the house neat. It was quite obvious she considered me as head of the household and did not consult the women very often or defer much to them. But it relieved them of household chores and they were glad to have her. The salary she specified was not burdensome.

Another thing I did in preparation for winter was to enroll in two correspondence courses with the University of North Dakota that would earn some credit for me as well as keep me busy in the evenings. One was in Beginning Spanish which was a foolish thing to take by correspondence and, before I was half through, several of my lessons had been lost in the extension machinery and I did not feel like sending in more until I had the others corrected. The other was a good course in magazine writing, ideal for a correspondence course, and I learned a great deal from it without doing very well. Professor Adams, who taught the course, was a straight-armed critic who showed me many faults in my writing.

The main incident I remember in the early part of the winter was the District Teachers Association meeting in Minot for which school was dismissed, and we were expected to attend. I cannot remember much about attendance as I made an appointment with Dr. McConnell there to have my eyes tested, and he prescribed glasses for me which I secured. That took up some of my time. Also Ruth was there attending from Grilley School in McHenry County. She was having a bad year and on her doctor's advice was having her tonsils removed. The doctor removed the tonsils in his office. I am afraid it greatly aggravated the throat condition she had been suffering from. At least she spent her time in that office trying to recover from the operation with the assistance of one of her fellow teachers.

All of us from that area left on a late afternoon train on Saturday to catch the branch line out of Granville. Ruth was with us and looking anything but well. I introduced her to my two teachers but that was the extent of our socializing. I was worried when she left the train at Deering. She later wrote me she did not get to school for a week, because her mother kept her in bed until that throat had improved. We were met at Mohall by one of our patrons and taken to Sherman that evening.

The rather short time between the District Teachers Association meeting and the Christmas vacation was a very busy time, and the fact that my car was out of commission did not help the situation. Repeated repairs seemed to be ineffective, and I decided to store it in a metal building nearby which the owner rented to me for very little. While preparing to leave for the holidays, our housekeeper told me she did not plan to return. I realize now that it was very lonesome for her as the women teachers were not too friendly and did not put themselves out to make her feel welcome. I suspect I did not do as much as I could have either. Anyway we made arrangements for one of our local people to take her and the primary teacher to Antler early the Saturday morning to catch the Rugby branch line.

The brother of the intermediate teacher, who was about my age, came over the evening before to get her and me to take us to their farm. From there I could easily get to the railroad at Lorraine and catch the afternoon train to Granville which in turn connected with Minot. From there I could get a Soo Line train to Velva to spend Christmas with the family. The brother and his father had decided that the weather was too cold to risk the Hudson car they owned, so he brought a team and buggy as there was little snow on the ground. Saturday morning it was below zero with a strong northwest wind which we had to face on the way to the farm. I cannot recall ever being any colder in my life. I drove occasionally to relieve him from facing the wind. It was a rough trip and a heating stove was mighty welcome when we reached the farm. We drove in a sleigh to town and I caught my train and got to Minot but had three or four hours to wait for the train to Velva. I was still chilled to the bone although I had a good warm dinner and then went over to the high school to see a basketball game. I recall meeting J. H. Colton, my old Sunday School teacher and school superintendent who was the principal of the high school at Minot, and had a short visit with him. I watched the game for most of the time but I began to get chills from the cold I had experienced that day. I could not get warmed up in the gymnasium so I went to the Soo Railroad Station where it was warmer, having a cup of coffee or two before the train came in. I got to Velva about 4 o'clock in the morning and walked to the house Dad had rented where Mother had a room prepared for me. I finally got to bed and got warmed. Fortunately, there were no after-effects of the cold after that day.

After a pleasant, if unexciting holiday, I returned by way of Sherwood, spending Saturday night in the hotel. Sunday the uncle and aunt of the primary teacher picked me up and with her drove out to the school in their car, a pleasant change from the trip in before Christmas as the weather was at least moderate.

In our renewal of our housekeeping arrangements after Christmas, there was some disagreeableness that grew out of the fact that the one teacher had a feeling that without our housekeeper most of the cooking would depend on her. But we finally settled into the routine of living more as we had the few weeks before the housekeeper came. Fortunately our winter was rather mild and we had no serious problems.

Looking forward to my summer I was decoyed by an offer from a school supply company to canvass both Bottineau and McHenry Counties and attempt to sell their line of everything from furnaces and playground equipment to textbooks, although no emphasis was placed on the latter. I had finally arranged for a garage in Mohall to repair the car. I had to have it hauled to town one Saturday, and my garageman worked until late at night getting it all shipshape. I have to give him credit. He did it where others had failed before him, and I was able to drive back to the school. For the next few months we had transportation of our own. After this I went to a meeting in Fargo of the salesmen for the Northern Supply Company, I think it was called, and spent a weekend at that meeting. I confess I did not have too much confidence that I would have great success, and unfortunately I was correct.

We had our school exercises according to the calendar. My high school students without exception made their credits by passing the state examinations, and the seventh graders were all moved on to the eighth grade. The plan was that there would be no high school the following year. But two years from then when the present seventh graders were ready, high school would be resumed.

After the other teachers left, I stayed in the teacherage for about a week, made some trips to neighboring school districts talking with rural boards who were farmers busy on their farming activities and all disclaimed any intention of making any purchases. The rest of the county did not prove any better, and the orders I took were about enough to pay my gasoline bill. So I soon retreated to McHenry County where I could stay at home. But here again my career as an itinerant salesman was a complete flop, and I soon gave it up as a bad deal. My father's work as administrator of this estate was about over and he was planning to campaign for election as county probate judge again. With this in mind, I rented space in a small garage and tried to put the car in first-rate shape so he would have it to use. I did a complete overhaul myself under the supervision of my garageman, ground the valves, and replaced many of the bearings in the crankshaft and really left it in the best shape it had been in since Dad had owned it.

I had time before the University of North Dakota opened where I had definite plans to attend, and I took a job on a threshing crew north of Velva. It was a poor season as it was rainy, and we did not average over two days' work a week. I finally quit and decided to go to the university a few days early and see if I could find some kind of a job. Someone drove me in the car to the Great Northern at Granville, and I caught the train to Grand Forks. A Velva boy had asked me to room with him as he had a rented room on the streetcar line toward town about a mile from the university. It was not a good location because you had to go on downtown or to the campus to eat which meant another streetcar ride.

I registered in a program which aimed at meeting the arts college requirements and also those for a teacher's certificate with a major in history and political science. Most of the Towner boys were in a particular fraternity, and they made an effort to get me to join it, but I knew that inexpensive as it seemed, it was too much for my pocketbook.

Chapter 8

A. B. University of North Dakota

I went through the Job Placement Service at the university without coming up with anything that was useful. The university student jobs seemed to be filled, and those listed from downtown had been assigned by the time I got down to inquire about them. One of my fellow high school graduates, Clifford Wilson, had found a job with a grocery store for a certain number of hours a week and I tried that angle, particularly I solicited the J. C. Penney Store. But these efforts were all unproductive and I grew fairly discouraged. The only jobs that I could find were selling jobs by canvassing, and I had no optimism on making any money in that way.

In the meantime my living arrangements were not too satisfactory although my roommate was a likeable person. I discovered Pete Berget had a room a few blocks from us and he was likewise dissatisfied with his arrangements. The location between town and university was inconvenient. I had known Pete for a long time and although he was older than I was we knew each other's families very well. In fact, his oldest sister was married to my cousin, Arthur, and his sister, Hazel, had been a classmate of mine.

After talking over our problem of location, we finally located a room downtown directly on the streetcar line, and we gave up our current rooms and moved down there. Pete was also looking for a job, and he got a temporary one at a restaurant waiting tables but it did not last very long. The other people rooming at the house were not university-connected although the husband of the woman who ran the house worked in the power plant at the university. This location was more satisfactory in the fact that one streetcar ride each way took care of our day's transportation unless, as often happened in the good weather of the fall and spring, I walked home after my classes were over.

The academic program I had was entirely satisfactory and I had a very good selection of teachers. My Beginning German in which both Pete and I were enrolled was taught by W. G. Bek who was more of a historian than a language scholar, but he was an excellent teacher and became a most delightful friend. I was in Clarence Perkins' European History course and while not a great teacher he was an interesting one and was very helpful to me by giving me jobs grading papers from time to time. I had originally signed up in a Survey of English Literature course but I dropped it for a course in philosophy with Dean Joseph Kennedy, who I found was a magnificent teacher.

Another course was in political science with a young man, Claudius Johnson, who had not finished his Ph.D. at the University of Chicago but was in the process of completing the thesis. He was not much older than I was, and through him I became acquainted with several of the younger faculty members.

I do not recall the sequence of all my courses, although I remember switching to American History the second semester, taught by O. G. Libby with whom I eventually wrote my masters thesis. He was an excellent scholar, generally unappreciated by students. I still kept close contact with Perkins and toward the end of the year, I, with some advice from him, asked to be examined in English History in which I had never had a course. We had Cheyney's standard textbook at home, and I knew it rather thoroughly. Perkins advised me to get some acquaintance with a couple of other texts that he recommended, which I did, and took that examination. I secured credit in the subject by that process which was not common but was used.

I was helped too by the fact that our neighbor at Towner, Horace Bagley, was a subscriber to the weekly *Manchester Guardian* which he was in the habit of passing on to me, and during my year in college he mailed it to me. Reading these regularly gave me a British orientation that was most helpful in understanding its history.

As I learned more about the university and became better acquainted with its library, I realized that if I was going to get any kind of job around the institution my best prospect, and one that I anticipated enjoying, was in the library itself. Consequently, the second semester I signed up for a course in library methods taught by the librarian. I thought that it would be an entry into one of the student jobs in the library.

As far as I was concerned, there was only one social event the entire year, except that I went home at Christmas. That was on Thanksgiving Day and the group from Towner High School pooled their food that had been sent from home for the occasion and we had a feast, ill balanced but very good food. Grand Forks had an early snow that fall and there was a foot of it on the ground at Thanksgiving. We all went to a movie, plowing through the snow that afternoon. I do not remember what it was even though it was the only one I saw that year.

Toward spring Pete, technically a freshman student, had a chance to get into Budge Hall, the only men's dormitory. As the cost would be less than we were paying, and it would give him a right to a place the following years, he took it. I had some difficulty with our landlady because she insisted I pay the entire room rent, but I objected so vigorously that she finally allowed me to finish out the academic year on my old rent.

Pete's living in Budge Hall was a great asset to me in one way. At that time books of tickets were issued to the dormitory residents for their meals at the University Commons which were far superior to what we could buy reasonably at downtown restaurants. There were residents of the dormitory who never ate breakfasts, and Pete and I had already been able to buy breakfast tickets at some price such as 10 cents a meal throughout the entire year. Now that Pete had a location in Budge he had a standing offer for me to anyone who was not going to use his dinner ticket. He would pay 25 cents for it, and I began to eat most of my meals at the Commons. This was especially useful the next year.

One of my courses that I have not mentioned was the Army ROTC. I frankly enjoyed this and became a friend of the master sergeant in charge of most of the detail of the unit. We were required to take ROTC while we were freshmen and sophomores but this was the only year required of me as I was already a sophomore. Two years more would have given me a commission. I was not tempted by this as I planned to finish in one more year and a summer session. I confess I wore the uniform a great deal in spite of the wrapped leggings. It was quite a trick to learn to wrap them neatly but once one learned the system, it was not difficult. I was not very well supplied with clothes and on the drill days I wore the uniform all day. Which reminds me of a visit from brother Earl. I cannot remember the particular reason but Earl was returning from a trip to Chicago. While in Chicago he had been induced by our sister Martha to buy himself a new suit of clothes. She had helped him pick it out and when he came by, he was carrying it with him but seemed to dislike it everytime he saw it. He finally said before he left he was going to give it to me, and to that I gave no objection because I did not have a good suit nor anything approaching it. But I did not like the suit either. It was a sort of a greenish color that certainly was not very attractive to most men. This was while Pete was still rooming with me and Pete liked it and wore it on several occasions when he wanted to dress up. I do not believe that I wore it until the next year. I never told Martha that Earl gave it to me.

I had made up my mind to go to the summer session at the university, as I was most anxious to make up the year I had lost. I took advantage of my acquaintance with the librarian who had been my teacher and managed to secure a part-time job in the library. The compensation was 25 cents an hour and I held that job all through the following year. In fact, I found it most interesting because I ran into a lot of books that looked interesting, and I read them. My enthusiasm was greatest for the works of George B. Shaw, and I read everything of his we had in the library. The same was true with the periodicals, and I worked in every part of the library except cataloging during that year and summer that I held that part-time student job. I tried to work about 25 hours a week which would pay for my board. I was very short of money. I had left my old car at Velva and Dad made good use of it during his campaign and was back in the courthouse in Towner on January 1. Brother Donald had kept the car in Velva until he finished his high school semester. When driving back to Towner, he was stopped by a blizzard. He put the car in a garage twelve miles from Towner, and finished his trip by train. In the spring I sold my car to the garageman who was storing it. He paid me $100 which was probably all it was worth, and I had to have the money.

I succeeded in getting a room in Budge Hall for the summer session, which was an advantage but it gave me no rights to continue there the next year. The summer session proved interesting as it was made up of older students, most of whom were active school teachers and a few of whom I knew. When the summer session ended in August, I went back to Towner and found jobs to replenish my capital as much as possible for the coming year.

When I returned to Grand Forks in the fall of 1923, I looked for housing closer to the campus now that Pete could get me tickets for my main meals at the Commons. But I found nothing I liked, and finally rented a single room in an old house a few doors from the streetcar line and only about a block from where Pete and I had lived the year before. There was one large double room that two students had rented who proved to be a nuisance to me. But my room though small was quite adequate for my needs as I spent all day on campus, either working or studying in the library or going to classes.

My classes were little different from the year before although I was taking more professional education. C. C. Schmit, a quite interesting man, was my main teacher and was a good one. I learned many things about good teaching by watching him perform. I also was registered in Practice Teaching at the University High School as that was a requirement. A Mr. Kazda, a large, heavy sort of a jolly fellow, picked on me because he knew I had had some experience to start on and after a week he retired me to the role of critic because he could see I knew how to handle a class.

One of the new courses my senior year was a course in geography that I had sold the dean on letting me substitute for one of my science requirements as I had one unsatisfied. It was a 10-hour course running through both semesters with a tremendous amount of good things to read, and I particularly read what I could find on the relation of history and geography. Much of it was translated from German which seemed to have been where the greatest interest was developed. I did not rate the class very highly as an experience except for the reading. The students all had quite different backgrounds than mine and the teacher, a Dr. Simpson, while greatly interested in the angle that I selected, was not himself well informed.

I had more history, mainly Constitutional History, with Libby as well as his Contemporary American, and a beginning course in metaphysics with Kennedy. I took the only course that was open to me in German as Bek had become assistant dean of arts. It was in German Conversation where we had a small group, most of whom actually spoke German at home, and I was hard put to keep up with them.

I was also in Introduction to Psychology by a teacher named Humpstone who to me was something of a fraud. Most of what I learned about psychology was from textbooks like Warren's that I found in the library. I had more work with Johnson, and the second semester I had a course with George R. Davies in sociology. I got to know Davies and liked him very much. He had a curious way of teaching. He was really interested in statistics and his assignments were never to be written or discussed but they were to be worked statistically illustrating sociological principles.

I did not get acquainted with the great sociologist John M. Gillett, the "Father of Rural Sociology," until the next semester. He was a very knowledgable teacher and was a good one but had a mean streak in him that would occasionally show in his treatment of a student who was unprepared. I had anthropology with him and found it very interesting.

The only correspondence I had during these years like the year at Sherman School outside of Ruth and the family was with Otis Lee. Fargo College had closed at the end of 1922 and Otis with many of the other students had gone to the University of Minnesota where he was majoring in psychology and philosophy and keeping up his violin playing. He was a steady correspondent and a most interesting one. The big event of the year for me in 1923–24 was when Otis came to Grand Forks to be interviewed for a Rhodes Scholarship that he had applied for from North Dakota. To my delight he got it, and we celebrated the occasion as best we could. One thing I recall was his looking at the textbook Kennedy had assigned us for metaphysics and saying, "Do you use that in the beginning course?" When I answered in the affirmative, he said, "It is our senior course textbook and I find it very difficult." I told him I was finding it plenty difficult too and without Kennedy's help, there was little in it I would understand.

Another connection I had with Fargo College, however, was in 1922–23 when I arrived at the university and found Vowels, my former dean at Fargo, was the Assistant to the President of the University, a temporary appointment. I had some good visits with him, and I was invited over to dinner at his home. He did not return the second year, and I lost track of him.

The only non-traditional enterprise I engaged in that year was for reasons that I cannot recall now. I signed up to take part in an oratorical contest. I had been on the debate team at Fargo College but I am not too sure that I had a clear comprehension of what an oration was. A most interesting part of it was the ratings of the judges. There were five of these including the speech professor, a couple of faculty members from the law school, and two others. For some reason the student paper published how each judge rated the speakers. I rated one first and two lasts and I do not recall where the other two were but I took some satisfaction in the fact that the speech teacher who did not know me was the one who rated me first. As the topics were mainly political issues I suppose that had a great deal to do with actual judging of most of the judges.

I was carrying the maximum load so I could complete my A.B. degree in the four years including the one I had spent in Sherman School. The correspondence course, the examination in English History, plus the summer session before had given me enough credits to meet the requirements. I had been registered with the Teacher Placement Bureau since we were in the second semester and had recommendations on file for a high school history teaching job. But no inquiries came my way and by spring I had decided I would go on and try to get a masters degree. Schmit had talked to me against taking a high school job. He kept pointing out that I had a special interest in history and government, and I ought to go ahead and specialize in those. "I frankly think you will do better," he said on several occasions. Bek and Perkins also kept urging me in this direction, and I saw quite a lot of the latter in spite of the fact I was not taking more of his courses. Instead I was completing my major with American history. I planned to start the graduate work in the summer of '24 in summer session again and made arrangements to move to Budge. As for commencement, I spent my funds on a ticket home, visited the family and went up to Deering and visited Ruth. I came back to start the summer session and to receive a fatherly lecture from Dean Squires for missing commencement.

When I made up my mind to spend the summer in graduate work, I confess I might not have done it if I had had a good high school job. But not having that I began to look for something to do the following year, and the idea of staying in Grand Forks appealed to me as I could push along my masters work. Through Phi Delta Kappa, a national organization for education students, I had met Superintendent Hays of East Grand Forks. I thought there might be a possibility there so one Sunday afternoon I went over to his house where he was in the back yard clearing up the debris of the early spring. I went back and talked with him. I told him what I wanted. We talked at some length about it, and he finally said he would have to study the problem but "Maybe I will have something for you." A short time later I received a contract from him to teach civics, algebra, and problems of democracy, as the senior social science course was called, in the East Grand Forks High School at a salary of $1,500. I signed it happily with the feeling that next year was taken care of. How much graduate work I could do evenings and Saturdays I did not know, but it proved to be substantial.

Chapter 9

High School Teaching and Graduate School

Grand Forks, North Dakota, and East Grand Forks, Minnesota, were divided by the Red River. I had expected in my year at East Grand Forks to continue to live in Grand Forks with the convenient street car transportation to the university, but I found my school board had a rule against their teachers living out of the state in order to prevent this sort of thing. I found a very comfortable single room at the home of a widow in a good part of town where two other teachers occupied a double room. Mrs. Newhouse was not used to keeping roomers, had had no children of her own and tried to mother us all. The two fellow teachers were companionable and one of them, a teacher of commercial subjects, was particularly friendly and helpful. It was Mrs. Newhouse's pleasure and ours too that the three of us always referred to her as Ma Newhouse.

The work at school proved very interesting and not difficult. I had two sections of freshman civics, which in the second semester turned into a course in occupations. This gave me an opportunity to give youngsters some help in taking thought about their vocational future, and I was pleased that I was able to induce many of them to take jobs the next summer in a field in which they might want to spend their career. Had I stayed with the school I was sure that I could have developed it into a very useful course. I had two sections of beginning algebra which I found after my previous experience at Sherman School and at Fargo College was a very easy course to teach. I thought I had fine success with my students as several of them confessed to me that they were previous failures in the course.

The one group of seniors in the Problems of Democracy was the most interesting of all, as we followed the Minnesota course of study and a textbook that tried to concentrate on the major problems of the country and to present objectively the various strengths and weaknesses of the alternative solutions. The only disagreeable part of the work at the high school was supervising study hall once a day. The study halls were made up of students from various classes and various subjects, and while dealing with their academic problems was not at all difficult, keeping their concentration on their high school work was. I will admit it tried my patience to the limit.

There was one matter outside of this work that was later to give me a great deal of concern. Ruth was not teaching but, with the money she had saved from the three years she had taught, she had gone to the Valley City Teachers College for the year. There she became ill largely from the back problem she had inherited from the old sleigh ride party, and finally was referred to a doctor in Fargo who had put her in a cast from the hips up in order to correct a deformity he saw developing where she had had a crushed vertebrae. This sent her home where she was spending what I am sure must have been a dull fall and winter until after early spring when that doctor removed the cast.

In the meantime I was taking some Saturday morning classes at the university, all in education, and working evenings on a masters thesis on a topic that I had worked out with Libby the summer before. Libby had pioneered a study of geographical influence on American political history in his own doctoral thesis at Wisconsin on the geographical distribution of the vote on the Federal Constitution which I had found very interesting and had talked to him about at length. I was taken by the methodology and influenced no doubt by the geography I was reading and I proposed to him that I do a thesis on the geographical vote on the minority agrarian parties after the Civil War. This became my topic and I did almost all my work in the Congressional Record at the university library. It was a subject on which I could work whenever I had spare time, and as an old employee of the library I had a free run of the building.

I had a graduate education course Saturday morning with Schmit, in which Superintendent Hays was also enrolled, and one with Humpstone in educational psychology that was not very satisfactory. In spite of this, I think that my main interest that fall was the Presidential campaign of 1924 when I would cast my first vote. In North Dakota the contest was entirely between President Coolidge and Robert M. LaFollette. The Democratic candidate Davis had little support and there was very little campaigning for him. I was embarrassed on one occasion when I went to a meeting of the students supporting the progressive "LaFollette ticket." Some of them insisted on electing me chairman. I protested that I was not a regular student but a full-time employee in the East Grand Forks High School. They paid little attention and elected me anyway, but I resigned by letter immediately and they elected a young man who was appropriate for their purposes. In the meantime, my election had got into the newspaper and caused me some embarrassment in my high school.

After I had registered for the second semester it was clear I would have an easy time finishing my masters in the summer session if the thesis made progress, and I was making progress on it. Living in Grand Forks on a salary I found was quite relaxing after my two years of hand-to-mouth living. I replenished my wardrobe, paid off the few loans I had made my senior year and I stopped burdening my mother with my laundry.

I had one course in sociology to finish up for the summer. When Libby asked me if I would teach the Survey of American History and I agreed to do it, the only instruction he gave me was "try to get though the Civil War." It seemed to be a general practice not to try to do much in the survey courses for the recent several decades. I followed the tradition of the department.

With some assured income for the summer, I felt more free than I had with my funds and invested in a diamond for which Ruth had waited a long time. She was not out of the woods with her difficulties although the cast seemed to give her comfort and helped her gain her strength back. She went back to Fargo to have the cast removed and more x-rays and I succeeded in getting some time off including a weekend and stayed with her at the Gardner Hotel. I thought I had a very bad cold at the time but I realize now it was one of the first attacks of hay fever that was to bother me the rest of my life. Not knowing what to do for it, I had a rather rough time myself trying to make sure Ruth did not catch the cold. Ruth's doctor pronounced her well and she came back with me to Grand Forks. In fact, Ma Newhouse insisted I bring her back with me as she had room to put her up and wanted to do the motherly thing. Ruth was not there more than two days before she became sick and Ma Newhouse called her doctor who was one of Grand Forks' best, and he pronounced she had appendicitis and should have surgery. This was hard for us to believe but she communicated with her parents and left by train for Towner to be under the care of our family physician. Dr. Craise was a Canadian doctor who had a special interest in appendicitis. She was operated on at the Lutheran Hospital at Rugby and recovered normally.

My problem now was that I still did not have a job for next year, and Ruth and I wanted to get married, which would be impossible without a job. I hounded the placement bureau at the university and talked to various of my university professors. The only sort of help I got was an offer for a late five weeks summer session position at the State Teachers College at Mayville. With it there was a promise that there might be an opening for the following year in history and social science. The president, C. C. Swain, whom I had never met, was going through on the train one afternoon and asked me to meet him at the station, which I did. We talked only about 10 minutes. I took the summer session job but he said that he would like to hold up on the other until after I was on the campus.

He went into great detail about how their students were mostly young girls and they often had trouble with unmarried men teachers. "President Swain," I said, "if I get that job, I'll be married before the college opens in the fall." He looked at me intently and said, "You're sure of that?"

The five-weeks session at Mayville was settled and I turned in the grades in my course at the university and went through my oral examination both on the thesis and on a research paper I had written for Gillette and Davies on the sources of the political strengths of the Non-Partisan League in North Dakota geographically. Again I missed commencement. Everything went fine, and I arrived at Mayville on an evening train putting up at a very poor small town hotel. I still recall that at the theatre across the street there was a one-man band playing for a dance. It was impossible to sleep until it was over as I could not shut the window because of the heat. The next day I found a room in a private home and started my classes which consisted of part high school and part college work.

I had been at Mayville only two days when Swain called me in and handed me a contract made out for the following year at $1,800. I did not tell Ruth we were to have a "shot gun" marriage, and I did not realize at the time that the $1,800 covered the 11 weeks summer session as well as the regular year so it was no increase whatever over my East Grand Forks High School salary. But the job was different and that was what interested me.

There was very little time between the close of the summer session and the opening of the fall term. I had talked this over with Ruth and we had agreed that we would cut out all the formalities and get married, if necessary, on a weekend. So I wrote her and suggested Friday night, August 14, as a time and Fargo as a place. She could get there during the day, and I could get there after my Friday classes. She immediately agreed, and I called Reverend Beard at the Congregational Church at Fargo and asked him if he could marry us on the evening of the 14th and got an affirmative answer immediately saying he remembered me, but I always had my doubts that he did.

I wrote my parents telling them our plans and asked my father to make out a marriage license for Ruth to pick up as she came through Towner. She spent a night with my parents, and my seven-year old sister Susan begged to be allowed to go with her and be present at the wedding. Since my sister Evelyn who was attending the State Teachers College at nearby Valley City was planning to attend the wedding, Susan could return to Valley City with her after the ceremony. So it was settled, Ruth and Susan met Evelyn at the Gardner Hotel where I had reserved a room, and the three of them met me when I arrived on the evening train. After leaving my bag at the hotel, we went out to Reverend Beard's. He gave us a little sermon, and then with Evelyn serving as Ruth's attendant and Susan as mine we were married. Susan held my hand all through the ceremony and with Evelyn witnessed the certificate afterward.

While on the way back to the hotel in a taxi, seven-year-old Susan raised the question, "Well, when does the honeymoon begin?" The real end of the ceremony occurred the next morning. Ruth and I came down to breakfast at the Gardner. As we came in, I noticed Reverend Beard was having breakfast there, and was sitting over on one side of the dining room. I steered Ruth to the other side hoping to avoid his observation. But we had just started to eat our breakfast when he spotted us and called out in a loud voice, "Oh, Mr. Ellis, you forgot your marriage certificate last night. When I left home this morning, I tied it to the doorknob. Go out and get it anytime today." Of course everybody in the dining room was amused excepting the Ellises.

We stayed in Fargo until Monday morning when we took the early train back to Mayville to meet my morning class. For the next few weeks Ruth and I were occupying my room and eating our meals in the very poor restaurants that Mayville provided.

Finding a suitable place to live was difficult, as it was very soon before the fall opening of the college, and the small community had few apartment facilities. The best we could find for that first year was a small apartment of three rooms, located on the main street over a barber shop, and heated by a large, hard coal base burner. The purchase of the necessary furniture exhausted our combined cash assets, which made family gifts much appreciated.

We had a pleasant surprise toward the end of that short summer session. One evening while we were eating dinner at the restaurant, in walked the A. C. Bergs. He was one of my old scout leaders, and they were well known to both of us. They sat down with us and, to our surprise, told us that A. C. had taken a job with the college and they were delighted that we were going to be there also. They had been living in Bismarck where A. C. had been working in the State Department of Education. His job in the college concerned the rural education program. They were unquestionably our closest friends during our years in Mayville.

Chapter 10

College Teaching

Neither Ruth nor I had been in Mayville before I began my teaching there. It was a small place although larger than Towner. Its population was overwhelmingly Norwegian, and when downtown one had the feeling he heard Norwegian spoken as much as English. It was different on the campus. Many of the students and faculty as well as the business and professional people downtown were of Norwegian ancestry, in fact, first generation immigrants. The college had recently been upgraded from a normal school to a teachers college so that it could offer bachelor degrees, but it was small and it had a small faculty. There were three of us in the social sciences, Hewitt Vinnedge, who became a close friend, was the other history and government teacher, and Carl Birkelo taught the economics and sociology. Vinnedge who taught the European History courses also taught the American Government, so I inherited the American History and the European Government. I also had a course in the teaching of the social studies and supervised some practice teaching which was done in the local public school. There were two people in education with whom I worked. One was H. D. Welte, later the long-time president of Connecticut Teachers College, and the other was Delbert Jeep. Both Jeep and Welte came from the University of Iowa.

The character of the population was probably pretty well represented by the churches of the community. While there were five churches, three of them were varieties of Norwegian Lutheran. The Catholic Church was a small beautiful structure which did not have a resident priest and held service only about once a month. I always suspected this was maintained only because of the students at the college. The other church was the Congregational Church which had several things of interest about it. One was that many of its members were also of Norwegian background, and the minister, an Armenian, was a very interesting person who went by the name of West, which had been his first wife's name. He had taken it in place of his own Armenian name that presented Americans with some difficulty. He had two boys by his first wife that were now grown, one of whom wrote at least two novels that did not attract much interest and was principal of a school in Los Angeles. The other one was an artist who did etchings under the name Lavonne West which was his baptismal name.

He later turned to photography in which he made a much larger reputation. For his photography he took the name, Ivan Dimitri, which I suspect was his father's name. Reverend West had a third child with his second wife. She was a young girl who was a student at the college and was in one of my classes. We were regular attendants at the church. We found West's sermons very interesting, partly because of his interesting background and partly because he had a curiously oriental approach to the validity of religion, in which he often wound up a sermon with the thought that whether Christianity was the true religion or not, there was enough evidence for it that you better play it safe for the sake of your life after death. This Congregational Church attracted most of the non-Lutheran churchgoers in the community as there were very few Catholic residents except for faculty and students at the college.

Still I have to rate that first year at Mayville as the worst year of our experience because of Ruth's illness. Things went swimmingly for us for a month or more until Ruth became pregnant and was miserably sick with pernicious vomiting. We had what proved to be a very poor doctor who tried to help Ruth by giving her injections of some hormone that was currently popular, but it did not relieve her at all. To add to that problem, Ruth's brother, Robert, was injured by a horse and our word from home was he could not live. Ruth went home immediately and this did not help her condition at all. It was impossible for me to go to Robert's funeral, officially because of my work, but actually because I was completely broke until my next salary check, and I had not yet set up any banking connections. Ruth was too ill to return to Mayville. She went to Towner and stayed with my parents to be close to her doctor. She grew rapidly worse and I left early at Christmas to be with her. A few days after Christmas Dr. Craise wanted her hospitalized. We took her to Rugby where he had the help of a second physician who maintained his practice out of Rugby. I stayed in Rugby sometimes going home over night with Dr. Craise, and my mother came up with Dr. Craise several times to be with us. The doctors decided that the only hope for Ruth was to terminate the pregnancy. Although it was too late for an easy abortion, it was done. But she did not get better. She began to have hemorrhages in her intestinal tract for reasons I never understood and was fed entirely intravenously for quite a while. They would feed her and a few hours later she would have a hemorrhage. This problem did not seem to be resolved readily. One day I had gone down to the hotel to get some lunch as there were no facilities for the public at the hospital. Craise and his collaborator had a conference on Ruth's condition after which he came down to the hotel to tell me that he did not have much hope that Ruth would live.

I hurried back the three-fourths of a mile to the hospital and saw that the medical staff had been told, as Ruth's room was filled with nurses singing Lutheran hymns. Mother was there singing with them. I sat down by Ruth's bed and tried to calm her as she was extremely nervous from the hemorrhage that morning or the singing or both. They stopped in a short time, and Mother and I did what we could to calm Ruth. And she did calm down and when I left that evening she was asleep. Mother went back home with Dr. Craise telling me she would call Ruth's parents.

Fortunately Ruth was better in the morning and had no hemorrhage that day. Her parents came and found her better than they expected, and the M.D.s grew more optimistic. A day or two later Craise told me that he thought she was out of danger and after waiting a few days, I returned to Mayville to resume my teaching.

Ruth soon moved from the hospital to my parents' home at Towner and later on to the farm. Berg told me at Easter time that they were driving up to Towner to visit old friends and if Ruth was well enough to come back, they could bring her. I went to Towner and she joined me there and we left Towner with the Bergs one afternoon and drove to Devils Lake where we stayed overnight in the principal hotel. Our room was on the second floor and as there was no elevator, I had to carry Ruth upstairs which indicates how slow she was in coming back. The next morning we got to Mayville and everything was satisfactory even if Ruth was still greatly handicapped.

In spite of these interruptions I had done pretty well with my teaching and Swain had given me a raise during the year. So academically I suppose it could have been called a plus year. However, Ruth was far from strong and during the summer we had a Broadway play put on in the city park by the regular Chautauqua program which we went to see. We sat near the edge of the tent fortunately as she passed out during the performance. I carried her outside and an obliging young fellow offered us a ride. So after carrying Ruth to the car we drove to our apartment and as she was still "out" I carried her upstairs. An amusing sidelight to this was that the next morning she felt fine and was full of energy and no problems. But I was so worn out with carrying her in the park and up the stairs that all my joints were stiff and I could hardly get around that day.

In the meantime the problems of finances were really serious. I had borrowed money from my father to pay the hospital bill, and I paid off Dr. Craise in installments before I paid my father. The summer session ended our first year at Mayville and our first year of married life.

Life at Mayville was much less hectic after Ruth regained her health. We moved into better quarters, an upstairs apartment which was quite satisfactory except for one thing. It had no private entrance. I also remember the bathroom had the oldest type bathtub I had ever seen. It was a wooden frame with a zinc lining heavily coated with paint. We lived there our second year, but for the summer session the Bergs had called our attention to the house next door to them. It was for rent during the summer, as the owners had moved to their farm. It was a new house, well-built and well-equipped, which helped tremendously. Then the third year we moved to the second floor of the Birkelos' home which had a private entrance. The Birkelos were very nice people and we enjoyed them very much, especially the two children. I felt like a neglected minority because all four of the Birkelos had red hair, brighter red than Ruth's, and I was the only one without red hair living there. Little Buddy, the younger of the two children, was a special delight to us, and he was continually bringing Ruth books to read to him. She lost her reputation as a magician one day when Buddy brought a book and presented it to her to read to him. "Why Buddy," she said, "I can't read this. It is Norwegian." He asked with astonishment, "Can't you read Norwegian?" She replied negatively, and he shook his head and said, "Even *Minerva* can read Norwegian." Minerva was his seven-year-old sister.

My teaching assignment changed but little. I introduced a course in American Constitutional History for advanced students, and as the normal school had become a college and had not yet graduated degree candidates, we needed courses for upper classmen. I taught it out of a casebook and lectured in between cases which I found an interesting method of teaching that I had never before experienced. My own understanding of American Constitutional History certainly increased.

Part of my time at the college was taken up with committee work as President Swain had made me chairman of the Curriculum Committee. There were a great many changes needed in the curriculum with the new status for the school, and Swain told me he wanted changes made. The older members of the faculty were very reluctant to make any changes. We broke the ice in a few places but not many.

I suppose the most aggravating committee assignment was membership on the Chapel Committee. Although a state school Mayville had daily chapel in which the students and faculty all assembled. Sometimes we had a local or outside speaker and sometimes chapel consisted merely of an announcement or two and a biblical responsive reading with which our songbook was equipped. Swain put me on the committee saying that it was an easy assignment because he knew the Curriculum Committee was going to be difficult. He said he always took care of chapel when he was home and when he was not, A. C. Berg liked to do it. As it happened, my friend A. C. was ill that year and went through a very serious operation. He was not able to attend his classes for virtually the entire year. It seemed to me Swain was absent nearly every day at that hour so

I found myself burdened with that duty, somewhat, I might add, to the delight of some of my friends on the faculty.

During these two years the State Department of Education decided we needed a new course of study. Bertha Palmer, the State Superintendent, asked me to serve on the social studies course of study committee for the grades, which I did with the help of a committee of faculty members in other state teachers colleges. Out of this grew a course on the state which I constructed myself, trying to get around having separate courses in state history, civics, and geography. We put them together into one course we called "Our State" and tried to take advantage of the interrelationships as much as possible. Afterwards I got the idea that it might be useful to teachers to make a workbook, which was a series of lesson sheets to be placed in the hands of the pupils, which would follow the organization of the course of study and assist the teacher in her work. I invited Welte who was on the general course of study committee to assist me, and we turned this out quite quickly and had it published by the principal school book publisher for the state at that time, the American Book Company. If we ever expected to make any money out of it, we certainly were disappointed as it did not sell in any substantial degree.

During these last two years I did some graduate work at Grand Forks with Libby. He had started the *North Dakota Historical Quarterly* for the State Historical Society which had its headquarters in Bismarck, and he had a number of things he thought that he wanted me to do. One was a rewrite of the reminiscent account of a Badlands rancher. He asked me to write that into a historical narrative, shortening it a great deal but getting in the more interesting and important events. This I did using many notes including some that other persons had written on the manuscript giving useful cross references. The main interest I suppose in the account was the fact that it was not the usual cattle ranch but a horse ranch, and also that the rancher had been a neighbor of Theodore Roosevelt and the Marquis de Mores. I did this and eventually Libby published it.

I had also got together, with my mother's help, my Grandfather Butterfield's letters that had been preserved in the hands of the family. I got permission from the different aunts who owned them to place them in the State Historical Society where they would be cared for and not lost or destroyed. Libby wanted the Civil War letters for publication in his review so Ruth undertook this editing job although neither her nor my name went on it. She transcribed all of the letters with the few notes that we got largely from Mother. I engaged in a few other activities, reviewed some books for the *Current History* magazine and also for the *New Republic,* one of which Herbert Croly, the editor, asked permission to use not as a review but for a lead editorial, which I readily granted. Both of these publications paid for their contributions so I was doubly pleased.

During the two years I also made a few public speeches, mainly school commencements in the spring. The most memorable was being asked back to Towner High School to give the commencement address. I was glad to appear before a home audience and enjoyed the experience. Afterward Judge Bagley gave me a few suggestions about public speaking and how to improve it which were useful to me.

I also was asked to come back to the university to talk at a ceremony marking Dean Kennedy's retirement. This I was particularly happy to do although the event was marred by the fact that the dean was unhappy at being retired. The State Board of Administration chairman, Robert Murphy, had come to see me shortly before that and urged me not to go. He said he did not think Kennedy wanted the ceremony at all. I communicated with the dean and he said he was pleased that I had been asked to speak and urged me to accept. So that was that.

The most memorable thing that happened during those two years happened in the summer of '27. After our summer session was over, Dad had planned to go to Moose Lake, Minnesota, to visit his brother Everett whom he had not seen for a long time. He bought a new Dodge car, the only new car he ever owned. He did not drive very well and had written me that he would like it very much if Ruth and I would go with him, Mother and Susan, and asked me to take over the driving from Mayville to Moose Lake and the return. A day or two before the scheduled arrival in Mayville I had a late night call from Mother telling me that Dad had died in his sleep from a heart attack. We went home by the first train we could make and were joined by all the children of the family. Dad had six sons to serve as his pallbearers which was unusual even in our rural area.

Then other problems came up and we stayed to help Mother until we had to go back to start my courses. In the first place there was considerable political competition for replacing Dad as probate judge, or as country judge as it was called in North Dakota. Among those who were anxious for selection to fill out Dad's term was his youngest brother Eugene of whom I was very fond and would have liked to get in Dad's place. But the County Commissioners were subject to other pressures and during a meeting sent word to Mother that they wanted her to be the county judge. She declined, I think, partly because she thought Gene might be chosen if she did not accept and partly because she may have been afraid of it as she had done no work in the office. Judge Bagley urged her to accept when the request was repeated, which she did. I accompanied her to the meeting of the Board of County Commissioners, and they invested her with the title and office. I remember the Monday morning when she took the office. I went with Mother because I knew much about her new duties, having been around the office more often. The first thing that happened before she really got settled at her desk was a lawyer from Rugby appeared with a will he wanted probated. I helped Mother swear him in to give his testimony and to present his copy of the will. I had to leave a few days later but I had told Mother that if she ran into any problems to call Bagley who was not only a lawyer but had been the probate judge before Dad, and to take his advice which she did. Bagley wrote me a few months later telling me how quickly Mother had caught on to the work of the office and there was nothing about her performance that anyone need worry about.

Back in Mayville in our final year, we were in comfortable and attractive quarters and had our best year as far as personal satisfaction was concerned. I had a good many friends among the students especially among those who were planning to take degrees and major in history. During our last two years Vinnedge married a very attractive girl who had been attending the college, and we enjoyed their companionship. Eventually they joined his parents in Milwaukee where he became a candidate for a doctorate at Marquette. Also, during the last year Duane Squires joined us, having secured a master's degree from the University of Minnesota. In fact, he took over my work when I left the next year. All in all, it was a busy year, and I was only seriously concerned with where I was going to do my advanced graduate work.

As I worked longer with the college, I became more intimate with President Carl Swain. Swain was a good administrator, and I learned a great deal from him although some of it was negative. He had a low boiling point and occasionally blew his top over some trivial thing but he normally had good judgment, and, as a member of the board of St. Olaf's College, he had outside experience. He was a frequent speaker at teachers meetings and at Norwegian Lutheran churches. I am still amazed at how good a faculty he was able to keep together on the campus with the salaries and facilities that he had.

As we approached the end of the third year at Mayville, I was convinced that I had gained all the experience that would be useful from that assignment, and more important I was anxious to get back to graduate work and take my doctorate. I combed the graduate catalogs of universities trying to find some kind of scholarship or assistantship that would see us through the first year at least. I calculated that we would have $1,000 in our bank account, and any amount I would get in the way of a stipend would perhaps carry us through the entire time.

The two largest fellowships that I found for which I was eligible were at Columbia University and the University of Chicago. I applied for them early in the spring of 1928. My references, of course, were largely O. G. Libby and Clarence Perkins at the University. Nothing came from either of these applications and had I known more about graduate education I would not have expected any. At any rate this ended my search for a stipend at that time, and my mind was pretty well made up to go to Minnesota where I had been on the campus, in fact, had attended a class with brother Bill when he was a senior student in business school there. I felt that I knew my way around Minneapolis and we probably would be more at home at Minnesota University. This plan was changed when H. D. Welte returned from Iowa University where he had been that year to teach in our summer session. He talked to me at length and urged me, by all means, to go to Iowa. I did not know much about the university, which was my own fault, and, of course, he did not know the history department, but he was very high on Dean Paul Packer of the College of Education. He told me that he had talked to Packer about me, and Packer was interested in my coming to Iowa. This did not quite fit. I hated to spend the money but eventually I wired Packer that Welte had recommended that I come down there for an interview, and I would appreciate any comment he had on that. I received a reply to the effect that Packer thought it would be in my interest to come. So before our summer session began I took a train by way of Minneapolis and Cedar Rapids.

When I arrived in Iowa City, I first looked up Packer who visited with me briefly and quite generously as I recall, considering how busy he was as it was registration time. He took me over to the history department and introduced me to W. C. Root, the chairman. I spent the rest of the morning with Root and some of the members of the history department, of whom I now only recall George Gordon Andrews. Root took me to lunch with Andrews and Packer. We discussed various things connected with the profession and in what field I wanted to work. Root told me I would probably work with Louis Pelzer who was not on the campus at the time.

Before I left that afternoon for Minneapolis, Root offered me a one-third time instructorship where I would assist him in the General American History course teaching sections, and which would pay 700 dollars for the nine months. I had a good look at the campus and visited the State Historical Society, which was in the same university building, and also the university library which was very badly housed in an old gymnasium. I took an overnight train back which got into Minneapolis in the morning, and then took the street car out to Bill's as the train to Fargo did not leave until evening. Bill was busy, of course, at his job. My cousin, Eileen Ellis from Moose Lake, was there staying for a day or two for a 4-H contest, and after lunch Brownie, Bill's wife, proposed that I show Eileen the city as she had only been there once before. This we did, winding up at a movie after we were worn out.

After I got home, I talked the matter over with Ruth and she was agreeable to my taking the Iowa offer. It was my thought, which proved to be correct, that we could live on the $700 and save our reserve, and if we did not like it at Iowa, go somewhere else on it the next year. There was one complication in this. Ruth was ill all that summer and I was not at all sure she would be able to make the trip to Iowa City. But she certainly pulled herself together at the end, and we took the train from Mayville to Fargo and Fargo to Minneapolis where we planned to spend the day at Bill's.

Early in the day my sister Martha and her husband Jack Zehringer and their baby arrived by car from Towner where they had been visiting Mother. They had brother Bob with them and were planning to send him to high school in St. Louis where they lived—Normandy to be exact.

After some discussion we decided that Martha would use my train ticket to Cedar Rapids. She and the baby would go on the train that far with Ruth, I would ride with Jack and Bob and we would meet in Cedar Rapids. The ride was a pleasant one, the first long one I had ever taken on a concrete highway. When we reached Cedar Rapids, Jack and I secured rooms in the hotel where I had stayed that spring. We then drove to the railway station, where in time the train arrived and we all moved to the hotel. The next morning the Zehringers were up before we were and left for St. Louis, and after breakfast we checked out and took the inter-urban to Iowa City.

Chapter 11

Graduate Work at Iowa

There were two other couples in Iowa City from Mayville. They were Aletha and H. D. Welte and Marian and Delbert Jeep, and both couples were good friends of ours. The Jeeps invited us to come to their apartment when we arrived, which we were glad to do. Jeep's field was education and he was working with Ernest Horn, who was certainly the best scholar in education at Iowa.

After we made an unproductive search for an apartment, the Jeeps finally talked us into sharing theirs, which we did reluctantly although it had been occupied by two couples during the past several years. Thus settled, I reported to the history office where I was welcomed by Root who took me in to meet Pelzer and Plum and later introduced me to many graduate students. The three students who meant most to me in the long run were Paul Giddens, who had been there in residence a year and had taught at Iowa State, Howard Anderson, and William Peterson. I suppose I was on closest terms with Paul Giddens although I had many common interests with Howard Anderson.

I worked out a program between history and political science. When Paul Giddens had asked me what I was going to do, I said I was going to work in political science and history. He looked at me rather peculiarly and said, "You can't do that at Iowa." When I asked him, why not, he said, "Well, they don't get along." My reply was "I will do it or I'll leave." As a matter of fact, I had about as much training in one as the other and most of my research could be classified as either political science or history. As I worked it out, I had over the next two years Root's seminar in Colonial History, Louis Pelzer's in History of the West, and George Andrews' Readings in Modern European History, in which the time was spent on the war guilt question, the German documents for which were just being published.

In political science, I had work in Constitutional Law with an unusual teacher. This was Benjamin Shambaugh who was as good a teacher as I ever had. I also did some work in political parties on an individual reading basis with Kirk Porter, and continued this the next year along with some work with John Briggs. I also had work with Harry Plum in English History. When he found I was interested in the farm movements of the '80s and '90s, he put me to reading on the cooperative movements in England. He was a very pleasant person, easy to work with, and not very demanding. Two other members of the history department with whom I did not have any formal work but learned to know quite well were Ross Livingston and Bessie Pierce, with whom I shared an office.

My teaching consisted of attending Root's lectures in the big introductory course and meeting some sections of it for discussion. It was fairly routine work and the material so familiar that it did not take much of my time in preparation.

The most important man to me at Iowa was Louis Pelzer. He was an interesting personality, a large raw-boned man who had lost an arm. He was exceedingly sensitive about it and one had to be very careful not to hurt his feelings. I had been warned about this but one day when we were going over some papers in his office, and he was having trouble in straightening them out with one hand, I reached over and helped. I could feel him bristle. He and Root were not on very friendly terms and this added somewhat to my problems as Root and Shambaugh were not either.

Another peculiarity that was interesting and useful to me was that the State Historical Society was really a part of the political science department and Shambaugh was in charge of it. It had a library that was more convenient and useful to me than the university library, and I had my desk in the society library for a time. Peterson was also working with Pelzer as he had developed a great interest in the history of steamboating on the Mississippi. Anderson taught part-time in the university high school. I had no contact with him, officially at least, and neither did Bessie Pierce although she taught the teaching of history courses for those planning to teach below the college level.

Another teacher with whom I worked was George R. Davies, an old friend who had taught me sociology at North Dakota. Perhaps I should say he taught me statistics by using sociological data, because his method of teaching at that time was never to ask questions, never to assign a paper, but solely to set a statistical problem regarding the data in the particular lesson. He had moved to Iowa as head of their Bureau of Economic Research and had a group of graduate students from the Business School. Because I was hoping to work on some aspect of the monetary problem in politics in the eighties and nineties, I knew I needed to know more about the economics of the problem and the statistical measures. I talked with him about it and he was glad to include me in what he called his seminar, which was really a special problems class. I took as my problem the building of a series of index numbers of the Iowa farmers' dollar during that period, taking data from the market pages of the newspapers for each year but selecting as I recall the January 1st prices. This made a very rough measure but it seemed the best we could work out without undertaking a great deal of probably unproductive work. I enjoyed working with Davies very much. He was an excellent statistician and he understood exactly what I needed to know.

This then was my program as lined up for my doctorate, and I proceeded to work it out, enjoying every part of it. Andrews' course was not a seminar but a course he more properly called Readings. We would not write a research paper but read the literature on the subject including the records and present oral reports to the class. I found it a very useful course for graduate students and used a modification of it after I went to Missouri with, I thought, considerable success.

Besides the courses there was the matter of the language requirements. Although I had a good basic knowledge of German from my work with Bek, I had been away from it for four years and had to brush up on that. I went to the library and found a German history book which I started to translate and found I could make it rather easily. Because of the reports of the particular difficulty of the examinations that were given in that area, I took great care to be prepared. I found in the end that I was far better prepared than I needed to be.

French was a different story because I had never studied French. In finding that the French Department had a course for graduate students who were in a similar situation, I joined it and met one afternoon a week for two semesters going through an introductory French language book at the rate of above five lessons a week. In order to speed this up because it was quite elementary, I got a French history of the Franco-Prussian War and began to translate it with the help of a dictionary. I did not wait until the class was over to go to the department and ask for my examination, which was not difficult and which tested only my ability to translate. Foreign language struck me as being a waste of time as the research in which I was going to be interested did not involve either language. Although I had use for the German later, I could very profitably have used the time I had used on French doing something more immediately useful to me.

My immediate problem was to work out a thesis subject because I foresaw this would be the time element that might delay me and would also make my Iowa reputation. I talked at length with Pelzer about it, and he drew back from too direct use of the monetary question, saying that he did not know enough economics to direct a thesis that involved it heavily. After considerably more discussion he suggested that I choose one of the political leaders of the Free Silver Movement and do a public career biography that would embody the politics of the problem. I agreed to this as it seemed the best compromise I could make, as I was running into further blank walls among all the historians when I got over into the economics of money. We picked two names. One was Richard Parks Bland of Missouri and the other was Henry Moore Teller of Colorado. I located the living members of their families and wrote them regarding records, private papers, and correspondence particularly. Judge Ewing Bland from Missouri discouraged me completely saying that his father had left no records. Apparently that was correct although there were some advantages that would have accrued to me from a study in Missouri because of my later career there.

On the other hand, Teller's younger brother, Judge James Teller in Denver, led me to believe there were a great many records of his brother available and useful. I am sure he did not purposely deceive me but his assurance was based upon his ignorance of historical methodology. At any rate, in one of the early bulletins of the Colorado Historical Society I did find a former secretary of Teller's, named Dawson, had brought in a collection of Teller papers to the society when he became its director.

As far as the local materials were concerned, I stayed close to the general political sources, especially the *Congressional Record*. As Teller had become a senator when Colorado was admitted to the Union in 1876 and had served until 1909, except for three years when he was Secretary of the Interior in Chester A. Arthur's Cabinet, the *Congressional Record* was the basic record but tremendous in size.

The first year was a very busy one, as the courses I took were interesting, and I enjoyed the companionship of the faculty and graduate students. Root especially put himself out to be agreeable and took me to lunch twice with some special friends of his. One of them was Henning Larson from the English Department, whom I liked very much and later saw often when he was dean of arts at the University of Illinois. I attended the meetings of Phi Delta Kappa, an honorary education organization, where I often saw Packer. Welte was Packer's student and also a member of his class in college administration. I went to the class two or three times during the year with Welte and found them interesting and sometimes stimulating.

Towards spring a new factor entered the picture as Bessie Pierce took a position at the University of Chicago to fill a chair in Chicago history that the department had established. As I apparently was the only graduate student who had taught the course on teaching history in high school, Root chose me as a temporary replacement, no doubt with Bessie's approval. He talked to me about the new work and considered it about another one-third time job but at a higher level. He made the offer with an increased pay to $900 and the academic rank of Lecturer in

History for the next year. I was pleased by the additional money but more by having an independent course rather than teaching sections with an occasional lecture to the large group when Root was out of town. Root was not completely happy though as he could see that I was avoiding European History and putting the emphasis on political science. I think as a result of this he offered me a summer job of teaching Andrews' undergraduate course in Modern European History for the summer session. I was completely familiar with the course having taken it first as an undergraduate in Fargo College with Correll, my first college history teacher.

The compensation was also really welcome, as I could see that if I followed up my thesis subject after the summer session by visiting the Colorado sources I would need a car. Consequently, I put our savings into a new Model A Ford Coupe. We made some preliminary inquiries at the University of Colorado and the Colorado Historical Society, and as soon as the summer session was over, we packed our new car and started for Colorado. The standard mode of auto travel at this time was to spend nights in the newly-developing cottage camps that were quite inexpensive, but you had to supply your own bedding. The camps had a central bath house and the cabins usually consisted of a very small room with a place between cabins for automobile parking. We spent the first night in Nebraska and reached Boulder the next afternoon. Summer session was over at Boulder and it was easy to get nice quarters near the campus. Professor James Willard, the chairman of the history department, was in town and treated me very generously by telling me what they had in the library that was peculiar to Teller, much of which he had collected from Teller's old law office in Central City although his own field was British history. After working through those materials, we went to the Historical Society in Denver, where we met LeRoy Hafen, the Director. Under advice from him, we went east of the library and found a room in a decaying mansion that we thought we could live with and went to work in the society library. To my amazement, Hafen had not heard of the Teller papers that I had seen cited in one of the early publications. He opened the room to the manuscript papers and said, "Help yourself, if you can find them." They were not mentioned on any index card or in the card catalog, but after some searching, we found them. It was a group of items that Dawson had preserved from the Teller papers mainly centering on the campaign of 1896.

We went to work on these and did as much with them as we could and searched for other things, particularly other papers that might have correspondence with Teller. But the collections were not very big. We also looked up Judge James Teller who was very agreeable and pleased that we had chosen his brother to write about, but he had no documents of any importance. However, I did get from him names of people in Denver and names of Henry Teller's family who might possibly have some papers. This work cleaned up, at least superficially, we decided we would have to go to Central City to see what we could find there before returning home.

There was not a good road of any kind to Central City at that time. Following directions from Denver we drove to Idaho Springs on Highway 40 and asked about the road up Virginia Canyon that led to Central City. A narrow gravel trail was pointed out to us that seemed to me to run right into the mountain. We started up the trail and by the time we got far enough on the road to see what it was like, I could not turn back. It was our first experience in mountain driving and really a hair-raising one. When we were about halfway up the mountain, Ruth remarked that if there was not a better way down, she was going to spend the rest of her life in Central City. There were a few turnouts where you could stop. Fortunately we met only one vehicle, a pickup truck. Finally we got to the "pass" where we had another problem. The road down into Central City was wider but very steep. We reached the main street, where we found the Teller House, which was the big hotel. Here we met Henry Teller's son, Harry, who with his wife was boarding a group of miners who had re-opened an old gold mine.

The depression had stimulated the independent mining enterprises that were subsistence in nature. I visited some with Harry Teller but received no information regarding any family records. Next we went to the newspaper office where we found most of the files of the *Miner* which had been at various times a weekly, bi-weekly, tri-weekly, and had several different titles. Now it was a pretty thin weekly paper. As the paper was useful but more easily researched in the historical society which had a complete file, there was nothing to delay us in Central City. Fortunately I found that there was a better road back by Boulder Canyon. We drove down the gulch through Blackhawk and on over to the head of Boulder Canyon which quickly put us in Boulder where we spent the night. There seemed to be nothing of any importance in Central City for us and, except for some miscellaneous things which we discovered later, this proved to be true. Labor Day weekend was ahead of us with the historical society and the university library closed. I appealed to our friend Willard, he gave me his key to the university library, and we spent the Sunday of the weekend working in the newspaper files which were not very produc-tive. The librarian was quite put out to find me there so I returned the key to Willard that night. We decided to take Labor Day off, and we drove up to Estes Park. We had a pleasant day, came back to our quarters in

Boulder, left for Iowa City the next day, and felt well rewarded for our trip and work in the university and historical society libraries.

Before we had left Iowa City we had moved from the Jeep apartment to one in an apartment where George R. Davies and Mrs. Davies lived. It cost more and was no prize but it at least was private. The Jeeps took in a graduate student who lived with them that year. I think we made the move with a minimum of problems.

I had less classwork and, although my teaching took more time, my main work was devoted to the public career biography of Teller based overwhelmingly on the *Congressional Record* and the relatively few personal papers I had been able to uncover. The university library had a file of the *New York Tribune* covering the period, which was another source that I used very extensively.

One change at Iowa in the fall of 1929 was that after Bessie Pierce went to Chicago I was alone in that office until Cornelius de Kieweit joined me. "Dick," as we came to call him, was a very interesting person. While Dutch-born, he had been brought up in South Africa and had his education at the University of Witwatersrand. He had also taught in South Africa before going to London, where he received his doctoral degree. He came to Iowa without any American experience, and he had some adjusting to do before he became really effective. He used to talk to me about his teaching and the failure of the students to respond to his assignments, which were largely the written essay-type that was fairly standard in British universities but were not used much in most American universities. I tried my best to suggest to him what his trouble was in adapting to his students, and years later he told me he really appreciated what I did for him in those talks. I had helped him to gradually change his procedure until he was enjoying his teaching. Dick was unmarried then and we occasionally saw him socially as he invited us to tea and we invited him to dinner at our apartment. Through the accidents of academic life after some years of work at Cornell, he became President of Rochester University and, as such, we were thrown together on national committees and organizations.

In December came my offer to go to the University of Missouri the next summer in a regular appointment, and this pushed my thesis writing still more. As I wrote the narrative from my notes and memory, Ruth typed it up in a tentative form and after revision, I submitted it to Pelzer. He found little to criticize but had a few very good suggestions to make, all of which I accepted. It was late in the spring semester when I had the manuscript finally completed, typed and approved, and then I was qualified to take the final orals. I had written finals the semester before but as these were definitely subject matter centered they were not difficult and the questions were not unexpected. The oral examination was interesting in a way. George R. Davies was on the committee, and they all deferred to him on any economic questions. The outside reader was a chemist who had found in my thesis a reference to the use of cyanide in refining gold ore which had affected its supply and consequently its value. This was the only thing that interested him and his questions entirely regarded this process.

After this was over I prepared my final examination for my course. It had been a semester course and this was the second time I was offering it, each time with a good size class, but it had been easier to teach the second time as I had been over it once recently. My brother Earl and his wife Thelma came to commencement from Aurora, Illinois, where Earl was managing a farm for Howard Thompson, a cousin of my father. We had a pleasant visit with them. They left immediately after the commencement, and as soon as we could pack up, we also left. It was a warm June day and the only thing that sticks in my memory about the commencement was that as our line of doctoral candidates approached the podium and the president was going through the ritual saying, "I confer upon you all the privileges and honors that accompany this degree. . .," someone up ahead was saying in a loud whisper, "What are the honors and privileges of a Ph.D.?" Someone behind me in a similar whisper said, "You don't have to take any more examinations!" He was mistaken!

Chapter 12

Beginning at the
University of Missouri

My first relation to a position at the University of Missouri was in late November or early December in 1929. I received a letter from Jonas Viles, chairman of the department of history, telling me that the department was interested in someone who could teach history and also teach courses for high school history teachers, such as the course that I was then teaching at Iowa. He asked me to come for an interview at some convenient time and gave me some possible dates. Dr. Root had told me that Colorado State Teachers College at Greeley was looking for someone in my field, and he thought I might be interested, but when I received this letter from Viles, he was all for my accepting the invitation for an interview. Apparently he and Pelzer had already written to Viles about me.

Transportation from Iowa City to Columbia was not easy. I took a train to Grinnell, where I changed to an overnight train which reached Centralia, Missouri, about 4 o'clock the following morning. I found there was no train to Columbia until 5 o'clock p.m. and I recall asking the station agent if there was any other way of getting to Columbia. He replied, "There is no other way but horseback." Upon arriving in Columbia I went to the Daniel Boone Tavern, where I had a reservation and immediately went to bed.

Later I had breakfast and made my way to the University, where I met the members of the history department who were there. I then spent some time with Dean M. G. Neale of the School of Education who was officed in Jesse Hall where the History Department was located. He appeared to be a very positive administrative type who seemed to know what he wanted. He took me to lunch at the Harris Cafe with the major part of the education faculty. I recall that the education faculty seemed made up of short, heavy-built people like John Rufi, Ralph Watkins and Charles Germane, although I did not yet associate the names with the right people. We had a pleasant lunch and I described, at the Dean's request, the Iowa Training School situation. That was all I saw of the people in education.

During the afternoon I visited with various members of the history department—Viles, Jesse Wrench, Assistant Dean of the Arts College, Frank Stephens, Michael Cochran, Charles Mullett, and Louise Trenholme. I also met a few graduate assistants. I was told that Thomas A. Brady, the ancient history man who was not there, was finishing his doctoral degree at Harvard. The department had dinner for me at the Harris Cafe that evening, after which we adjourned to Viles' living room where there was a great deal of talk of history and related matters. I took a late train and returned home by the route I came.

A week or so later I received a letter from Viles offering me a position. He had asked me before I left Columbia what I expected in the way of rank and salary. I had told him that, as I had five years of college teaching experience, I thought I ought to have an Associate Professorship and a salary of $3,000. When I received his letter, he offered an Assistant Professorship and $2,800 with a proviso that if my work was satisfactory I would be made an Associate Professor with a $3,000 salary in two years. The Iowa people wanted me to accept the offer but before I did I wrote to President T. F. Kane at the University of North Dakota who had once suggested that I return there. My letter was a personal one and I asked him what he thought I should do. He wrote back immediately and, knowing their poor financial prospects, he advised me by all means to take the Missouri offer. One troublesome provision in the offer was that I had to report for work in June. I had not planned to complete my thesis until the end of the summer session, but I suppose that Viles assumed that a little pressure would get me to do it more quickly, which I did.

As I reported before, we left Iowa City immediately after commencement. We had already shipped the few pieces of furniture we had brought from North Dakota, and as soon as we had lunch after the morning commencement, Ruth and I loaded the Model A and started for Columbia. We spent our first night in Missouri in Kirksville, as I was curious to see the campus of the college there. I had known people who had attended and taught there, especially George G. Andrews. We drove around the campus after dinner and the next morning drove down Highway 63 to Columbia. There was concrete pavement all of the way except a stretch near Moberly which was brick paved on one side only, an arrangement we had never seen before.

That day in June was a hot, humid day and we were very warm by 10:30 a.m., when we reached Columbia and drove immediately to Viles' house. Viles had by correspondence with us rented the Wrench house for the summer, as Wrench would be teaching at Rolla. Mrs. Viles went with us to show us the house, and complained bitterly that "Jonas had no business renting you that house because it isn't in good condition." It had not been occupied the year before as the Wrenches had been chaperones at a fraternity house. It was an old two-story house in a large wooded lot with a porch that looked like it might fall away from the house at any time. Anyway we decided to make the best of it. The summer of 1930 was a hot one, the house had no window shades, and it seemed to us tremendously hot. We had one neighbor, Walter McNabb Miller, a retired member of the medical faculty, who as a result of a larynx operation could converse only with an artificial voice box. In spite of his impediment he proved to be an interesting and helpful neighbor.

My teaching load for the summer was light, as I had only an undergraduate and graduate course for high school teachers of history. The attendance in the latter was surprisingly large as the work had not been offered before. Many of the graduate students who had wanted it had not been able to get it. I was assigned an office with the history department, usually after the first summer with Jesse Wrench, who made an interesting office associate to say the least. For the regular year following I undertook the Recent United States History which Viles had taught, but he did not let me have the Constitutional History course which was also his. I also taught one section of the American History Survey. I did help with the registration, advising social studies teachers although most of them already had other advisors. I was fortunate enough in the registration procedure to sit by Ella Victoria Dobbs, who was in practical arts, and I found her a very colorful and interesting person. She, too, was not very busy and gave me salty rundowns on the faculty we saw around the places of registration, so that I felt I knew a great deal about the faculty by the time the day was over.

During the summer we arranged to rent a house, which was the last one within the city limits on West Broadway at that time. It was a new brick bungalow—five rooms with a complete basement, a good furnace and in all a very comfortable place in which to live. Immediately to the west were farms, including that of our milkman. The city limit now extends many miles west of that and the country road is built up with houses, apartments, churches, shopping centers and the Shelter Insurance building and grounds.

In the summer of 1930, President Stratton Brooks was still in his office although he had been terminated as of September 1. I saw him occasionally in the University Club which was then in Tate Hall, and I remember my interview with him when Viles had taken me down to meet him. He was a rather blustery, gruff person who, when I was introduced, said, "Well, young man, what do you know about history?" There was considerable speculation as to who would replace him but when the fall came around Walter Williams was made Acting President and later President.

Bessie Pierce had induced me to read a paper at the National Council for Social Studies session at Columbus at the summer NEA meeting. When the time for the meeting arrived, I found that although I had my paper prepared I did not have enough money to attend. Rather than go to the bank where I had established a checking account, as I had not yet received a check from the University, I went to the Household Finance Corporation to borrow $50. I found that I could not borrow less than $80, which I agreed to take. Much to the irritation of the finance company, I paid the debt when I received my first salary check, thus ending my first and last business with Household Finance.

Upon arrival at the hotel in Columbus I met Carter, the Secretary of the Missouri State Teachers Association, and told him that I had no reservation at the hotel. He immediately accompanied me to the registration desk and make arrangements for me to have one of the MSTA rooms. Later in the day he asked me to talk to a member of the Board of Regents from the University of Idaho who wanted information about our Dean of the School of Education. I protested to Carter that I did not know enough about the Dean to have an opinion. But he insisted, as he could not find anyone else from the University, so I met the Board member from Idaho and explained again that I was not a good witness but I gave him my impressions. When Dean Mervin Neale later accepted the presidency in Idaho, I wondered if all administrators were picked on such poor evidence. I returned to Columbia the following day, after attending the meeting where I presented my paper.

As I recall it now, my education work took more of my attention the first year than the history did although when Dean Neale left to be President of the University of Idaho, I heard no more about the courses in the history of American education that I was to teach. Except for the summer, the School of Education did not take the projected half of my time. I started the Recent U.S. course the next fall, taught one section of American History, had my undergraduate teacher training course, and took charge of one university high school class, although it was not in my schedule, and I did not give it full time. I would choose two of the more mature practice teachers who were in my course to observe me while I taught the high school class the first month. Each of them worked up succeeding units and at the end of the month, one would take over the class, and I would merely supervise it by visiting it two or three times a week and hold post-mortems with both of the practice teachers. Of all the high school students I had at Missouri, Chester G. Starr, Jr., became closest to me in after years, although I remember pleasantly many of them. One of my practice teachers was James Kelley, who became a state senator and later President of the Kemper Military School. Several of these were graduate students who needed professional education credit to get a certificate to teach, one of the few places where there were some jobs in 1932 for college graduates.

I kept the class, American Problems or American History, under my charge until I received the Guggenheim Fellowship and had '39–40 as a sabbatical. This also constituted considerable work in organizations, as the Social Science section of the State Teachers' Association put me on its program the first fall, and I became active in it as one of my duties as a member of the University faculty. With a group of St. Louis County teachers, particularly Julian Allrich and Howard Cummings, and with Francis English, principal of Carrollton High School, we changed it into a State Social Studies Council affiliated with the National Council as well as the State Teachers' Association and promoted district groups in St. Louis and Kansas City. This led naturally into the National Council and we were able to bring it to Missouri—Kansas City or St. Louis—for its meetings on several occasions, and I began to meet with it regularly and serve on its committees.

The second semester of the first year I took over a section of Wrench's Introduction to History course where he gave the lectures, and I with several graduate students supervised the "laboratory" where he had a large number of exercises for historical learning set up that required the use of historical records. Some of these were very good teaching devices. Some seemed to me to be merely busy work. One characteristic that stood out as a bad aspect was that while he added a few new problems each year, he rarely dropped any. Consequently the number had become so large that the students could not do first-rate work on most of them.

The history department had been increased by the addition of Tom Brady who had returned from Harvard, and he proved to be an enjoyable colleague. I continued to give my undergraduate course in Teaching Social Studies at least one semester. If the demand required it the second semester I offered both it and the graduate course. In the summer session I offered both courses if we had undergraduate students who needed it to complete the work. Otherwise, I gave only the graduate course plus a history course.

The composition of the department was interesting. Viles was a Massachusetts Yankee who had had all of his work at Harvard but had spent one year in England doing some kind of historical work immediately afterward. He and Mrs. Viles had two boys living, Charles who was married and working, and Philip who was attending the University. They had a fine comfortable house on Rollins Road in the sorority and fraternity neighborhood. They were very sociable people and entertained the members of the department often. Jonas edited a few things, had written a grade school history of Missouri, and had written extensively for the

Dictionary of American Biography. He certainly knew good history when he saw it, but in spite of this he lacked the imagination to be an effective teacher. His lectures were generally soliloquies on the aspects of American History he was interested in and often had little connection with the course. While he could ask very probing questions, they did not seem to be the kind that could stimulate students in answering them. He was generally liked by his colleagues and certainly treated the younger men with great consideration. He undertook no real research during the years I knew him. The nearest thing to it was a high school state history he wrote with some pedagogical help from me. He also edited a volume on the history of the University, the first half of which he wrote himself and on which he worked hard. It is a very general picture that summarizes his views on Missouri history and Missouri society in the past. He wore a beard, walked with somewhat of a stoop, and was a devoted gardener.

Jesse Wrench was the color man in the department, indeed in the University. He wore his hair long with a hair net to keep it under control. Later I discovered it was partly to keep his bald spot covered. He had a handsome Van Dyke beard and until shortly before I came had always ridden a bicycle. He dressed for color with a blue beret, a Dante-like cape and golf knickers. Associates told me that when he rode that bicycle with that cape streaming out behind him he was quite a sight. Shortly before I came he had acquired a second-hand Whippet car and drove that everywhere. His language was colorful and students loved to tell stories, some of them accurate, about remarks he had made. Among his other peculiarities, he rolled his own cigarettes which would pile up in a big ashtray in a day, hardly any of them with more than a few puffs taken on them. Around the department we used to say he smoked matches. Wrench was a strange person for a scholar in many ways. I am sure as a young man he had been an excellent teacher. He had been a student at Cornell and Wisconsin and even as an undergraduate he had gone to Palestine with Nathaniel Schmidt to do some excavating. This interest in archaeology was never lost, and, in his years approximately following my arrival at the University, he rather lost his interest in history and devoted himself to archaeology. He and a sociologist named Brewton Berry founded the Missouri Archaeology Society, and he devoted most of his spare time to its promotion.

A few years younger than Viles was Frank F. Stephens who, as Assistant Dean in the College of Arts and Science, had given up most of his teaching, although he occasionally taught a section of American History and regularly taught American Diplomatic History which was his field of special interest. He was an unusual person in every way, an excellent teacher, except that he tended to grade all of his students alike. He worked very hard at his job in the Dean's office and the small amount of teaching that he did. Occasionally he had a masters student, but most of them wrote with Viles or with Cochran in European History.

Louise Trenholme was in charge of the general course of American History and also taught a course in the History of the South. Louise was the widow of Norman Trenholme who had formerly been the senior man in the department, an English history specialist, but who had died in the middle '20s. Louise had course work at Columbia and had been teaching at North Carolina College for Women when she met Trenholme whose first wife had recently died. Louise had not quite completed her doctoral degree at Columbia at this time.

Mike Cochran was an interesting personality and something of a scholar in Modern European History. His learning was wide but rather scattered, and he was intensely interested at this time in the World War I guilt problem which absorbed most of his time. He was a very poor classroom teacher, did not work at that to any appreciable degree, and was getting to the point where he was suffering from psychiatric problems.

Charles F. Mullett had been brought in a few years before to take over Trenholme's courses. Like Louise Trenholme, he had not completed his doctorate at Columbia, but was publishing a series of articles in the journals relating to various aspects of English and Colonial History.

The newest member of the department next to myself was Tom Brady, who had been at Harvard the year before and who was to take his orals and receive his degree during the Christmas holidays. Tom had done a masters degree at Missouri as well as a bachelor's, had been an instructor in history and had transferred from there to the Harvard University Law School. One year of law and the experience with Ferguson's *History of Roman Law* turned his attention back to history, and he completed his work in Ancient History in that department. Tom was the only unmarried member of the department except for Louise Trenholme. Eventually Louise Trenholme and later Mullett completed their doctorates at Columbia and published their theses.

Technically a member of the department was the Dean of Women Bessie Leach Priddy, a Ph.D. from Michigan. She taught one course that I later acquired. She was rarely with the department and no one knew much of her work in history.

We spent two years in the house on West Broadway. During the first year we were in Columbia Frank Stephens' wife, Blanche, died leaving him alone in his large house on Thilly Avenue. He had asked us to join him in the house for the year '31–32 including Ruth's younger brother Aubrey who lived with us while attending the University. We had talked this over and decided it was not a wise thing to do at that time. The following spring he again asked us to share his house with him, and we agreed to do it, as both of us had become fond of Frank. It also made a difference that Aubrey would not be with us during the year. Ruth took over managing the house, with Frank's longtime maid doing the cleaning and the laundry.

At this time we were not aware that Frank was interested in remarrying. Probably as a way of letting us know that possibility he invited us to take a trip with him on an October Saturday when the Missouri trees were at their most colorful. He drove down to the Ozarks where he owned an interest in a cabin. On the way out of town, we picked up Louise Trenholme. We had a colorful and pleasant drive down to the cabin where we had a picnic lunch and then drove back, spending most of the time looking at the scenery. It was dark when we were coming into Columbia from the south and just before we reached the city, at a curve in the highway, the headlights picked up a stray horse or mule in the road ahead of us. Frank was driving at a high rate of speed and he turned into the left lane to pass the animal. From our back seat I recall having the thought in mind I would have stayed in our lane and used some of the shoulder. We passed the animal but in getting back into the right lane the car began to skid and eventually caught and we turned over three times. On its original overturn it came down on the left front corner of the top and the door by the driver flew open. Frank was thrown out on the last turnover and landed directly in the path of the car. When the car stopped it was right side up and the rear wheels were in the ditch.

When I stood up in the car my head went through the soft roof that was standard on cars then, and I clambered out to see Frank who was out cold. I went back to see Ruth who had been asleep when it happened and found she was conscious but in great pain. Louise was also in considerable difficulty. I had some blood on my face from broken glass. People came along in cars and we were soon in two cars bound for Noyes Hospital at the University which was not much over a mile away.

When Ruth was carried in, she was x-rayed, and it was found she had two fractured vertebrae in the upper part of the back, and her left arm was broken just above the wrist. Frank had regained consciousness and was not badly hurt, even though he had ugly gashes on his head and hip. Louise had injured both knees when they had hit the dashboard and had a fractured collar bone. Ruth's arm was set and put in a cast and she was placed in a fracture bed. She was hospitalized for a month before I could bring her home. Both Frank and Louise were in the hospital for a week. The doctor put some adhesive tape on my face where it had been cut. To add to my personal handicap I had lost my glasses. The next morning I found them at the scene of the wreck with one lens broken and the frames badly bent.

The publicity following the accident made all of the acquaintances of Frank and Louise very much aware that they were seriously interested in each other. Four months later they were married and on an extended European wedding trip. We had moved out of the house when they returned.

Although our social life and my teaching were primarily with the history department, professionally I was much more active with the training of the high school social studies teachers and with the National Council for the Social Studies, working with them both state-wide and nationally.

The older generation of leaders of whom Bessie Pierce had been one was becoming inactive while a newer generation of Edgar Wesley, Howard Wilson, Allan King, Mary Kelty, Howard Anderson, who had been at Iowa with me, and others were assuming the leadership, and I became part of this group. That, with the state leadership that went with my university position, became a source of a great deal of interesting experience for me in our meetings and publications. I contributed one review to the first yearbook of the Council which was edited by Bessie Pierce. Eventually I edited the seventh yearbook myself and contributed to some others. I am sure the most significant thing I published was my presidential address in 1937, where I tried to sum up my point of view on history teaching and the place of teacher opinion in social studies teaching. I recall that Howard Wilson expressed his disagreement with my point of view which was all very friendly.

Later Francis English, who had joined the department, and I collaborated on another article for one of the yearbooks and in general Francis took over my work in the Council including serving a term as president.

The history department had definitely become my home, the center of my operation. I not only was officed there but was budgeted there and largely I suspect because of the surplus of staff in Education brought on by the depression no new courses in the history of education were established. I continued though to give my undergraduate course one semester. When I gave it twice, I gave both it and the graduate course in the summer but if the majors in Social Studies were taken care of in the first semester, I would give the graduate course the second semester.

After the first year at Missouri I did not teach the General American History course again, but shortened my Recent U.S. course to begin at 1898 and introduced a new course which I named Foundations of 20th Century America, which covered the period from the end of the Civil War to 1898. A few years later I introduced my graduate course called Readings in Recent U.S., first for one and then for both semesters. At first one was enough, but later enrollment was such that it was desirable to give it both semesters and keep the number down to 10. Dean Bessie Priddy retired and left her course in Social Forces in American History. I never knew what this course meant to her as I did not know her well. I do know she used Faulkner's *American Economic History,* and I suspect that is what it was, but when I inherited it I tried to make it an intellectual history based on a structure of education, religion, and literature—especially popular literature. At least these were my lectures. At first the class used Nevins, *American Social History as Recorded by British Travelers.* Later it studied Gabriel's *Course of American Democratic Thought* which was an extremely thought provoking book for them, and we discussed the ideas it presented in considerable detail. I believe it was the most thought provoking undergraduate course I ever gave even though it stopped before 1900. Later on I dropped one of my reading courses in favor of a more traditional seminar in Recent U.S. History to give some students a chance to find their thesis topics. A few masters candidates came my way in my second year although these were generally assigned by Viles and they were not free choices of theirs nor mine. Later when we decided we would do doctoral level work, these students chose their own theses director or chairman, and it worked as far as I was concerned exceedingly well. I acquired some very good students with whom it was a great pleasure to work.

In the meantime I was not neglecting my Teller. What I had done in the thesis was a public career narrative largely written out of the *Congressional Record,* newspapers, and the work we did in Denver and Boulder in the summer of 1929. As soon as our first summer session was over in Columbia, we started for Denver and spent the next month between Denver and Boulder trying to supplement these sources with other material. At the beginning of the Christmas holidays I left immediately for the Library of Congress and put in all the time I could in the manuscript division and the newspapers files, exploring the material that was there. Before returning I went to Boston where the American Historical Association was meeting. Tom Brady was there to take his orals, and we roomed together. I also was in touch with Otis Lee, who was in the Harvard Graduate School finishing up his doctorate. We spent one very pleasant evening and part of another day together. Otis had changed very little from our days together at Fargo College.

I listened to some of the papers at the meeting but mainly I got acquainted with people and visited with the few I already knew. Tom passed his orals, and we left at the same time but I stopped in New Britain, Connecticut, where H. D. Welte, now President of the Connecticut State Teachers College, had invited me to spend New Year's with him and his family. They had a New Year's Eve party with some of his faculty and I spent the next day with them before going on home.

The work on Teller continued in this manner. I am sure we made at least one more trip to Denver and three to the Library of Congress before I induced the department and the College of Education to let me have the summer of 1937 off. We had rented a summer cottage from Teller's daughter, Mrs. Emma Teller Tyler, at Shawnee, Colorado, about 50 miles from Denver. We drove out there taking my mother and my sister, Susan, with us. Susan was now living with us, and my sister, Grace, joined us there later. We made one or two trips to Denver each week to work primarily in the Western Collection of the Denver Public Library which proved to have some interesting materials. By the end of the summer I had the book pretty well completed. Ruth had typed it, and I began to look for a publisher. Allen Nevins had asked to see it as he was editing his series of American political biographies, mainly of presidents. He felt it did not fit his series so rather than take the time going around to other publishers, I tried the Caxton Printers in Caldwell, Idaho. They agreed to publish it on two conditions: One, that I reduce the length by about 100 pages, and two, that I agree to purchase at the wholesale price 100 copies. I found this a very disagreeable way to reach publication but rather than wait, I went ahead with it. The only bad part of my relations with Caxton was that they let me have only one proof and a few errors crept into the copy from the resetting changes I had made in the original proof. It received good reviews except in the case of the American Historical Review which did not review it. For various reasons it was delayed and finally the editor asked me about my wishes. It was so late that I suggested that he forget it.

All in all, I had every reason to be satisfied with the production. In fact, later it got on some lists of better books in western history. But frankly, there was not much color in Teller's personality, and it had little attraction except as straight history, certainly little or none for the general reader.

Chapter 13

Building an Academic Career

During my first few years at the University, although I worked mainly with the National Council for the Social Studies, I also became involved with the Mississippi Valley Historical Association which later became the Organization of American Historians. I attended the meetings regularly, became acquainted with the historians who were mainly interested in my own field, and enjoyed many friendships that lasted a long time. The organization had the original slant of its founders, which included such old teachers of mine as Libby and Shambaugh, and definitely had a state history association flavor. This changed slowly to a university flavor because of the sheer numbers of members and the amount of research going on. We usually met at university campuses including the University of Missouri where, although our facilities were not adequate, we were able to entertain the group with complete satisfaction. Their meetings were in the spring while the American Historical Association meetings were held immediately after Christmas. I found myself more interested in Mississippi Valley than in the latter, but attended both.

I presented some papers to the sessions of the Association growing out of my Teller research. The *Mississippi Valley Historical Review* published the first of these, "The Silver Republicans in the Election of 1896." Later I read one on Teller's relation to the Cuban policy of the United States but never submitted it to the *Review* for publication as it did not seem to merit separate publication.

The most important of these articles was one on "Public Opinion and the Income Tax, 1860–1900." In working on my Teller material I had noticed in congressional debates and other places a mass of intemperate discussion of what seemed to me an ordinary economic-political issue, and I began to make notes on the subject. Later I worked on it directly and took advantage of an opportunity in the summer of 1936 to use the Widener Library at Harvard which had a fine collection of economics textbooks for the period which added substantially to the article. This article was republished in books of readings at least two and possibly three times. Before these articles I had written one out of my Teller research for *Colorado Magazine of History.* Leroy Hafen, Director of the Colorado Historical Society and editor of the magazine, had asked me to write an article from my research on state history. I chose the unsuccessful statehood movement in which Teller had been heavily involved and titled it "Colorado's First Fight for Statehood." It was mainly from public records and newspapers as I had little manuscript material, but it was an interesting political fiasco.

I gradually developed another interest which was almost accidental in its development into a research project. This was the writings of Finley Peter Dunne, the author of the popular Irish character Mr. Dooley that Dunne used in his dialect essays. I had enjoyed these very much, and read many of them in connection with my research when working with newspapers that carried the syndicated column. I had also picked up books in which Dunne had republished many of them. I used short quotations from them to illustrate or to enliven lectures in my Recent United States History course. The college representative of Scribner's, himself an Irishman, learned this and talked to me of his own interest in the dialect stories. He called my attention to the fact that Scribner had been Dunne's last publisher. To my surprise, not long after that I had a letter from Charles Scribner, Jr., informing me that they were planning to publish an autobiography of Dunne and would like to revive interest in him before they brought out the autobiography, as he had been out of print since 1924 and almost completely since about 1916. He suggested that he would be glad to pay me a fee if I would edit a group of my favorite selections, providing Dunne would approve it. I did not know then but Scribner told me later Dunne had always refused to let anyone edit any of his material. I busied myself with this, using materials entirely from essays that had been republished in books. This was done as these had been selected by Dunne for republication and were more likely to have his approval.

When I had prepared about 100 pages of manuscript, I sent it to Scribner, who sent it on to Dunne and later reported to me that Dunne liked it and wanted me to go ahead with my work. In the meantime I opened correspondence with Dunne, who was living in the Los Angeles area, and he agreed to have a meeting with me at the St. Louis airport on his way to New York. However, he wired me from Salt Lake City that he was too ill to see me and the meeting would have to be postponed. He went on to New York and a short time later died of a cancer-caused hemorrhage in his throat. This ended the prospect of an autobiography and, while I had the anthology virtually complete, Scribner paid for it but did not publish it immediately. I presume they were evaluating whether it should be published since it was not going to be followed by an autobiography. Eventually, however, it was published. It had been held since our original proofreading of it. (I say "our" because Ruth who typed all of the material was the expert in the dialect 'especially the spellings'). When it was finally published, it had one disappointing typographical error of a complete line inserted about 12 lines out of place.

I suppose the important thing which the anthology did was to get me so interested in Dunne that I decided I would do a book about him. Tom Brady who had a Guggenheim Fellowship for a year's study in Athens urged me to apply for one. When this was granted, it made a rather curious situation in the University. Three of us, Karl Bopp and Elmer Wood, both in the Department of Economics, and I received Guggenheims. We had a sabbatical plus a fellowship which was to meet our costs of the year and we left immediately after summer session for Chicago. My sister Susan was still living with us, and my mother came to Columbia to be with her while we were gone. We moved them into a small apartment where the responsibilities would be less than in the house we had on Ross Street. We spent about three months in Chicago looking up Dunne's old friends and family, finding all the correspondence and records we could about him which were in private hands. The best group was held by his sister, Charlotte. We examined all the materials available in the Chicago Historical Society, the Chicago Public Library, and the University of Chicago Library. Several old newspapermen in Chicago who had been friends of Dunne's were very helpful as were some of his non-journalistic friends. From Chicago we went to New York where we went through a similar process, making appointments with various people who from other leads we knew had known Dunne, and using both the Public Library and Columbia University Library for materials we had not found in Chicago. I am sure the most interesting experience I had in this connection was with Mrs. Charles Dana Gibson who let me borrow a series of delightful letters that Dunne had written her when she was with her family in Virginia and Dunne was living in New York in the Gibson apartment with Charles Dana. Charles Dana did not want her to let me borrow the letters but she was not one to be told what to do.

On Christmas Day 1939 we left New York City and drove to Washington, familiar grounds now around the Library of Congress for research. We secured a small apartment and began to use the resources of the Library of Congress and to make appointments with several people who had known Dunne. Mark Sullivan was one who, while he was never close to Dunne, was active when he was and a great admirer of his writing as shown in his *Our Times*. Before the end of January we had exhausted Washington resources as far as we knew. We left by car stopping for a week in Chicago to clear up some details and then to Columbia. We stayed there a few days and then drove south to Highway 66 and followed it nearly all the way to Pasadena. From Oklahoma on we did considerable sightseeing, driving through some of the Navaho reservations, the Petrified Forest, the Grand Canyon where we spent a night, and then to the Hoover Dam, where we left Highway 66. We spent one night in Las Vegas, which in 1940 was a dirty, dusty little town. Its only noticeable feature seemed to be the gambling places which were open twenty-four hours a day. At least they were still open when we ate breakfast in the morning and cut across the desert to California. We established ourselves in an apartment in Pasadena about a block off Colorado Avenue, made our contacts at the Huntington Library in San Marino and then went across to Hollywood for an arranged lunch with Peter Dunne's widow, Margaret Dunne, who was considerably younger than he. I told her I would appreciate it if I could keep his papers in the Huntington Library while I studied them. She willingly agreed to this, and we established a regular routine of having lunch with her on Monday and spent the rest of our time working on the family papers of later years than those in Chicago owned by Charlotte. One evening during the first month, Philip Dunne, Peter's second son, had us with his mother to dinner at his home in one of the municipalities about Hollywood. We had a delightful time. I found him in some ways a better source of information than his mother, although it was clear the children did not know their father well. He had been away from home a great deal and the mother had raised the children.

The Huntington Library had a collection of newspapers on microfilm with the type of reading equipment that was just coming into wide use in libraries. We were able to locate a number in which "Mr. Dooley" had been syndicated and Ruth typed copies of those we did not have. On certain dates I was able to find some additional informational material that was useful other than that in standard reference works. The Huntington had very little to offer us in the way of research as its emphasis was in different fields, but it was a pleasant and convenient place to work and we enjoyed our months there very much. The other researchers and library staff were pleasant people to work with. We ate lunch regularly with them and saw something of some of them after hours. The material Mrs. Dunne had was useful but limited. After I had gone through it and taken notes on the material, I started writing. I wrote steadily in long hand while Ruth typed these copies. Then we made revisions until I had exhausted my materials.

Outside of the library and the work in it, we did have several pleasant weekends in Southern California. Ruth's mother's sister, Olivia, a widow, lived in the town of Orange south of Pasadena. We visited her several times and on one weekend we took her with us and drove to San Diego, going through the Spanish buildings and the old city of San Diego. We came back through the Imperial Valley which even in February was exceedingly warm. We went to other places around Los Angeles that gave us a wider view of Southern California and on the whole enjoyed it very much. My mother's widowed sister, Esther, was living in the Los Angeles area and we took her to dinner one Sunday and spent a pleasant day.

Frank Stephens' brother-in-law was the pastor of the local Congregational Church in Pasadena and we went to his services on several occasions and got acquainted with him and Frank's sister. Among the other trips we made was one to the UCLA campus where we spent some time in its library which was not useful to us in our work but was interesting in other ways. The most interesting thing to us about southern California were the remains of the Indian-Spanish Period.

Late in June we finished the manuscript of the Dunne biography and sent it off to Knopf who had asked for it. That done we packed up our car and went north, going into the Sequoia Forest where the largest of the redwoods were, and spent a day looking over the General Sherman and the lesser giants. We spent the night in Bakersfield in a motel that was extremely warm and the next morning we left for San Francisco. Many features of the World's Fair of 1939 in San Francisco were still in existence, especially on Treasure Island, and we spent part of a day and one cold windy evening at these exhibits. It was there we ate our first Indonesian meal in the Indonesian Pavilion which was still welcoming visitors. We also visited the University of California campus and then started for home east on Highway 40 stopping at Davis to see the unit of the university which, as I observed it then, was wholly agriculture. We had a night in Reno, another plus a day in Salt Lake where we visited the Temple Square Lot and had a guided tour of the Mormon monuments. Our guide was a local lawyer who, as many other Mormons in Salt Lake City do, donated a half day a week to this service. I was interested that the emphasis was all on the heroic history of the Mormons, their persecution and the Brigham Young leadership that led them to Utah. There was no emphasis whatever on Mormon religion. A sidelight was that I wanted to locate the site where Young had first seen the site of the city and had declared from his sickbed, "This is the place!" But at that time it was little noticed and we had some difficulty finding it although we eventually did. Some years later when we came through Salt Lake it was marked with a fine monument.

After our short visit here we drove on east going part way on 30 in southern Wyoming but then back down to Denver where by pre-arrangement we met Mary Brady and the two youngsters, Susan and Tommy, who had been visiting Mary's parents, the Leslies. The stories of the heat on the plains were very unpleasant to contemplate and the night before we left I bought a large chunk of dry ice, wrapped it in newspapers and in a blanket, and put it in the trunk of the car. We started early the next morning and the sun lived up to the reports we had over the radio and in the newspapers. About 10 o'clock we stopped and I unwrapped the dry ice and put it on the floor of the front seat under the scoop ventilator that blew air over it. Opening the small windows in the back of the car, we went on. How much actual cooling it did I do not know, but I do know it had some psychological value. When we stopped in Kansas for lunch I noticed a thermometer registered 100° but I did not tell Ruth and Mary. We spent the night in eastern Kansas in a good motel and were home early in the afternoon of the following day.

Our new house on South Glenwood, which was being built for us under an architect's supervision by young B. D. Simon, was almost ready to occupy and after a couple of days we were able to do so. It was the only house we had built for ourselves, and it was one we later left with a great deal of regret as it was ideally designed for us.

Naturally my work was not all teaching and research and I began to find that I had administrative types of assignments coming to me from the university and the arts college. It was Dean Frederick Tisdel who started in 1931 to use me as a member of the Junior College Visiting Team. This was a group of faculty members who visited the junior colleges in the state and evaluated them for approval. The system went back to 1907 or 1908 and had a great many merits, but its great defect was it made a great deal of work for members of the university faculty who had other work as well. It brought me in touch with the junior colleges of the state, and I enjoyed it. My colleagues on the committee, especially Dean Tisdel and C. A. Phillips in Education, were full of information about the educational background of these schools and in the case of Phillips about Missouri history as well. Other members were Herman Schlundt in chemistry, later succeeded by Herbert French, and eventually H. Y. Moffett in English succeeded Tisdel. The second year I was made chairman of the visiting sub-committee and later chairman of the entire Accredited Schools and Colleges Committee which included the work of accrediting the private high schools as well as all of the junior colleges. I served on this committee for about 10 to 12 years, most of the time as chairman. We had monthly meetings, usually in Registrar S. W. Canada's office who served as secretary of the committee. Dean Tisdel was in many ways an interesting person to work with and the person I reported to from the committee. He went on many of the trips with us and had a fine dry sense of humor that was completely lost upon his faculty who did not see him at this close range. He seemed to the faculty and had to me before this time a rather distant and austere person with little sparkle, and his brief remarks to the faculty in presiding were usually rather colorless. He had once been president of the University of Wyoming but had been squeezed out by politics and had come to Missouri for a position in English literature. Later when the arts college deanship became vacant, he moved into that position where he was a rather conservative but fair-minded administrator.

It was during one of our trips that Tisdel told us a little story of his experiences at Wyoming that greatly amused me. Shortly after he assumed the presidency there, he was asked to speak to a luncheon club downtown. He reported he made the expected speech of a new president on the cultural influence of an institution of higher education on a community. It was well-received he commented, but when the group came out into the lobby of the hotel they found a suspected horse thief had been lynched in the street while he had been speaking.

The function of the accrediting committee in evaluating the private high school was as important as that of the college, but it was administered in a different manner. A faculty member from the School of Education visited each private high school and reported to the committee. This person was J. D. Elliff who was near retirement. My first experience with the name Elliff occurred the first year I was at the University and before I knew him. In the summer session of 1930 one of my graduate students who was from Oklahoma was active in the Oklahoma State Teachers Association there. She made a request to its staff that I be invited to speak to their social studies teachers section.

As a consequence I received an invitation to appear at the meeting which was held at Enid and to give two speeches, one to the social studies teachers and one to the general assembly which was primarily to superintendents and principals. I was surprised at the invitation largely because of the second assignment, but I realized later it was a way of bringing in outside talent and using it in two capacities. I do not now recall much about the remarks I made to the general assembly but no doubt it would have related to the relation of the social studies to the high school curriculum in some way. The surprise that hit me was in a conversation with the secretary afterward. He admitted that they had expected an older man from the university and on quizzing him further, I discovered that the name recommended to them, Ellis, was so close to being Elliff that they thought they were getting him when they carried out the request of the Social Studies section.

I reported this to Elliff later, and he enjoyed it I think as much as I did. Elliff and I became rather close friends and one of his duties that interested me was that he was on the Board of Curators at Lincoln University and, as he was to reach retirement age at the university, his reappointment to that position was unlikely. He asked me if I would take his position if he could get the appointment made as his successor, and I told him I would. I already knew the history people at Lincoln and was interested in the problems of the segregated racial system I was working in for the first time. I know Elliff tried to get me named in his place, but I was not surprised when he did not succeed as the board there was heavily involved in politics and the members appointed were those who had political influence of their own.

When Elliff retired he was replaced on the accrediting committee by John Rufi in the College of Education. Rufi was certainly one of the outstanding members of the faculty who was responsible for the direction of the training of many of the outstanding people going into school administration, although his program was specifically designed for the high school principalship.

Another administrative job was wished upon me by Dean William Robbins of the Graduate School and also Chairman of the Department of Botany. Professor Lloyd Short of Political Science had been serving as acting dean every other summer while Robbins had the summer off. Short left for a position at Minnesota and Robbins asked me if I would take over the graduate school deanship on alternate summers while Robbins had his vacation. This I suppose was a more typical administrative experience. I found that I enjoyed working with the graduate students and the faculty who were their advisors. Unfortunately he had a secretary who seemed to think I was too young to make those decisions, and she was always trying to make them for me. Robbins and I hit it off fine, and we worked together well. I have forgotten whether I was already on the graduate committee or whether he appointed me, but from this time I served on the graduate committee which was largely made up of deans of divisions which did substantial amounts of graduate work plus a few professors from larger departments. I served as Acting Dean the summers of '36, '39, and '41. In the meantime Henry Bent had become dean and Robbins had left for the New York Botanical Garden. I learned a great deal about the strengths and weaknesses in the faculty in administering the Graduate School. There was a small group of faculty making sacrifices to take care of graduate students in summer session and a larger group who showed little interest. The graduate work was growing during this period because we were adding doctors degrees in some fields where we had only given masters.

Another committee assignment that I found most interesting was a library committee which was a new committee with only three members of which I was one. Dean Robbins and Arthur Fairchild, Professor of English, were the other two. The library was hard up for space, its budget was very small considering the needs, and there was a strong tendency to have branch libraries. This is always true but it is worse when you lack space in your main library. The work of the committee was primarily to distribute the funds that were allocated to the library for books and journals and here again the difference among your faculty and departments came out. Some of them were more aggressive and usually the ones who were doing the most work were always asking for money while others that were less alive seemed to make little attempt to build their collections. Our tendency on the committee was to turn over substantial funds to the librarian with instructions to keep these fields up in spite of the departments where we thought they were important departments that would some day be significant to us.

The two most interesting assignments, however, in connection with the library were selecting the new librarian and planning a new wing. The librarian choice was first, and in the end we picked Ben Powell, then an assistant librarian at Duke University. Ben was young for a head librarian but he impressed me very favorably with his knowledge and philosophy of library building. He became my candidate but I must admit at the time of the interview, I nearly lost him because of a sporty little hat that he wore of which the older members of the committee did not approve. It was a jaunty little pork-pie hat which seemed to turn him into an undergraduate student. Ben had a masters degree in library administration from Columbia and considerable work on his doctorate which he later completed. He was a fine librarian and did a lot for the University.

The second matter was the building of the west wing of the library, where again the committee played a large part in passing on the plans with Mr. Jamieson of Jamieson and Spearl Architects. Because of our tremendous shortage of lecture rooms, we provided for one large fine lecture hall in the library as well as seminar rooms for graduate classes and carrels in the book stacks. The result was a fine addition where both the University and State Historical Society libraries became adequately housed for the next several years.

Another committee assignment that was interesting that we later developed further was a personnel committee for the College of Arts and Science either just before or just after Tisdel retired as Dean and was succeeded by W. C. Curtis. Either Tisdel or Curtis set up the faculty personnel committee to review with him department recommendations on salary and rank. The original committee was made up of Edward H. Weatherly, Mitchell Tucker, myself and the Graduate Dean Henry Bent. I am not quite sure the Graduate Dean was a member; at least he was asked to be present and comment on these recommendations. Later he asked to be relieved of the duty because of the complaints he was receiving from the people who thought they were not treated generously enough by the

Dean of Arts. Although there were many ad hoc committee assignments, these were the standing committees on which I served and from whose work I derived a great deal of my reputation in the University and considerable satisfaction in some of the work we were able to accomplish.

A change in my situation at Missouri was made in 1941 when the history department at the University of Wisconsin made me an offer of a position there. I had gone to Madison on their invitation for an interview and while I already knew the American history people I met many others and saw nothing I disliked. The offer was a substantial increase in salary and had many other attractive features. Ruth and I had already talked about the possibility and the pros and cons were well rehearsed. I informed the department chairman and he informed the dean and President Middlebush. I was asked not to accept the offer until I talked to the dean and the president. In the end I was urged to stay and an alternative offer of change in my position was proposed. The big change was that I would be relieved of my work in education and be solely responsible for my historical work. This was not a matter which I suggested but was freely offered. In fact, I would have many regrets in giving up my work in training teachers but it was obvious to my colleagues that I could never carry the load of two positions and do really top level work. In the end Missouri offered to equal the Wisconsin salary, to give me an office by myself and to provide some stenographic assistance. With these terms it was up to Ruth and me and we decided we would prefer to stay at Missouri.

I believe my first real contact with top level administration at the University of Missouri occurred at New Year's 1942. For a long time the University of Missouri had had an annual inspection committee called the Governor's Board of Visitors. It had apparently been established by the legislature at one time as a check on the Board of Curators—not a check on the authority but a check on the information they gave the governor and the General Assembly. The Board had some very distinguished members over the years and one of them, John Dalton, became governor and played a very important part in higher education. My contact at New Year's 1942 was almost accidental. The chairman of the Board of Visitors at that time was Allen P. Green of Mexico, Missouri, President of the Green Refractories, and one of the very wealthy men in the state. He was also a very unusual and unique personality that you could not help but admire as you got acquainted with him. At any rate he was not a person to have charge of a committee and make a routine report. For this report he had convinced the Board it was highly desirable to survey the building needs of not only the University but all the state colleges and devote the report to the great lack of facilities in higher education in Missouri.

It was the last day of 1941. Leslie Cowan, Secretary of the Board of Curators, called me and told me he would like to talk to me. When I got to his office, he said that he and President Middlebush had been working with the Board of Visitors and that Green had asked for some help in drafting a report. He had already rough drafted something but had no confidence that it was in proper shape. Cowan said that Middlebush suggested that I might be willing to go over and help him. We had no special plans for New Year's Eve or New Year's Day and after checking with Ruth, I agreed to go. I drove over to Green's office at the brick plant. The plant was closed down of course but his office was open and he made me welcome and showed me what he had done. Well, it was a bigger job than we could do in an evening so we agreed that I would come back in the morning. In the meantime I would read all of his draft. I returned in the morning with a recasting of the early part of his report, which seemed to please him, but I found he was not an easy person to write for. He had very firm ideas about certain expressions that he wanted to use. So the task became not one alone of making the report intelligible but of doing it within the framework of a number of his pet words and expressions. He did have a large number of charts that he now exhibited to me. He seemed to have somebody in his office who was good at this and he used these to good effect. What he actually proposed was a great expansion of the physical facilities of all the higher education institutions based on a bond issue that would cost over $90 million. I had no confidence that this was a reasonable possibility within Missouri's finances but of course that was not my problem.

My problem was to put it in readable English which I proceeded to do within the limits that he would allow me freedom to operate. We got along on a very friendly basis because he was that kind of person. He gossiped at great length about his relations with Middlebush and how he had taught him to hunt quail and his criticism of the way Cowan and Middlebush were conducting the university. Anyway at the end of the day we had a manuscript of the report that I thought was passable, but of course he had to submit it to other members of the Board. Before I left he reached back of his desk and took down from a shelf a new copy of Webster's *Dictionary of Synonyms* and after inscribing it, he presented it to me.

The Board met the following week and after they had made their revisions I was called in to "bind up the wounds." It was a most interesting experience, and looking back at it historically the basic list of needs that he and his committee had arrived at were what we were following 10 and 15 years later. It is perhaps needless to say that the General Assembly paid little attention to the recommendations, and I doubt that the governor did.

As I write this in the 1970s two interesting thoughts occur to me. Green's grandson, Governor Christopher Bond, is establishing a pretty clear record for being the least interested in promoting public higher education of any governor during my life in Missouri. The other relates to the work of the Board of Visitors itself. I have looked over the list of structures planned for each institution, and there is a remarkable correspondence, considering all factors, between what was proposed and what we later built. Built, I might add, at much higher cost, while during that long interval thousands of students and faculty suffered from inadequate facilities of all kinds.

Chapter 14

History and War

The beginning of the war with the probable involvement of the United States in it had a tremendous effect on the University of Missouri as it did at all campuses. While it was true before, it was especially true after Pearl Harbor. The students, especially undergraduates, subject to the draft found it difficult, if not impossible, to stick to their work, and to measure up with their usual quality. Graduate students who for the most part were older had less difficulty, but many of them as did some of ours joined the Navy officers' training rather than wait for the draft and go in as a private. This was all part of a larger picture of great unrest in the public at large and the campus participated in it.

After our entrance into the war the regular enrollments declined very speedily and the University began to develop programs for the military services, the first of which was a diesel motor school developed under Harry Rubey in the College of Engineering. The younger members of the faculty began to enter the services, and the Air Corps particularly was aggressive at recruiting faculty members as teachers for their schools and training programs. Many colleagues such as Raymond Peck and Willoughby Johnson were caught up in that program while others joined the Navy. Among them was Assistant Registrar Harry Rummell. As he had gone through his basic training and was involved in other work, he wrote to me and urged me to follow suit. He said he was in an office where he knew I was wanted to administer a Navy School. I was more than a little intrigued by the idea, I presume partly by the psychology of having been too young for World War I while many of my friends and brothers, Bill and Earl, had enlisted in the Marines and Army. Eventually I followed Harry's advice and made a trip to St. Louis to talk to the Navy people there. They were all enthusiastic until they tested my eyes and found I had only 4/20 vision without my glasses which they said would not qualify. I told them the duty to which I thought I was to be assigned but it seems the Navy was following rules for deck officers. They called me back some days later, the officer in charge saying that he thought he could get the Navy to break that rule in my case but he never succeeded.

Shortly before that time the Army began to recruit for military government teams. It seemed to be looking for experienced people in engineering, fire and police officers, city attorneys, persons with local government experience, and a very few people for school administration. The theory was that these teams would be assigned to military occupied areas to restore order and services and get the civilian government operating in good order again after the military had moved on. The idea was fine in theory but actually it did not work out that way as the war developed. I put in an application along with Conrad Hammer who was in Ag Economics. I knew Conrad had applied since he had asked me to write a letter of recommendation to accompany his letter of application. Not long afterward I was called to Jefferson Barracks, south of St. Louis, for a physical examination and an interview in which I was asked flatly what kind of rank I expected. When I replied that I was not interested in rank but was interested in getting into that branch of service, it seemed to please the officer very much.

I kept the dean's office as well as the department informed of my plans. A little to my surprise just as summer session was starting in '43, I came in from working the garden on a Saturday morning and found a letter addressed to "Captain" Elmer Ellis, notifying me that I had a commission and to report to Jefferson Barracks between such and such hours on a certain date. Later I found that Conrad Hammer had received the same orders and had a major's commission. It seemed to embarrass Conrad as I who had written for him had a lower commission. It seemed quite appropriate to me as he had service experience in both the Navy and Army. We combined our forces and reported in at Jefferson Barracks together, although Ruth and I drove to St. Louis and spent the night before reporting with my sister, Martha, and her husband.

Con and I had equipped ourselves with uniforms as instructed and, after reporting at Jefferson Barracks, we did virtually nothing but listen to a few informal lectures on military courtesy. The two or three days' delay there were completely unnecessary, but one morning we had orders to report to Camp Custer in Michigan which was a military police training station near Kalamazoo. There we found we had arrived for a four-week training program that had already gone through two weeks of the four. We barely got acquainted with our associates when we were informed that since we had arrived so late, we would stay over for the next four weeks which displeased us but was best for us in the long run. We were now better informed in what would happen in our training, and found that we would very likely go to the University of Pittsburgh for three months of language and area training, which turned out to be the German language and the Balkan area. With this in mind, I encouraged Ruth to come to Kalamazoo and I went in one Saturday night and met her at the hotel where I had made a reservation. The next morning,

Sunday, we went looking for an apartment and eventually found a house and moved in. She drove me back to camp early Monday morning as we were on a six-day training schedule and this was to be the next to the last week of our program at Custer. We wound up our program two weeks later on Saturday night with orders to report to Pittsburgh.

Ruth picked up Conrad Hammer and me at the camp and we started for Pittsburgh, arriving there Sunday afternoon. We found an apartment about four blocks from the Cathedral of Learning, while Conrad lived in a hotel as did most of the men whose wives were not with them. I then began regular classroom work, German language training all forenoon with a standard teacher plus two native speakers who took us in turn, while afternoons were devoted to area study with a great variety of professors, natives of the Balkans and others who knew something about the region. On the whole, I thought it was well done. I found myself delighted particularly with the German language work. I went into the advanced section, the only member of the group it turned out who had never sometime in his life spoken German, a credit, I suspect, to Bill Bek's teaching many years before.

I found the University of Pittsburgh a very interesting place and made friends with a few members of the faculty. I saw the Chancellor on several public occasions. I became well-acquainted with the advantages and limitations of the one skyscraper building, jokingly said by many to have 57 floors to correspond with the 57 products of the Heinz Company, one of the large donors. The Carnegie Institute was nearby and we made some use of its library. The Hebrew Young Men's Association let us have access to its recreational facilities, and we swam there two or three times a week. We also went up to a university gymnasium on a nearby hill where we played basketball or sometimes baseball. Our apartment was quite adequate although, typical of downtown Pittsburgh, one had to scrub the table before every meal in order to get rid of the soot coming largely from the steel mills which were not far away.

Soon after we arrived, Conrad Hammer had orders to report to the Pentagon. He was immediately sent to Africa with our invading army there to serve as an economics consultant in agriculture that led him to a career both with the Army and later the State Department. I do not recall seeing him again until we visited the Hammers in Bonn, Germany, in 1952.

The work was interesting, and I improved my German conversation ability tremendously. I was amazed at how much I had forgotten since 1924 when I last had instruction or since 1929 when I passed my test in German at Iowa, but it came back under the intensive instruction and study. After about ten weeks of this, I had a letter from the Pentagon saying that the Army was setting up a historical branch and inquired if I would be interested in joining it. I replied that I would have been but since the Army had spent so much money on instruction for military government, I thought I should stay with it. A few days later I received orders to report to an office in Washington just a week before my twelve weeks were over. We packed the car and wound up in Washington that night. The next day I reported to the old Munitions Building and was directed to the Pentagon where I met Colonel John Kemper and Lt. Colonel Charles Taylor. Kemper was a West Point product and had a masters degree in history from Columbia while Taylor was a medieval history professor from Harvard—both very fine people as I learned to know. We had some general conversation about what I would do in this work. According to their present plan, I would be stationed in Washington and would make periodic trips to Europe for various tours of temporary duty. These preliminaries over, Kemper conducted me to a big room where there were about a dozen desks occupied by men in uniform. He took me over to a corner where sitting at a desk was Chester Starr, my old high school and college student. I think Chester was more surprised than I was. Without realizing that we recognized each other, Kemper said very formally "Major Starr will instruct you in your duties." Chester, who had an ROTC commission, had been in Ft. Benning training infantry before being transferred here. We exchanged information very quickly. He invited Ruth and me to his apartment for dinner and the evening and he gave me instructions for how to find it. He was unable to call his wife Gretchen, as they had no telephone, so it was a surprise to her to have two strangers arrive at her door, not knowing who they were nor why they came. But everything turned out very well, Chester soon arrived, we had a delightful evening, and we and the Starrs became very close friends.

During the next several days we secured an apartment not far from the Starrs in Parkfairfax, Alexandria, after which I reported for duty and really assisted Chester in completing a tactical study of the Buna-Gona campaign from the combat records of the army and auxiliary services. Our apartment was unfurnished and since we had no desire to move furniture from Columbia we went to a new large Sears, Roebuck store, where we purchased the necessary equipment.

In the meantime, I was getting acquainted with many of the people around the historical branch, the most interesting one being Robert Livingston Wright, a civilian. He turned out to be a brother of George Wright who was a textbook representative for one of the publishers. George was quite a different person from his older brother. Robert was distinctive looking because he had no hair on his head including his eyebrows. He was a professor of Turkish at Princeton and had been president of Robert College in Istanbul. I found him most interesting and delightful, and a person who had few illusions about the way government operated. When you needed to get something done, he was a good advisor. A number of the other military people around were also men whom I had known before as they were trained historians. I suppose my best friend in the group was Bell Wiley, who was over in the ground forces history section then located in the Army War College. With him were two others that I knew by reputation, Robert Palmer from Princeton and Robert Greenfield from Hopkins.

The Air Corps was working on somewhat different kinds of military history than the Army was. As we were general staff and G 2, presumably we exercised some supervision over these units, but until much later when I got orders to have a history of army training prepared, it was not in any sense direct. Starr and Harris Warren, another historian, were soon sent to Europe to form part of a team for the 5th Army in Italy which Starr was to command. I had expected, according to the way I was instructed at the branch, that I might follow Starr and Warren to Italy. A short time later, just before Christmas, I suddenly had orders to report to San Francisco for service in the Pacific. This certainly changed our plans because there was every indication that I would spend the rest of the war there with the 7th Division.

During the few days before leaving we were unable to dispose of our furniture so I had the Army transport it to Columbia. Perfect timing was impossible, and after the furniture left by truck our friends Sam and Frances Wennberg invited us to stay with them during the several days before the order came through permitting me to leave the Pentagon. Upon its arrival we left for Columbia where I would wait for further orders. After a week in Columbia I received orders to leave for San Francisco. Leaving Ruth in Columbia, where she began working in the recently organized Western Historical Manuscripts Collection, I took the train to San Francisco. Following my arrival there I went by ferry from Fort Mason to Fort McDowell, which was on Angel Island. The one stop made between Fort Mason and Angel Island was at Alcatraz.

I had fully expected to spend two or three days at Fort McDowell and then ship out probably by plane. As it turned out, I was there a full month before I had orders to leave. During that time I did nothing except qualify myself on the rifle and pistol range with all of the standard weapons and wait. Fortunately for me, I was joined a few days after I got there by Corporal James MacGregor Burns who had been sent out by the Pentagon. He had to stay in the barracks while I lived in the BOQ. To keep him out of K.P. and other duties of that kind, I filed a statement that he was in training in his field as a historian and was under my supervision. He spent most of his time in the San Francisco public library. In later years Burns made an impressive record with his publications. I still had, of course, a great deal more freedom, and every day after the day's orders were posted and I was sure there was nothing for me, I took the ferry over to San Francisco and either went to the public library or to the lobby of one of the big hotels around the square where I read or wrote or both. I found it too difficult to get to Berkeley to make that a worthwhile trip so my regular routine was to go to San Francisco for my lunch and dinner and return in the evening. I also gradually ran into a few other people with whom I had some connection. One was a Colonel at Fort Mason who was alumni secretary at Central College. I spent one evening with him and his wife and had a delightful time. Shortly before I left, my brother Bill showed up in San Francisco as his company was transferring him to Oakland and, as long as we both were there, we had dinner together. Finally, I was ordered to report to Fort Mason for a briefing session. I found that I was with a group of other officers who were told we were to conduct troops to Hawaii on a troop carrier, without any time being stated. My troop turned out to be exactly 100 men including Burns who were stationed at McDowell. When I returned, I found non-commissioned officers there already training the men in various exercises, mainly suiting them for travel. The exercises looked for the most part to me like routine time-killing procedures and surely the men knew everything that they were being taught, some of them actually having been in the Pacific on earlier tours. My group consisted of a miscellaneous group of "casuals" which meant they were replacements from various services, and I believe nearly every branch of the army was represented.

Late one afternoon we reported to the dock with our packs. I had by this time been issued a carbine with some live ammunition, and we boarded the ferry which took us directly to a ship which was docked in San Francisco next to the long bridge over the Bay. As we disembarked from the ferry, some Red Cross women served us coffee and donuts which turned out to be our evening meal. Then we went aboard the *George W. Julian,* a liberty ship which was pressed into service as a troop carrier and manned by the Coast Guard. I found myself quartered with five other officers in a cabin in double decker bunks and my men all in the No. 4 hold where they were in six-level bunks. The first night out the first of a series of nightly developments happened that made the trip most unpleasant. The shower and toilet facilities the men used were obviously faulty and the water would cover the floor of the men's quarters. It became almost routine for Jim Burns to come up to our cabin and wake me up around 2 or 3 in the morning to tell me that they were in trouble again. I would take a look at it, then go up to the Army Commanding Officer and wake him up. Then he would argue with me about the fact that the plumbers were not army personnel and they got overtime if they worked at night. However, I held my own on this, and he would eventually call the plumbers and we would get through the night without serious difficulty.

My biggest surprise was when I found the first morning that each of the four companies had to supply its own cooks. I took a rapid census of our men and naturally could not find one who would admit he had ever cooked. I finally picked a watchmaker from Philadelphia. Over his protesting, I made him chief cook and let him pick his own help which did not make him too popular. He did very well for a watchmaker.

Sometime before noon the next day we were moving and went out under the Golden Gate Bridge. I think most of my men, like me, had never been to sea before. The long swell made the ship roll a great deal, and by night there was hardly a man on that ship in my company or any other who was able to eat dinner. Nearly everyone was seasick. When we had gone beyond the bridge, we were joined by a group of vessels none of which carried troops and one was an LST. We had one destroyer escort and two planes above us. We also had a World War I liberty ship that burned coal and could make about three knots, which set our speed and accounted for the fact that it took 13 days to reach Honolulu.

When we were three or four days out, I ran into a First Lieutenant who thought he was part of our team. He turned out to be Edmund Love, a school teacher from Michigan, with a masters in history. I put him to work helping with the men since he had seen quite a lot of army service and was agreeable and efficient. Other than these developments and the usual nuisances that go along with about 900 people crowded in a little space, things went smoothly enough, certainly as smoothly as I expected. We landed in some confusion late one evening because my men of different services had different orders, but there were people at the dock to assist them. The Corporal, the First Lieutenant and I were transferred to what was really a quarantine quarters for Camp Scofield, the big military post on Oahu, the largest peacetime post in the Army. The next day we were visited by Lt. Col. S. L. A. Marshall who came over to meet us and made every indication that he expected to stay with us for some time. This interested me because I had been told before I left Washington that I would replace Marshall and he would come home for a new assignment.

We were in quarantine three days as I recall and then were moved to the headquarters of the 7th Division where we were attached. We wound up in a small office on the ground floor which was equipped with a couple of battered typewriters and all the office supplies we needed. Shortly after that Colonel Marshall took us with him to an "interview" with a group of 27th Division troops who had been on the Eniwetok operations—the operation I was to accompany had I gone directly to Hawaii. At least that was what the men thought in the historical branch in Washington. Colonel Marshall did go and apparently had enjoyed himself immensely, and now was delaying his departure in order to wind up the narrative of the operation. Marshall had a unique method of approaching this combat history. He was interested, as the entire branch was, in small unit operations and his methodology was one of getting together a group of people who had been in the operation, usually a platoon, and having them recapitulate it to him and answer questions that he might ask. I was interested in his methodology as the Colonel was a newspaper man, not a historian. It had some distinct advantages and a great many weaknesses. He method was to open the matter with a question, ask for volunteers, and let each one say what he wanted to. Then he would dictate a version of what he concluded had been the consensus to a typist who would type it out. Often it was easy to see that if the platoon lieutenant was there, he did not always agree with what some of the men said and with what the Colonel dictated. Furthermore, Marshall would take this typed manuscript, read it over several times, sit down at his typewriter, and type a new version throwing the original one away. And this became his story of that particular operation unless there were other units involved who were also interviewed, and as a result there might be some conflicts to resolve there.

A short time later I felt I earned his displeasure (as a professional historian I am afraid I was suspect anyway) by suggesting to him that it would strengthen our procedure if we would get a stenographer to take an accurate record of the questions asked as well as the answers and that would become a part of the permanent record.

Before I left the Pentagon I had been given another task to do that a Captain Drummond in the office was working on from the record and that was the Attu operation. Two of the regiments of the 7th Division had participated in this and I had been asked to interview them—those still with the units—and try to clarify some of the problems involved. Colonel Marshall agreed and assigned that to me and kept Jim Burns and Edmund Love with him, although Lieutenant Love was given special assignments from time to time with units like the landing craft and others. The men I was to contact were located in a different part of the island about five miles from where we were headquartered, but as jeeps with drivers were always available I went over and introduced myself to the officers involved. They rounded up the men who had been with the Attu operation who were still there. It was surprisingly few, but I went into this problem with the men. The first thing I learned was that no daily records had been kept but had all been written up after the operation was over. After the main operation was over, a group of sergeants got together and worked out the records as best they could remember them. Nevertheless, I started with these records for the questions and would read the entry, sentence by sentence, and ask for comments much as Colonel Marshall did for the Eniwetok. In a series of these group interviews which I wrote up myself I was able to send back to the branch materials that Drummond needed. In fact, this was my main work in Hawaii. I found it a fascinating bit of history as the unit had never been under fire before, had been trained for desert warfare and suddenly was shipped to Alaska.

In the meantime, I wrote a guarded letter back to Colonel Kemper, realizing it probably would be censored and Marshall might see it, in which I made it as clear to him as I could that Marshall was not coming home in a hurry and asked him for instructions for further duty beyond those I was taking from Colonel Marshall. The answers were noncommittal because as I found the people in the branch were frankly afraid of Colonel Marshall's influence. He was a veteran of World War I, had been around the Army a long time, and had started writing these histories before the branch had been organized. I now turned my attention to helping with the Eniwetok matter and did what I could to assist Colonel Marshall. Nevertheless, it was easy to see he resented a professional historian second guessing him on what he was doing. He did go home finally after the Eniwetok account was virtually complete.

Not long after Marshall went back to the branch, I received orders to report to the Pentagon. The orders were that I could take any available transportation and as this was an opportunity to have some experience with flying I asked for air transportation and reported one morning, much earlier than needed, to the air base at Pearl Harbor. We took off about 9:30 in an unarmed bomber. I do not remember whether it was a B-24 or B-25 but I think it was the former. My fellow passengers were all returning pilots going back to fly out other planes and there was an enormously large damaged motor lashed down in the front part of the cabin. It was almost midnight when we arrived in San Francisco and came in at the south end of the Bay and flew up to an airbase north of the Bay. We spent the night there and the next morning a bus took us to Fort Mason where I was able to get railroad transportation on the Santa Fe to Kansas City. I called Ruth to have her meet me at Kansas City and called Bill who was now living at Oakland who met me when the train went through and we had a short visit. Traveling all night, the following day, and part of the next night I arrived in Kansas City and found Ruth was there to meet me. A few days later we were on the road, driving our car back to Washington.

Upon my return to the branch, I was officially instructed that I had been brought back because the chief of staff had ordered a history of military training during the war and it was thought I was the only one on the staff who had a good background to do it. I was never sure of the whole reason because I suspected Colonel Marshall had a finger in it. He was still in the office when I got back but never spoke to me. A short time later he took off to England where he had set up a history team—many of the men I had trained—to follow the Normandy invasions into France and Germany.

Because of the number of people coming through the office for various lengths of time before they were assigned to the field, on my own I started a seminar on writing combat history. Formerly they had come in one at a time and had been tutored. So for the next year, I generally managed this as well as supervised the writing of the military training history which was to be written by the different services—air, ground, and service of supply. I think it is fair to say that all resented having to stop and do it, because they were all busy with what seemed to them more important work. This was particularly true of the ground force. It took direct orders from the headquarters to get the service force to perform at all.

We were able to get a furnished apartment in Parkfairfax which was in the same building where Gretchen Starr and her baby Jennifer were living. Jennifer was born a few months after Chester was sent to Italy. The other people in the apartment house were all service-connected people, and except for the Washington summer heat and the inability to get more than a small rations of gasoline without cheating, we had a pleasant time. In the meantime Louis Geiger, who had been recruited by me, was sent over to join Chester and his team. I also was able to recruit Boyd Shafer to come into the branch to help me with this history of army training and when I left the next spring, he took charge. In the meantime my commission had been changed to Major.

One of our most pleasant experiences living in Washington was an association with Sam and Frances Wennberg and their two children. Sam was in one of the economic agencies and later when he was assigned to go to England to do some work, Frances went to Chicago with the children to stay with her family while he was gone. Of course, Sam's travel orders like everyone else's were indeterminate and he spent several days with us after the family had left. In fact, Sam would come home at night carrying his suitcase and leave with it again in the morning, expecting orders. For several days he came back every night. It was certainly a frustrating experience for Sam but we enjoyed his time with us. Our second bedroom was pleasant to have because of visitors. The Weatherlys who spent the winter at the University of Virginia spent some time with us. Ed came up once to work in the Library of Congress on his own while Anne stayed with the children who were in school. We visited them once and the first thing five-year-old Ted pointed out to us was the road back to Columbia. Sam Davis, who was teaching not far from Washington in a navy school, spent several weekends with us as did several other friends, including Tom Brady on one occasion when he was in Washington for a meeting related to Missouri's area and language training. The work at the Pentagon was interesting and I became well acquainted with the fine qualities of Livy (Robert Livingstone) Wright who was our civilian chief. He certainly knew his way around government and taught me how to get in to the Secretary of War's office without going through channels. Secretary Stimson had a civilian aide, a New York lawyer named Goldthwaite Dorr who wore a beard much like Jonas Viles'. As he seemed to have no particular title, I found it always possible to get to him and get any orders sent down to the lower echelon that I needed in order to get my training history underway.

I think that back of the desire to have this training history written was the fact that the American Council on Education was planning to have one written and the Army was very concerned about that. Therefore the Army wanted one of its own. Boyd Shafer eventually completed this in a manuscript which I read and thought was very good, but in the end it was never published. The Army history we were working on ran into too many volumes then, and this was one that was left out.

Along in late February or early March I had a letter from President Middlebush asking me to meet him in New York. He said the University was anticipating some great problems in the immediate post-war period, and he needed to talk to me about them. This was when the war was obviously ending in Europe and the Pacific. I met him there at the University Club. Leslie Cowan was with him. Middlebush proposed that when I came back I would take a job that he had labeled Vice President with the very awkward title of "For Extra-Divisional Educational Activities." He had visualized this taking off his desk a great many of the administrative tasks, such as the library, the general extension, admissions and registration, R.O.T.C., student health, counseling, and many others that the Army would have called bits and pieces of the organization. He said he had already contacted one of the senators, I believe Bennett Clark, who had assured him that there would be no trouble in getting early discharge under those circumstances. He also told me that Curtis had only one year left in the Arts Dean office and if I preferred that job, I might move to that when Curtis left. I told him I would respond after I had talked to Ruth and had thought about it a day or two.

As a result sometime in March, I was discharged, the branch having extracted a promise from me to come back for the month of August and recheck the progress of training history. In the meantime the seminar on combat history had virtually dried up, as we had now sufficient staff to handle the field units. McArthur's command had been a problem because he had insisted on picking his own and no one wanted to dispute his authority to do so.

We cancelled out our apartment by letter to our friends from whom we had rented, paid the rent, and helped find a new tenant for them. When the orders came through, we loaded the car and drove home through Peoria purposely to see sister Susan, her husband Bob and their children, Carol, David and Rob who was very ill in the hospital. We spent a weekend with them and except for little Rob's illness, we enjoyed seeing them. Later, after Rob's recovery, they moved to San Diego where Bob had a job with the *San Diego Tribune*.

Back in Columbia we reclaimed our house, and soon I was established in an office on the first floor of Jesse Hall across from the President. Aside from going back to Washington in August and carrying out my obligation to the history branch to wind up my duty there, I was busy at the University trying to build this office into what Middlebush wanted it to be. In January Dean Curtis decided to resign early and I took over the Arts Dean office along with my old friends, Frank Stephens and Vera Ward, and in time to meet the post-war flood of students returning from service. Tom Brady succeeded me as Vice President and continued building it into a very useful organization.

Chapter 15

The College of Arts and Science

The College of Arts and Science was an exceptional Division of the University in that about one-third of all the faculty on the Columbia campus were members of that college. Nearly one-half of the students were registered in the college, which is misleading because the large number of students was due to the large number of freshmen and sophomores who registered in the college for two years, and then transferred to one of the professional schools such as journalism or law or education. I believe I had been largely responsible for changing education from a "school" to a "college" because it seemed to me a practical way of improving our student counseling. Still many students who eventually went into education for their degree stayed one or two years in the arts college in spite of this change. With this large group that virtually involved all the university programs, the problem of managing was substantial.

My experience on the Personnel Committee of the College began with Curtis' appointment as dean. The college had suffered from misadministration in some departments, where poor chairmen had become senior faculty members and the tendency was not to replace them. The committee was able with the help of the dean to cure some of the worst of these problems by advising the dean on personnel problems in the department when they differed from the chairman's views. I presume the greatest effect we had was on mathematics, at least in the beginning. I discussed these remaining problems, however, with the various University committees, and eventually we changed the system considerably by introducing a more democratic government in the departments. Many of them adopted rotating chairmanships or three-year terms of office for the chairmanship so that in most departments the chairmanship became virtually elective, although the departments differed substantially and some neither wanted nor would have profited from an elective chairmanship.

Nevertheless, with the Personnel Committee developing as it did, the chairman eventually became elective in most departments. This led to some difficulties—the one that I recall most painful to me happened in the Department of Zoology where Mary Guthrie was chairman, having replaced Curtis when he became dean. She was a very able faculty member, a very good scientist and she was the only woman in the department. Early in my administration I was besieged by the department as each member came to me individually asking for a change. It was striking to me that none of them promoted anyone as a successor, but with such overwhelming sentiment in the department, I could see every reason why I should make a change, which I did. By the next year Guthrie resigned to take a position elsewhere which was no doubt due to her replacement as chairman. From the standpoint of efficiency in my office, her leaving did not improve the department, as her replacement was not as efficient, at least in the bureaucratic sense, but it was a happier department.

One incident that always remains in my memory occurred soon after I became dean and Gustaf Wahlin became chairman of the mathematics department. A member of the department, while at a national meeting, called Wahlin and informed him that he had an offer from Notre Dame which he was going to take unless the University of Missouri met it. Wahlin immediately came to my office and repeated the conversation. Knowing the person involved I said to the chairman, "He hasn't an offer," and he agreed. I said, "He is a person we would find it difficult to replace. You call him and tell him that we will not consider outside offers unless they are in writing. If he will bring this offer in writing, the dean will consider seriously what we might do to meet it. But we would not take any action on the basis of oral offers." Wahlin reported soon afterwards that his professor was greatly disappointed but did not promise to bring a written offer and when he returned, did not have one. This was the only case of this kind that ever was on my desk, but I suspect other people who may have been tempted in this way realized that it did not work with their chairman or dean or president.

I believe that none of us anticipated the great flood of students that came in the fall of '46, although we knew it would be large and we were recruiting faculty wherever we possibly could. When the group finally did come, we found we had too few faculty and there was almost no supply of additional ones. We had already done away with the worst of our rules, preventing both husband and wife employment at the University, and now the rest went by the board, the only exception being if there were administrative relationships involved.

English and mathematics proved to be great staffing problems immediately and we experimented with math in some large classes as part of the answer. In both fields we recruited faculty wives from the University, Stephens College, and Christian College by approaching them directly if they had proper qualifications, and in math using several bachelor level "assistant instructors" for the beginning courses which were really high school level courses. This proved to be the worst problem although the problem of classrooms and housing was also tremendous. Barracks buildings from army posts were brought in and re-erected, and housing trailers which had been used at war plants were grouped in three large areas. The difficulty of faculty housing was relieved to a large extent by bringing some temporary officers' quarters from Fort Leonard Wood, re-erecting these with some improvements, and using them for faculty housing.

Student advising also was a problem but as most of the veterans were older than the usual student and some had been in college before, they needed very little help in advising. This did not become such an acute problem until we began again to get the students directly from high school. The problem of getting the students registered in the fall of '46 was one of the roughest we had to surmount. I recall one specific instance when a group of faculty and I met with what we assumed would be something less than 500 students in the Waters Auditorium, where with the large supply of registration material I planned to go over the program with them, as they were all starting in the arts college. In the meantime they would fill out their registration forms and would take them to a faculty member for checking, and we would handle them in this whole-sale fashion. When they ceased coming, there were over 700 and we had seats for 500. Ed Palmquist found that the auditorium in Mumford was not in use, so he with some of the staff took all who could not find seats in Waters and led them to Mumford. I suppose that was one of the roughest nights of registration and some of the poorest advisement that we ever did at the University. But the maturity of the students saved it from being a debacle. I recall that we had already postponed registration a week to get prepared adequately for it, but even then we were exceedingly short of staff who were experienced in this work.

As I moved into the Dean's office I made an attempt to continue some teaching, especially my Recent U.S. History lecture course, but it proved to be impossible. I was so busy with my administrative duties that I found myself going to my lecture some mornings wondering what I would say about the subject. I did continue my seminar and supervised a few doctoral theses particularly for people like Louis Geiger, Gilbert Fite and William Settle. In each of these cases I was ably assisted by Lewis Atherton. Atherton had been my first doctoral candidate and had been such an able teacher and scholar that we retained him in the department.

One of my students, Clarence Roberts, had taken a job at our campus at Rolla, and I induced him to change his research into something that would fit his probable future in a technological school. With the help of the head of ceramic engineering, we got him interested in the history of brickmaking. This changed to firebrick making as we got further into the subject, because there was little written that related to it in American historical writing. Although he did a very respectable job and published from it, my planning was all of no real moment because, as soon as he got his degree, he took a job in a liberal arts college and spent the rest of his career there.

The most difficult problem in the college as I saw it except for the staffing problem was student advising. In many departments it was difficult to find people who would try to do good advising, and sometimes I wondered why some of them went into teaching at all. In order to do a better job we began to preadvise in advance of registration and did a great deal of it in our office particularly with the beginners. Thomas Harris, an English instructor, who was a marvelously good advisor was induced to join our staff and become an assistant first to Frank Stephens and later to Francis English, who replaced Stephens when he retired.

Stephens retired at 70 and as I knew he would be at a loss for something to do with his time I started early to discuss with him the possibility of writing a history of the College of Arts, which he decided to do. We gave him a small office and stenographic help and he really went to work. After he had produced three or four chapters, which Tom Brady and I read and commented on, we had a little seminar on the subject. We decided that since Frank was finding it difficult to separate the history of the arts college from the history of the University he should develop it into a history of the University, a task that took almost ten years to finish. It was quite painful to have to talk him into cutting out large sections of what he had written on the grounds that it had little application today. For instance, he had a full chapter on the "Missouri grading system" which we had abandoned and which had never been fully effective anyway. But to Frank, who had lived through it, it was something of great interest and importance.

The choice of Francis English to succeed Stephens was a most fortunate one but one I disliked to make, because Francis was doing so well with the Western Historical Manuscript Collection and with the development of Missouri history as a field of study in the department. With the retirement of Viles, Stephens, and Wrench, the department was undergoing very substantial changes. While Charles Mullett continued to teach his full load and Tom Brady, with his administrative duties, continued to do some teaching, Lewis Atherton began to carry the bulk of the American history work, aided by Walter Scholes and later by James Bugg. Harvey DeWeerd, who had been John Wolf's replacement, was soon to leave for full time research. David Pinkney was his replacement.

I found that my work in the Dean's office was without any particular training and I profited immensely by annual meetings that were being held by the arts deans of the Mississippi Valley state universities. About 25 deans met at different campuses each year and usually without any formal agenda talked over our common problems. I found these most interesting and educational as some of the older deans had had a great deal of experience. They could analyze an idea that some of us might have thought was new but they had tried before, and at least sketch for us the weaknesses as well as the strengths of it. I found Henning Larsen of Illinois, whom I had known at the University of Iowa, especially helpful.

One incident developed early in these meetings when the Missouri Valley Conference of Deans met in Albuquerque. Dean Lawson of the arts college at the University of Kansas was there. It was the first time I had met him. He was a lively person of Swedish descent with a good sense of humor and a terrific tease. He picked me as a natural enemy, being new and from Missouri, and all through the forenoon session he made adverse remarks about Missouri and what he called its pretension. As we walked to lunch Henning Larsen remarked that Lawson was riding me rather hard and suggested a plan which I agreed might be useful. The first time after lunch that Lawson made a crack about Missouri, I asked, "Dean Lawson, do you know why Kansas has so many Swedes and Missouri has so many mules?" He answered, "No, why?" Again following my script, I said, "Missouri had first choice." He never bothered me again.

It was during this time I became involved with the American Council on Education through its Instruction and Evaluation Committee, which was first chaired by T. R. McConnell and later by Ralph Tyler. I was their successor but fear I did not give the same quality of leadership as chairman. I doubt that there was anything particularly notable about this experience except that I came to know some very fine people and learned a good deal from some of them.

The most important work in the college during those years was securing faculty. Our salaries were low and after 1950 we had no retirement plan except social security, which made it difficult to secure first-rate people. In general I think it is fair to say we had our best luck in recruiting new Ph.D.s from state universities. We found Ivy League graduates difficult, especially as some colleges hid their top graduates from us. We had to use a spy system to find out who their best graduates were. Then too, either the teachers or their wives frequently yearned so much for the East that it was useless to recruit them from some universities so we virtually quit trying.

University income, however, never kept pace with the growing need in numbers nor in programs. Moreover, we were restricted by our low salaries to recruiting new and, largely, inexperienced members, which in itself is not bad if you have good applicants from which to recruit. Two exceptions that I personally recruited from the Ivy League were Stubbs Brushwood from Columbia and Albert Brent from Princeton. In each case our departments involved were very weak in leadership.

Next to the difficulty in recruiting faculty was our lack of buildings. Outside of the sciences, I do not believe a single member of the arts faculty had an adequate office and certainly many of those in science did not either. This was so bad that in the post-war period we tried to make greater use of the classrooms and the laboratories we had by scheduling classes on the half hour. The main purpose of this was not to start a half hour earlier in the morning but to make better use of the noon hour which had been virtually impossible to use with noon meals at dormitories and fraternities set by habit and economy at 12:00 and not easily subject to change. We found, however, that students would take an 11:30 or a 12:30 class. We tried not to schedule a student under any circumstances in both these periods. It increased usage substantially, and later after enrollments began to grow again we had to revive the system. It is still in use.

One of the major improvements that I saw possible as arts college dean was a program for the improvement of teaching. Not that Missouri's teaching was worse than elsewhere. It probably was better, because in several departments there existed a definite and deep interest in good instruction. But during my many visits to junior colleges where I visited classes and occasionally visited a class of a former instructor of the university, I saw enough poor teaching to realize how much improvement was possible. I have no doubt that I carried over much of my experience with high school social studies teaching into my attitude.

The first year when it fell to me to set up our committees for the arts college, I set up one on the improvement of instruction and put on it some of the best teachers that were known to me. The chairman was Edward Palmquist of the department of botany, who taught what I had reason to believe was one of the best introductory botany courses being taught in the country. We started the program as an arts college affair, and the next year agriculture followed our example when Dean John Longwell appointed a similar committee for the College of Agriculture. There was some cross fertilization of the two programs but not as much as I would have liked. We began at least ostensibly with the new instructors, presumably those who had no supervision or instruction in teaching and were doing what most college and university teachers do—imitate the professors who had been their teachers.

The arts college committee set up a series of lectures on the improvement of teaching which most departments in the college required their instructors to attend. Everyone was invited and many did attend. Then we had conferences with departments and urged departmental activity in this regard suggesting particularly that new instructors be invited to visit the classes, especially when they were multiple sections of the same class as in freshman English, to see how the more experienced hands handled the teaching. There were a few instances where we knew we were assigning an instructor to a teacher who had fallen into slovenly habits of instruction and this was done with a purpose. I expressed to department chairmen that I felt nothing could improve the experienced teacher who was not doing his best like telling him you were sending some young instructors to visit his class to learn how the craft was practiced in his department. I had repeated reports and some other evidence that the teaching of some of the older faculty members had improved immensely on being told that they were now not only teaching students the content, but they were also teaching instructors how to do the same thing well.

As far as the series of lectures was concerned, I started it with a lecture of my own on evidence of good teaching which I think, coming from the dean, made some good impressions on at least the instructor and assured him that at the University of Missouri good teaching was valued highly. I remember calling on Dean Theo Irion of the School of Education, an educational psychologist, to discuss motivation in college classes which he did ably but a little too technically for some of our people. Loren Reid from the speech department had a good presentation on improving lectures, and Robert Daniel from psychology had one on improving teaching. Tom Brady presented a discussion of the teacher and student discipline that was useful and well received although a bit aside from our main purpose. The attendance at these lectures was comforting and the response was favorable, so much so that we published them in a pamphlet, *Toward Better Teaching*. In this pamphlet we placed a list of teaching aids available and their location. Such information as slides and how to have them made, projectors and tape recorders available as well as service from the testing and counseling service seemed much appreciated by new instructors to the campus, and grew and improved as time went on.

Out of this, together with the junior colleges' experience we had, I hit upon an idea that I discussed with several people. We could perform a service in the state by putting on a state-wide program, if we could find financial support for it, because what we were doing was needed in all colleges and universities. I discussed this with President Middlebush and finally made an application to the Carnegie Foundation for the

Advancement of Teaching. We worked out the application and presented it as a plan asking for a grant of $50,000 to carry on a program throughout the state. It fell first in the hands of Oliver Carmichael, who was the director of the Foundation and a friend of President Middlebush. He wrote Middlebush an enthusiastic letter about it and said it would go to his board with his approval which was very encouraging.

The news of the Carnegie Board approval of our plan came by wire to Middlebush. We were to start the fall of '49 and run for five years and were granted the full $50,000. The program was not to be concentrated on our campus but was to be state-wide. For administrative purposes we had to have a University committee. After consulting with me, Middlebush appointed one which consisted largely of deans of divisions. We felt this was important because if we could not get the deans of the colleges interested on our own campus, we had little chance of being effective out-state. We worked mainly at home on our main campus the first year. Then in 1950 we set up a group of state-wide conferences on the subject, the first on the campus and later at St. Louis and Kansas City. These conferences constituted a major force for our entire improvement program. We started with general conferences and wound up with conferences in subject matter fields or areas. Besides Columbia with its central location we used St. Louis and Kansas City most of the time, but did include some in other parts of the state usually basing it at a state college. For the conferences we used outsiders whom we thought had contributions to make and whose names would lend prestige so as to attract the attendance of other college people. Among the people I recall using were Dean Theodore Blegen of Minnesota, Ralph Tyler of the University of Chicago, Fred J. Kelly of the Office of Education, Robert Pace of Syracuse, and Dean Hayward Kenniston of Michigan. Dean T. E. McConnell of Minnesota and Gilbert Highet of Columbia were others who made substantial contributions.

Of course all this had to have someone to direct it, and after making a search for such a person, we found it exceedingly difficult to get an able person for the job with no promise of continuation of it after the length of the grant. At this time, 1949–50, we were negotiating with a young man to take over Moffett's work on the teaching of English, who was teaching at Colorado State at Greeley. His name was Donald Drummond and he had creative writing talents as well as teaching talents. He had a good personality and had good training at Stanford for exactly what we wanted. So in the end we fell back on him, cutting his teaching load to the basic course for high school English teachers which would not cover Moffett's complete program of teaching in the area. But this was temporary in our thinking. Drummond was appointed not only assistant professor of English but director of the program for the improvement of instruction. He made a good impression on our local faculty and on faculty members outside generally. In fact, it was overall a very fortunate choice as I could not devote the necessary time to it, nor could Francis English who served on the university-wide committee. Ed Palmquist would have been a very useful director but he had too much at stake in the Department of Botany at that time to take this one.

We made annual reports to the Carnegie group and Carmichael himself made several visits to us to see how we were operating and expressed himself as highly pleased. The original mimeographed piece on ways to better teaching was improved, revised, and published under several different editors' names at different times. It was given to each new instructor who came to the University and was distributed to the entire faculty. We sent free of charge copies to instructors throughout the state where a substantial interest developed and lasted a considerable time. I was particularly intrigued by a request from a Philippine institution. The last revision was made in 1970 I believe, after neither English nor I nor Drummond nor Palmquist were in active service, but the demand has continued and it steadily improved in content under new editors. Drummond was invited to many campuses in Missouri and made several presentations himself on the problems. Ed Palmquist and Francis English did also.

In addition to the *Toward Better Teaching*, we published several specialized pamphlets that were made up of the presentations of the programs on the specialized subjects such as writing and speaking, and social studies. These were distributed in a similar way and were in substantial demand within the state. During the year 1951–52 when I was in Amsterdam, Drummond with Francis English's assistance kept the program moving at a desirable pace. On the whole I could see the Missouri institutions received it very well and we had many compliments from them.

One of the more popular items in our production was a teacher rating scale, which was really only incidentally something of a teacher's evaluation but primarily a device for showing teachers how their students reacted to their teaching, giving indications of where they could improve it. I had some evidence, too, that it increased students' confidence in a teacher by having their advice sought in this way. They were instructed strictly that their names were not to go on their rating scales. Another factor is that this rating scale was one I had started to develop years before in my history teaching and had revised and used in my large courses. A revision of it is still in use. We avoided completely the attitude that I had found in use in the University of Michigan College of Arts, and a few other places where student ratings were used for administrative purposes in evaluating the teacher. We were convinced that this gave a wrong psychology to the whole matter and the value of the rating scale was lost. The teachers used the ratings themselves and only occasionally would one submit one to his chairman or dean, and that was strictly voluntary and not encouraged.

Other things that we encouraged included the use of some training films that were made by Paul Klapper of Chicago and by Edgar Dale of Ohio State. These were used with considerable success and teachers generally acknowledged they profited from the presentations. As a carry-over from the complete program we hoped to encourage the development of a friendly attitude toward the importance of good teaching, a belief that its improvement was possible with every teacher, and that by thought and study each teacher could improve himself. We did not make records of this but several college deans testified that they had committees on improvement of instruction and that they followed our example in this respect. They continued at Missouri and still exist. I think that Drummond, English, Palmquist, and I, to mention only those that I am confident of, were convinced that the real maintenance of good standards of instruction depended almost wholly upon the department. If it valued superior instruction, it got it. If it did not, the instruction tended to deteriorate and the general program was best aimed at keeping the departments conscious of their problems here and the administration also.

Dean Curtis had left me a problem that I never completely solved. He had instructed the science departments that top-notch universities failed approximately half of their freshmen in their beginning science classes and that was the test of a quality university. It affected several of our departments for a time but it mainly had its effect in chemistry where Dean Henry Bent was still in practical charge of the freshmen work although he taught only a small part of it.

This came to me from the College of Agriculture where chemistry was required of all freshmen. Their faculty complained about the situation and I learned that some of their extension agents were advising students planning to come to the University to go to a state college first, and take chemistry as freshmen and then transfer to the University. I had conferences with Bent about this and he was in complete agreement with Curtis and defended his theory of grading freshmen in any science. I pointed out what was happening as a practical matter and that prospective agriculture students were being directed to start in a state college and many of them stayed there. The second conference I had with him was due to the fact that I found he was putting the freshmen who had had high school chemistry in the same sections as those who had no chemistry and taught them as if they were beginners in the field. I told him I thought this was very poor judgment and that it induced freshmen with high school chemistry to take it easy in the course as they assumed that they would have no trouble keeping pace with students who did not know any chemistry. He showed me figures later that he had compiled which in his own section showed that the high school chemistry students did no better than the others in passing the course. I suggested to him that was largely due to the fact that they were misled by being in a group which knew no chemistry to begin with. I apparently had no effect upon him although he was a good classroom teacher. Later after I became President I discovered that Agriculture had solved its problem by adding its own freshman chemistry course from its department of chemistry.

I should add a special word about freshman English instruction which was in the charge of Willoughby Johnson. The University had a special system of handling this when I joined the faculty and with very few exceptions stuck to it steadily. They took largely recent M.A. graduates, frequently high school instructors, and employed them to teach these courses with a three year tenure. In some quarters which knew very little about teaching, there was criticism but the criticism overlooked the realities of the situation. Freshman English with us, as with every university, was essentially a course in remedial high school English. It was extremely difficult for the teacher to keep up any enthusiasm, especially after one had taught the same course many times. Two or three times I had explained this system to my fellow university arts deans and always got from them expressions of envy as they said this course on their campuses was staffed by middle-aged and older people who had grown, as one put it, "harness worn" in going over the old materials. Consequently, they considered their English teaching some of their worst.

The post-war period at the University of Missouri seemed to coincide generally with a replacement period in faculty staffing. It seemed then, as it seems now as I look back, an older generation was retiring and replacements had to be made. It was not of course absolute, but it was general. This problem of recruitment of these new people was very serious to us, because with our short budget it was exceedingly difficult to find those top people you wanted for your departmental leadership. With us in the College of Arts and Science, I felt our large departments were particularly vulnerable, except in English where we had excellent leadership with Edward Weatherly and some of the recruits he was getting around him. There were some exceptional instances that I look back on with great pleasure. In accordance with departmental wishes department chairmen in English limited themselves to a three-year term, and Weatherly retired from the chairmanship to turn it over to Harold Moffett who was older than Ed and close to retirement himself. However, Harold was very able and he and Ed were very close friends so there was no real change in the administration. Two unusual things happened. One was he came to me one day and said, "Did you know that Hardin Craig is retiring at North Carolina?" I replied that I knew he had gone there after he had retired at Stanford but I had not known he was retiring again. He said he would like to try to get Craig to come and spend a few years with us at Missouri. I asked, "How old is he?" As I remember he was already 70, but Harold who had Craig as a teacher had kept in touch with him and assured me that although he was past retirement he was full of vigor and youthfulness. He was a widower and popular with his colleagues in the field of Shakespeare studies. I told Harold I thought we had problems if we took on new faculty past retirement age when we were retiring our own. He admitted that but thought it was worth doing. He happened to have a particular problem because Charles Prouty, our replacement for Fairchild, had been enticed away by Yale and we needed someone more than a youngster for the Shakespeare field. I asked Harold if he thought Craig would come on half-time and possibly teach only Shakespeare. Harold said he would ask him, and the result was that Craig did come on half-time and stayed with us 11 years. I suspect he was one of the best bargains the University ever had. I became well-acquainted with him myself and had no doubt whatever we had a genius of a teacher. His Shakespeare course was taken or audited by many of the faculty wives including Ruth and Anne Weatherly. Craig did not limit himself to teaching. He was heavily involved in research, published at least one book every other year, and spent his summers at the Shakespeare Theater in England. I asked him about our library, and he said we had a magnificent library in his field. He had a carrell in the library and had found a good place to live, but ate his meals downtown at a cafeteria where he could maintain his odd vegetarian diet that he had lived on for a long time. After we moved into the president's house, I saw more of him. He usually ate a late Sunday dinner, and when walking back to his room, he would frequently come in and visit. When visiting with us, he did not dwell on his field of Shakespeare but recited Robert Burns and other Scottish ballads in a very fine Scottish dialect. He took me back to my childhood and my first Sunday School teacher, Jean McNaughton Stephens. Craig was an unusual genius who did not seem to grow old. However, I had to end his tenure after he came to my office one day, and I noticed that his dentures were giving him a great deal of difficulty in talking. I sent for Charles Hudson, who was then chairman of the department, and told him about my experience with Craig. I told him that I would not reappoint Craig unless he had his dentures attended to. I feared his students would start to imitate his speech and we could not have that. "Talk to him," I said, "I think he will understand." However, Hudson was in such awe of Craig that it was beyond his ability to talk to him about it. I told him that my statement stood—that if he did not get him to fix his teeth Craig was through. Hudson told Craig that I would not reappoint him. It was only a day later that Craig was in my office. "I don't blame you a bit, Elmer," he said, "I have been expecting it every year." At that point, I found I did not want to complain about his teeth either. Then he told me Missouri was an ideal place for him and he wanted to stay here. He asked, "May I keep my desk in the department and the carrell in the library?" I told him that as long as he was around he would have full privileges of a professor emeritus. To my surprise he was back the next fall using his University facilities and lecturing at Stephens College. Moreover, he had had his dental work done. He taught at Stephens until he had a stroke, and his son who was a historian at Rice University took him home with him. It was not a serious stroke and he was soon over it. I had a letter from him saying, "Don't let anyone take over my desk or my carrell. Those doctors were wrong. I didn't have a stroke. I just fainted." I assured him his place would be here, but instead of coming back he went to his alma mater Centre College in Kentucky. While I do not think he did any teaching he wrote a history of the college which I know pleased his colleagues there very much. Iron man that he was, he was not indestructible. He died a great character, and I think the best bargain we had academically. If he had a competitor it was another man whom we gambled on.

Harold Moffett and our sometime dean of journalism Frank Mott were great admirers of the poet John G. Neihardt. I was familiar with some of his western poetry on the Indian wars and had heard him lecture, as Neihardt gave public lectures at universities for several years. He appeared at the University of Missouri soon after I came here. I attended the lecture and enjoyed it very much. I also was reading the *St. Louis Post-Dispatch* where Neihardt was editing the book review page in the Sunday editions, writing many reviews himself and editing a very reputable literary page for a daily newspaper. Moffett and Mott had recommended Neihardt for an honorary degree. It seemed very appropriate to me and I was glad to support it. The degree was conferred by President Middlebush in due course. But it was not long thereafter that Moffett, full of enthusiasm, came to see me. "Did you know Neihardt has moved here?" he asked. No, I did not. "He has bought a piece of land north of town and he and his family are moving here." I knew that he had been living down near Lake Taneycomo in a fine resort area that apparently was not exactly what he wanted. Finally Moffett got around to where his enthusiasm was and said, "Maybe we can get Neihardt to do some teaching." I asked, "Do you think he can teach? I know he gives a fine lecture but I have a feeling he might give a few top lectures and run out of steam." Moffett replied, "We could try him." I was encouraged by our experience with Craig and decided that if we could get him to teach half-time or less, we would hire him, which we did. He was more colorful than Craig, which is saying a lot. We set his main course on his own poetry, and while that style of poetry was no longer popular, it had real merit that deserves comparison and classification with Longfellow and other writers of that epic style. He also taught a course on the writing of poetry where he made a great many converts to his style. It was at this time that Fred McKinney in psychology was making a great impression with his lectures on our television station, where he gave his beginning course in psychology. We recorded it at the same time, and it was borrowed by other educational stations and used by them as a course. Neihardt was obviously a prospect for a similar plan, and he used his poetry as a basis for a course taught by television. I listened to his lectures whenever possible as they were broadcast in late afternoon, and understood better why they were so popular. He was truly a great teacher.

The high success of our experience with Craig and Neihardt encouraged a similar experiment. Tom Brady brought in Jakob Larsen, who had retired from the University of Chicago and was one of the leading scholars in Ancient History. While his teaching was competent and even distinguished in quality, I am sure the illness of his wife during most of his period with us prevented his becoming the force on campus the two people in English were. Still he was a fine addition at a level where we needed maturity.

In discussing this, however, with some of the people who had been involved, the possibility of doing this on a regular basis appeared impossible, since it is only a rare individual who would care to spend his retired years as Craig and Neihardt had. And the rare individual was a matter of chance.

Another individual who had some importance for the college was a new Dean of the School of Journalism, Frank Luther Mott. Mott was a historian of journalism—a very unusual teacher and a fine scholar. He had read a paper at the Mississippi Valley Historical Association when I was active in it, and I knew him more than casually. When he was selected as dean and came to Columbia, I tried to make him welcome. I knew he had been ignored by the history department at Iowa when he was there, in spite of the distinction he had in the history field. Ruth and I had a reception for him soon after he came, inviting all members of the history department which pleased Frank very much.

The place where he was probably most helpful to the college was in promoting the cause of a University Press, which William Peden in English and I were trying to promote as a desirable addition to our functions. The University had at various times published books; particularly it published a research series, a paper bound University of Missouri Studies in which Professor Belden of the English Department had been a moving spirit, but that had died down with Belden's retirement. While the term Press had been used on a few publications, there was no Press and no one to whom a scholar could submit a manuscript for publication. Eventually Peden and I, with Mott's help, got an appropriation in the University budget and Peden became the first Director of the University Press which grew into a very valuable asset to the University and to the state. We had every reason to be proud of the work that it did and the publications it sponsored. In time Peden's work in the English department grew so that he had to give up his directorship and we went on with other directors. Both Mott and Peden kept a strong interest in the Press and served on its directing committee.

Frank Mott continued to write, particularly his monumental history of American magazines which he brought nearly down to date before his death. Peden was very active in teaching creative writing, especially in the field of the short story, and in addition he was a substantial historical scholar and published on his favorite subject, Thomas Jefferson. He wrote a beautiful pamphlet on the Jefferson Monument, the original marker on Jefferson's grave that stands on the University campus today. Even after retirement both Mott and Peden were active in University affairs and in scholarly endeavors.

Elmer Ellis *(standing far left)* during a Boy Pioneers Campout. The knapsack he shouldered had been used by one of his uncles in the Spanish-American war.

Elmer Ellis *(fifth from the left)* played on the 1920 Towner High School championship basketball team.

Elmer Ellis during his undergraduate days
at the University of North Dakota, circa 1923.

This 1929 photograph of Ruth Clapper
Ellis was taken in Iowa City.

Frederick A. Middlebush and Elmer Ellis during a 1956 Commencement.

President Ellis and Mrs. Ellis with Harry S. Truman during the former U.S. President's 1959 visit to the University of Missouri.

Dean Curtis Wilson, Mrs. Wilson, President Ellis and Mrs. Ellis at the 1960 Faculty Reception held on September 14, at the University of Missouri–Rolla.

University of Missouri Board of Curators, 1960. *From left seated:* J. A. Daggs, Lester Cox, President Ellis, J. A. Finch, Jr., Oliver B. Ferguson. *Standing:* Robert Neill, Henry Andrae, Randall Kitt, Boyd Ewing, Doyle Patterson.

President Ellis and Mrs. Ellis at the 1961 Orange Bowl, where the Missouri Tigers defeated the Naval Academy, 21–14.

From left: President Ellis, Chancellor John Schwada, Paul A. Gorman, U.S. Senator Stuart Symington, Dr. Blanche Dow. Gorman, president of Western Electric, Senator Symington and Dr. Dow, president of Cottey College, received honorary degrees during the June 1965 commencement exercises, held in Columbia.

From left: W. Francis English, Winterton C. Curtis, Frank F. Stephens, President Ellis. English, Curtis and Ellis all served as Dean of Arts & Science. Stephens, at one time, was Associate Dean.

University of Missouri–Columbia Administration, *1966. From left:* Ray Bezoni, comptroller; Brice Ratchford, vice president; President Ellis; Raymond Peck, vice president; Dale Bowling, business manager.

University of Missouri Administration, *1966. From left:* Chancellor Merl Baker, Rolla campus; Chancellor John Schwada, Columbia campus; President Ellis; Chancellor James L. Bugg, Jr., St. Louis campus; Chancellor Randall Whaley, Kansas City campus.

President Ellis and Mrs. Ellis at their Campus home, May 1966.

University of Missouri–Columbia Summer Session Commencement, 1966.

From left: Chancellor John Schwada, Mrs. Thomas A. Brady, President Emeritus Ellis at the 1967 dedication of Brady Commons, named for Mrs. Brady's late husband, Dr. Thomas A. Brady, former Dean of Extra Divisional Administration.

Dr. Thomas A. Brady.

President Emeritus Ellis received The State Historical Society of Missouri's Distinguished Service Award from Society President William R. Denslow during the Society's 1978 Annual Meeting Luncheon.

Chapter 16

An Education in Europe

Before I accepted the vice presidency, I had cleared with President Middlebush that I would not lose my sabbatical rights. I intended to write another book and do the major research on it in that year. In the fall semester of '50 Middlebush told me that the Association of American Universities recommended a scholar each year to teach in the Netherlands. He said that at their recent meeting they had all been asked to recommend candidates to the committee, and he asked me whom he should recommend. More in a teasing vein than any other, I said, "Why don't you recommend me?" He replied, "I will." After some more conversation, I left. When I returned to my office, it occurred to me that Saul Weinberg had wanted to spend a year in Amsterdam. I immediately called Middlebush and said more seriously that Weinberg had this interest, and I was sure that he had some connection at the University of Amsterdam. I said, "Recommend him!" He said he would recommend both, and as far as I know that is what happened.

The next step in these efforts was a letter from the secretary of the Association asking me to file a Fulbright application and, on inquiry, it seemed that the grant was funded entirely on the Fulbright teaching grants and that all applicants had to secure a Fulbright. So without taking it too seriously, I filled out the application, gave the references, and sent it in.

A few months later President Middlebush learned that the grant had gone to Professor Raymond Moore at K.U., a fine geologist whom I learned to know later. I thought that settled the matter, but to my surprise I received a notice in the spring that I had received a Fulbright to teach in the American Institute at the University of Amsterdam. My first word was a letter from A. J. den Hollander, Director of the Institute, congratulating me and telling me they were very happy to have me.

As this was my sabbatical year, it was not difficult to make out financially on the sabbatical plus the Fulbright. It appeared to be a very attractive prospect to both Ruth and me. Ruth had never been in Europe, and I had been there only approximately two weeks in 1949 on a Navy cruise. We thought this would be a new and interesting experience, and I believe that it turned out to be the most interesting year of our lives, although the previous sabbatical with the Guggenheim on which we wrote the Peter Dunne biography would be a close second. The problem of what to do with the deanship during my absence was a serious one. Francis English, who was assistant dean, offered to do both jobs for the year, but I told him that was impossible and that he would kill himself trying to do both. Finally, Francis and I decided that I would ask Mitchell Tucker, who had served with me on the personnel committee of the college and who was chairman of the Department of Botany, if he would do it. He agreed to take over for me, and the most difficult decision to make was passed.

Through friends who had spent some time in Europe and reading books on the Netherlands, we learned many things that we needed to know and proceeded to make our plans. We decided to make the year as educational as possible. We would spend a few weeks in England at the beginning and at the end of the year, and during the year we would visit the countries north of Spain and south of Norway. Unfortunately Ruth became quite unwell in the summer of '51, and the one unhappy thing about our whole year was that she was not at her best during a part of it. We booked passage on the *New Amsterdam* which sailed from New York in early August and made reservations in a small family hotel, the Glendower, in South Kensington, London. Our plan was that we would stay there, do what Ruth felt like doing and no more. The trip on the *New Amsterdam* was most interesting. We were traveling cabin class and soon after boarding my old friend, Robert Greenfield, from Army history days showed up. We immediately made an agreement that we would request a table for four for the trip, hoping our fourth companion would be a pleasant one. Bob taught at Johns Hopkins, was a specialist in modern Italian history, and had been in Europe many times. He was also a handsome bachelor and had every intention of enjoying himself on this trip. The fourth companion at our assigned table was an older Dutch woman who had left the Netherlands 20 years before, was now a widow, and was returning to Amsterdam with the idea that she might live there with her brother.

After a very pleasant trip we arrived at Southampton, checked some of our luggage on to Rotterdam, left the ship and boarded the London train which was situated conveniently by the dock. We got our first picture of the English countryside and were impressed by the amount of flower and vegetable gardens visible from the train. That and the large number of smokestacks that arose from the many dwellings left the most vivid impressions. We arrived at Waterloo Station and took the underground to South Kensington. Our hotel, the Glendower, was just two blocks from the station. It proved to be a quiet but interesting area which was very appropriate to our needs at the time.

The Glendower's nearness to the South Kensington underground station was a great asset. We immediately began making trips around London. We took regular tours in buses, learned to use the underground which we found the fastest and generally the most useful method of travel, and became familiar with the public monuments and historical buildings as well as the museums. We decided the second city we would like to see in Britain would be Edinburgh, but when we tried through the American Express to get a hotel reservation in Edinburgh, we were unable to do so. However, the clerk said, "If you take our tour of North England and Scotland, I think you would find it interesting." There were rooms reserved in Edinburgh for the people on the tour. We had been set against organized tours by our friends at home, but after thinking this over, we decided to do it and had an extremely interesting time. We left by bus from a central place where we could leave our extra luggage. Bill Rowan, our guide, was a delightful person who classified himself as half Scottish and half English. He had served in the Scot's Greys and was very proud of that. Our trip north took us to Stokes Poges, Cambridge, York, Ripon, Newcastle and finally Edinburgh.

We stayed at the North British Hotel, which was one of the railroad hotels. Many of the better hotels in Britain were part of the railroad stations. The day we arrived, an incident happened that amused me. Those on the tour who admitted to having any Scottish ancestry were taken out of the bus by Rowan just as we reached the border. Then, before they were permitted to cross, he required them to get down on their hands and knees and kiss the soil of Scotland, as he did, before they set foot on it. Of course neither of us admitted any Scottish ancestry although Ruth probably has some. We got back at Bill by telling him how much more his R's rolled the closer we got to Edinburgh. We heard none, we insisted, in London. The night we arrived, I took a long walk up Princess Street, where I ran into a street meeting addressed by a Scottish nationalist who was really ripping into the English, to the delight of the crowd. There was a second and larger meeting by a revivalist.

When leaving Edinburgh we crossed South Scotland to Glasgow, crossing Loch Lomond on a large boat, and the tour bus picked us up at the other end. From Glasgow we turned south, stopped at Gretna Green, and then on to the lake country. The lake country was beautiful, but we had a slight rain which prevented us from taking full advantage of it while we were there. We spent a day in Chester, staying in a very old hotel which was a historic building itself. We walked around on the city wall and visited the museum of local Roman antiquities. From there it was on to Stratford for the play at the Shakespeare Theater. The evening of the following day, during which we made a stop at Oxford, we were back in London.

We had to leave London immediately as we were due in Holland two days later at the orientation session for the exchange teachers and scholars. We secured our checked baggage and took the train to Harwick where we got the ship overnight to the Hook of Holland. We arrived very early in the morning at the Hook and from there we went by train to Rotterdam. We secured a room at the Central Hotel, which was almost the only prewar building standing in the central area, the station and surrounding buildings having been destroyed by German bombing at the beginning of the war. About half of the hotel was gone, but the rest had been put in good shape. The next day we went by train to Amsterdam, where we checked the baggage to be left there, ate a lunch at the station restaurant, and took a train to Arnhem. A short bus ride took us to the small village of Oosterbeek. The orientation session was to be given at Huise Pieterberg, a very fine estate outside of Oosterbeek. Our room, which was in a dormitory-like structure, was fairly new, very spartan and very cold. The group at the session consisted mostly of high school teachers and graduate students who had Fulbright grants. We were the only exchange professor couple who attended the entire session, although several others dropped in for short periods. The high school teachers and exchange students were required to attend.

The orientation session was the beginning of our close association with many of the Fulbright group. I believe we became better acquainted with the high school teachers than any other group. Our learning sessions consisted of half-time on Dutch language and half-time on orientation in the Netherlands—not too different from the Army Language School at Pittsburgh in 1943. There were two sections of the language and we chose the beginners' group, largely because we were much attracted to the teacher. She was Ida Reesink, who became the best friend we made in the Netherlands and whom we were to see many times later in Amsterdam, as well as on our return trips to Europe and once when she and her husband, Henk, visited us in Columbia. They lived nearby in the small village of Brummen. He was a wholesale hardware merchant, and she had been a high school English teacher and also had been Queen Julianna's tutor in English language. This work of teaching Dutch to Americans was a labor of love for her. She brought to it all the enthusiasm that a great teacher should have. We had in our group high school teachers who had never studied a foreign language before and were probably the worst language students I ever heard. The lectures for the afternoon sessions were given by interesting people, all of whom had useful knowledge about the Netherlands. The one we came to know best was the head of the Economic History Institute at the University of Amsterdam, Dr. I. J. Brugmans. He was not in the regular history department, nor was den Hollander, who was a sociologist and head of the American Institute. When the session was over we all took off by train. We found that several graduate students were assigned to Amsterdam. The only high school teacher assigned there was Pauline White, who was to teach physical education in a high school. She attached herself very closely to Ruth as she really needed companionship. When we finally found an apartment in Amsterdam, which consisted of a large handsome living room with a fireplace and gas plate, a very small bedroom and a bath, she took somewhat similar quarters on the top floor.

The greatest disappointment I had was in my schedule in the university. Den Hollander had written me that I would have two courses and I could teach anything I wished relating to the United States, as it was not in the examination schedule. What was to be two courses turned out to be one lecture a week. This met at 11 o'clock on Thursday; I had a conference hour before it, and that was my program. When I argued that I could just as well be giving another course, I got the answer that there were no vacant hours at which to give a course. So, in the end, I adjusted to a light teaching schedule and took on all the lecturing that the United States Information Service and the Netherlands Foundation could develop for me. This was in addition to the lectures I gave at the Dutch universities which was part of my regular assignment, and included at least one lecture at each university. I also was told that I would lose half of my students at the Christmas holiday to study for examinations, and I would lose half of the remainder at Easter. This I was told was the normal way lectures went. Mine did not follow that pattern and part of the reason was I had a great many special students, people who were not studying for a degree in any sense, but were employed in local banks and export businesses and who wanted to know more about the United States. One of them entertained us at one time, and I found that his mother had been born in Joplin, Missouri, and had married his Dutch father during World War I when he was stationed in New York. I was assigned a desk in the library of the American Institute which was in one of the miscellaneous city buildings that had been assigned to the university. Across the hall from our entrance was the welfare office, where, each day when I arrived at the Institute, applicants for relief would sit waiting to be admitted for interviews. The library actually was rather good on recent books and, after I returned to Columbia, I took some pleasure in building up its back files in history and in sociology. I had the help of the Missouri departments and also the help of the history department at Lincoln University. Eventually we built the files back several years in the professional journals.

Den Hollander was a very pleasant, very polite person who put himself out to make you feel you were part of the team. He gave me an assistant in my onerous task, a young man named Gerald Lulofs. The first morning I went to meet my class, he wanted to carry my briefcase. There were other practices that gave me some amusement and also gave me some problems. Lulofs did not want me to go to class until after all students had arrived. He said if the students would come and see me there, they would feel they were not paying proper respect to the teacher and would not come in. They also wanted to stand when I came into the room, and I quickly dissuaded them of that practice. I told them it was my practice to get to class early as I usually had something to put on the blackboard and I did not want to waste their time while doing it. If they were actually late, they should come in anyway. I also found them very reluctant to ask questions. I had to work hard to develop any kind of give and take. I lectured, of course, in English, and I was very careful to speak slowly when I started my lecturing until they got accustomed to my way of speaking. Like everyone with a foreign language, they understood English better than they spoke it. After a time I told them to ask their questions in Dutch if they wanted to as I thought I would understand. I gave my lectures on the economic and political history of the United States since 1876, which was really the heart of my Recent U.S. course, but far briefer and more given to generalization.

While it had been cold when we arrived in Amsterdam, it soon warmed up and we had some beautiful fall weather. We quickly settled into a fairly routine existence. I went to the Institute nearly every day, took great care in preparing my lectures, and read several books, particularly on American foreign policy, that I had not had time to read at home. I went to Rotary on Thursday noon and probably learned more about Amsterdam from the people I met at Rotary, which included I. J. Brugmans, than I did from those at the university.

The programs were always in Dutch, although the conversation at the tables were frequently in English or in part English and part Dutch. The one exception was the time when there was a visiting delegation from England of probably a dozen men, and our Dutch speaker decided to speak in English.

Our apartment at 26 Paulus Potter Street was about a block from the city art museum, two blocks from the Rijks Museum and three blocks from the Concertgebouw. We were fortunate to get tickets to the concerts through the help of Wobbina Kwast, who was secretary of the Netherlands-American Foundation and whose office was less than a block from our apartment. The seats would not have been considered good by musicians, as they were not in front of the orchestra but behind it. They were much above those that were in the body of the auditorium. But to us this seemed to be an advantage because we could see every member of the orchestra, and we faced the conductor, Eduard van Beinum, as he directed. These were really added values for at least this one season's experience. Almost every week we visited the national museum and we came to know every picture on exhibit. Less often we went to the city museum which was very enterprising with its modern art exhibits. What interested us most in the regular collection were the Van Goghs which we enjoyed more than the ones we had seen at the museum near Arnhem. The last special exhibit was a fascinating one on counterfeiting—everything from money to paintings—Vermeer being the great example.

As our apartment was in Amsterdam, and while only a few of the exchange teachers were located there, most being scattered around the country, it became a sort of weekend center for the friends we had made at the seminar, particularly the high school teachers. Consequently, there was not a single weekend that some of them did not appear at the apartment Saturday or Sunday or occasionally Friday night, staying with Pauline White in her fourth floor apartment, and having "American" coffee with us. The people at the university were thoughtful in inviting us to dinner or more often to evening tea. The den Hollanders and Brugmans were perhaps the most generous in this respect.

While our single gas plate was very useful for preparing breakfast and lunch, we quickly decided that we would depend on restaurants for our dinner. Amsterdam had many fine places to eat, and we and Pauline White soon chose a small, friendly restaurant close to the Concertgebouw, called the Kaiser Bodega, as our favorite place. The waiters learned to know us and were eager to recommend their favorite Dutch dishes.

One of the most difficult things for us to get used to was the short distances. It took an hour by train to get to Rotterdam, for instance. In doing so we went through Leiden, Haarlem, The Hague, and Delft, any of which were, of course, a few minutes from Amsterdam and all were cities we wanted to know. Urban transportation was largely by street car which was old but serviceable. Taxis were not very expensive, but if you could get to a place by street car, it was much simpler. The closeness to other cities encouraged us to take a few trips on weekends. So, reinforced by Pauline White and two other high school teachers, we ventured to Brussels one Friday afternoon, found we were in a good hotel and had it almost to ourselves as the tourist season was over. We took the typical city tour with a guide who at the end of a visit to the museum said, "If you want to see our best art, you have to go to the Louvre because Napoleon 'liberated' it." Brussels is a beautiful place with a most interesting square with handsome facades of medieval and early modern types which represented the guildhalls of the old craft guilds. We also had the good fortune to witness that Saturday morning an interesting marriage ceremony. We were taken to the city hall as Saturday was a morning when marriages were performed free and many of the poorer people waited for that day. I should add that in Belgium a civil ceremony was required, and was usually followed with a religious service. This morning there was one of the not necessarily free ceremonies, as a diplomat's daughter from somewhere in South America was marrying an Italian businessman. There was a very large wedding party in formal clothes. The mayor, or mayoress rather, performed the ceremony and then gave a little lecture to them in French on married life and what it required, all in a very humorous vein.

That evening we went to Antwerp and the next morning we took the train to Bruges and spent most of the day there. It was difficult to believe that the colorful and interesting but small city was once the most important commercial center in Europe. The cathedral, the other public buildings, and the facades of the city square were all most interesting. We also wanted to see something of Ghent, so we stopped between trains in late afternoon and hired a taxi driver to give us a quick overview of the city. He spoke Dutch, as we were in the Dutch part of Belgium, but no English and no German. I sat in the driver's seat with him and tried to carry on a conversation as best I could in my pedestrian Dutch and we got along better than I expected, much to the astonishment of the other students of Dutch in the back seat who, like Ruth, knew as much as I did but lacked the courage to use it.

My memories of Ghent are very faint although it was a modern commercial city which grew out of the older city and not a museum piece as was Bruges. Our driver was intent on taking us to an old people's home, a type which we found was quite common in Belgium and the Netherlands, and was almost invariably founded by a church. It was not a home, but a series of small houses built facing each other around a rectangle of grass with a pump for a water supply in the center. It provided dignified living for elderly people with a minimum of labor. It seemed to us to have been a quite practical and very useful philanthropy.

We returned home by train that evening. We followed this trip with a similar one to Cologne on a very cold Saturday and Sunday. Cologne had been heavily bombed and the cathedral was one of the few buildings that had escaped serious damage. The main transept of the cathedral was walled off with a temporary wall as repairs were still being made. The guide we had on our city tour was quite bitter toward the American army because of some of the damage. One interesting sidelight of the bomb damage was that it uncovered the remains of a Roman building which had been on this site before. The city had excavated this and in it was a marble floor with an interesting design along with other relics placed in the underground museum.

After church at the cathedral in the morning, we took an early train in the afternoon and stopped at Dusseldorf for a few hours, walked around the city which was full of local people taking a Sunday afternoon walk in the brisk weather. It was a rather unpleasant group of people, for they bowled along giving you no choice but to get off the sidewalk or bump them which, after a time, I began to do. We had our dinner at the railroad station while we waited for the evening train. I ran into a situation that I was to see later in Europe which to an American was amazing. I went down to the men's room, and it was very busy as a crowd of men was coming and going. But over at one side was a young woman standing at a sink with one faucet for which she had the key. If you went over there and gave her a pfennig, she would turn on the water while you washed your hands. It was all completely open and everyone seemed to be used to it.

We got home late Sunday night and were glad to be back in our cozy apartment. The only other unusual event that I recall in this period was Thanksgiving Day when the various organizations, which were trying to make the Fulbrighters feel at home, arranged for a Thanksgiving dinner in Leiden. We all went over by various modes of transportation, chiefly rail, and had a church service in Leiden that was really an interesting talk about our pilgrims in Leiden by Eleanor Allen of our embassy. This church had existed at the time they were there but it was not their church. It was a handsome building and cold as ice. I think all of us were glad to have the service over although the presentation was very scholarly and very interesting. We then went to a fine restaurant where a dinner had been prepared which took a great effort by Miss Allen. She had secured turkeys and enough canned pumpkin to have pumpkin pie, pie itself as we know it being unknown in the Netherlands, for all of the Fulbrighters plus a number of Dutch people who were active in these groups. It was interesting for me to note that many were Dutch men who had American wives.

In the meantime we began to make preparations for the month long Christmas break. We had planned early that we would take a trip to Paris and Rome and we had no difficulty in making the arrangements. Pauline White and Louise Goodson, a Missouri high school teacher, were accompanying us, and there were numerous other Fulbrighters with whom we joined forces from time to time. Paris at Christmas time in 1951 was a very cloudy, foggy place. We both agreed when we left that we had not seen the complete Eiffel Tower at any one time. We had seen the top and we had seen the bottom but always one part was hidden. We spent the time up until Christmas day sightseeing. We visited museums, the opera and did all of the regular things that most tourists do. It did not look much like Christmas in Paris or in any other place we saw in France. There was not that Yuletide decoration motif that we have come to associate with Christmas, which I am told is not very evident in Britain either. The only drawback in our interest was that we both developed "turista" toward the end of our stay. I was so ill one day that we had the hotel call a doctor who, after examining me, said I had eaten either ice cream, shellfish, or an egg dish. I answered that I had eaten all three. He gave me some sulfa pills to take and said I would be all right, but it was several days before I got over the effects of the food poisoning. On Christmas day we and Louise Goodson left Paris by bus for a trip to Nice. Pauline White, who had decided to spend Christmas with her brother and his family in London, would join us in Rome. Besides the three of us, there was only one other passenger on the bus. It was an interesting trip as we went down the Loire and Rhone valleys. In spite of the fact that it was winter we saw women washing clothes in the streams, and we doubted that there was any heat in many of the houses as people were sitting out on the sunny side of the houses. We found that also true in Italy. Our last night out we spent at Avignon and had a good tour of the city, which was an interesting place. We then went on to Arles where the old Roman arena still is in use for bullfights of the French kind where they, unlike the Spanish, do not kill the bull.

From here we went on through Canne to Nice, two of the few places in Europe I was already familiar with from my trip in 1949. They looked much less interesting in the winter than they had in the spring. We enjoyed the Riviera. It was rather amusing to me to find that many of the hotels, including the one we were in, had two entrances—one on the beach and one on the streetside, and they operate under two different names at two different prices, the beach one being the more expensive.

On New Year's Day we started out with an Italian busline, and now had six passengers. The first stop, where we spent the night, was Pisa. We had a most entertaining driver who looked so much like Mussolini that among ourselves we called him that. He spoke no English, and none of the passengers spoke Italian. We followed the coastal road from Pisa and when we reached the turn to go inland to Florence, the driver made a great effort to make us understand that we might see something of great interest if we continued south. We were not sure what it was but we went. It was Puccini's home, where he was buried within the wall. The house had been kept almost as it was when he died. His hunting boots were standing on the floor by his bed. The guide at the place spoke no English but I have never seen anyone so handicapped, express himself so well. By speaking very slowly and by making a lot of gestures, even for an Italian, he could make you understand what you were seeing. We found it a very pleasant side trip, and upon leaving, our driver took us back to the road to Florence.

Florence was certainly no disappointment. All the praise that we had heard and read proved true. Although the weather was very sharp and cold, the museums were unheated, and you moved faster than you liked going through them. On the first organized tour we took we had a guide who was especially able. He knew how to teach and he knew we needed teaching. He would move us quickly by certain objects to see other things, and with that background he would come back to the originals which now we could understand. I talked to him a little on the side and learned he was a retired school teacher. When the tour was over, I tried to tip him. He would not take the money, which was the only time I can recall in Europe that a guide turned down a tip. He told me he loved the work and he certainly performed like he did. I tried to locate him for a later tour but I was unsuccessful. A few days later we took the bus again, this time for Rome. This was the tourist bus, now almost full. We stopped at Assisi and the main attraction there, of course, was the St. Francis Cathedral where St. Francis is buried and where many of his relics are exhibited. It is on three floors, with the entrance on the ground level. The members of the Franciscan Order of the church had made an enormous creche, the largest we ever saw, and they were very proud to show it. After spending a couple of hours here, the bus departed for Rome where we arrived after dark at the Albergo Imperial.

Rome proved to be as full of interesting things as Paris, even more so with the ancient ruins. We took the usual assortment of conducted tours, and to our disappointment none of them included ancient Rome. I suspect we were so close to the Marian Year that it had been replaced by the Christian monuments. We did this tour on our own with a guide book, spending a full day going through the interesting relics and remains. That a great city like Rome could go through so many destructive episodes and periods and still retain so much of the ancient city seemed amazing. Of course, the Renaissance art and architecture were tremendous, and it was interesting to see so many places where obviously ancient columns and other stone work had been used in the construction of the Christian churches.

We made our last weekend in Italy a trip to Naples, where we saw the beauties of the Bay and also took the day trip to Pompeii. We conferred with our guide about seeing Herculaneum. He said there were no tours to Herculaneum but if we wanted to get off the bus before we got back to Naples, he would give us directions on how to find it. In one of the most frustrating experiences that we had on the trip, we could not find it. Worn out and hungry, we walked to a railroad station and went back to Naples.

We returned to Amsterdam by train, changing trains at Rome for an overnight trip to Milan, where very early in the morning we and three other Fulbrighters boarded a train for Bern, Switzerland. Unfortunately, it had no diner and we had had no breakfast. At the stations where it stopped the only "food" one could find in the stands was candy and wine, which did not look very attractive for breakfast, especially when what we all really wanted was a cup of coffee. The train ascended quite high in the Alps, and we saw the snowcovered peaks, ski slopes, snow-sheds and extremely long and dangerous ladders where some construction was going on. As the sun was shining brightly, it was a beautiful day and a beautiful trip. The train did put on a diner to serve lunch and we were the first in line. But for some strange reason the waiters would not give us coffee until we finished lunch. We had a full lunch and then finally had our morning coffee.

We arrived in Bern early in the afternoon, went to a "terminus" hotel, and were well-housed for the night. The next day with the help of a guide book we toured the city, visiting the House of Parliament and the great Protestant Church, which had one very interesting window which showed the angel of death coming to fetch the prince and the beggar and people of all stations in between. There seemed to be some fixation with death among these Swiss. Years later at Lucerne, we saw their famous old wooden bridge where the paintings under the roof at every few feet were mostly concerned with similar themes.

I went to the Rotary Club at noon and listened to a Switzer-Deutsch speech that was so different from the high German that I knew that I could hardly make anything out of it. It was a pleasant group and I talked to my table companions, chiefly in English. That afternoon we went to Basel, traveling in a clean but spartan railroad car "third class" that had wooden seats. The route was across rather flat land where there was little scenery worth watching. We were soon in Basel where we checked our next morning tickets for Amsterdam before going to the hotel. When we arrived in Amsterdam the next evening after having had a colorful trip down the Rhine, our apartment seemed extremely pleasant and comfortable.

The next day I reported to my class as scheduled. I felt something was wrong from the time I entered the building. When I got to my room, two students were there. They were very apologetic as they said, "We were afraid you would come. After you left, the university declared an extra week of Christmas holiday."

In the period after the Christmas holiday I did a great deal of lecturing in the Netherlands. I lectured at all of the universities on American history subjects, except the "Free University" of Amsterdam, and to many private groups frequently arranged for me by either Miss Allen or Dr. Swan of the embassy staff. Toward spring the elections in the United States became of great interest in the Netherlands because of our European policies. After I gave one lecture on the approaching election, I found it so popular that I talked on it exclusively to these public groups. The Dutch were concerned that we would become isolationists and pull out of Europe, and they were much afraid that Robert Taft might come out the victor. It was easy to see that, while Dwight Eisenhower was their favorite for the Republican nomination, most of them would feel safer with a Democrat.

I also started visiting high school classes now that my Dutch had improved so that I could understand what was going on. Generally these were history or geography classes, which I found quite interesting. I began to collect high school textbooks in history. From my standpoint the classes tended to be excessively factual, and the procedures largely oral tests of what had been in the textbook assignments. But the teachers made good use of the blackboards and the classrooms were well equipped with wall maps. Almost without exception I visited the secondary schools of which there were three kinds: H.B.S., Lycee, and the *hochschule*. The latter was strictly a university preparatory school and all were government schools. Many of the other two kinds of secondary schools were controlled by churches or voluntary organizations, as the Dutch let any group of families of a certain number which would build a school building have its teaching staff paid by the state. As I observed it, this was a very wasteful method because many of the schools I visited had very small classes, and nearby was another school with small classes also. Either one could have handled all of the students. The Netherlands also had a very large assortment of trade schools with various periods of training. I was interested to note that in most of the church schools, each class opened or closed with prayer, which seemed to me a lot of prayer if a child had five or six classes a day, as often happened.

One of the most interesting trips we made in the spring was a trip to Zeeland and Dordrecht. I had a standing invitation to visit a school in Rotterdam, where Katherine Alley who was a Fulbrighter taught, and I think she was chiefly responsible for it. At any rate she arranged it so it would be a day that Pauline White could come with us.

We left for Rotterdam early in the afternoon where we had reservations at the Central Hotel, which was where we had spent our first night in Holland. Katherine met us at the train and, after leaving our bags at the hotel, we took a tour of the harbor going up the north side and coming back the south side. One could see it was much larger than the Amsterdam harbor, with shipping and shipbuilding very actively going on. From the dock we then took a tram to Katherine's place, where we met the family she lived with. The gentleman was the superintendent of schools or what corresponded to that. There were three very tall boys and a younger girl in the family. The wife spoke no English. We had tea with them while we visited. They seemed to live on the scale of a high school teacher in the United States, and were keeping Katherine for a ridiculously low price. He had a car for his work and Katherine reported that the family had lost everything during the war. After a light supper at the hotel, the four of us walked to a circus that we had passed earlier in the afternoon in a bombed-out area. It was strictly a one-ring affair but to me it was excellent entertainment of that type. I was particularly taken with a performing bear—a big black fellow who danced and rode bicycles and did all of the tricks that performing bears have done in circuses. When it was over we walked back to the hotel wearily, where Pauline secured her bag and went to spend the night with Katherine. Then we went to bed most gladly.

The next morning Katherine called early and said she had arranged for me to attend classes beginning at 9 o'clock. We left our packed bags at the hotel, joined the women, and walked to school with them. Katherine introduced me to a young man and a woman teacher. I visited the man's class first, a fourth form class of 15 girls. He asked if I would mind if he would conduct the class in English because he thought it would interest his girls who were all studying that language. I feared he was doing it for my sake, but I agreed and almost all of the girls participated, falling back on Dutch when stuck for vocabulary. He also used Dutch a few times when he saw an explanation he made was not clear. He knew his students very well as he had taught them for four years which he said was unusual. The students indicated they had studied the text before class. After class I went to the history library which the teacher said had been built by donations of pupils over several years. There were probably 300 volumes in the library. The rather astounding fact he told me was that it was open only about one hour a week. We broke up in order for me to attend the woman's class. It was in the same room and on the same topic. She also had 15 girls. Unlike the other teacher she sat at her desk. She stated or recited a summary of the lesson that seemed to be the very words of the text. After two or three sentences she hesitated for the students to supply the next sentence. They did this with considerable confusion, often several talking at once. I rated the man as a top-notch teacher and the woman as certainly below average. After the class we gathered in the teachers' room for coffee. Ruth and Pauline, after some sightseeing, had returned to the school, visited a physical education class, and joined us for coffee. We met several teachers and a very able-appearing principal who welcomed us, praised Alley's work to me, and told very happily of her visit to America after the war.

After lunch the four of us walked to the Boymans Museum, a new building erected since the war. It was well designed for showing paintings, and the collection was interesting with good representations of Dutch painters. We returned to the hotel, picked up our bags, caught the train to Dordrecht, where we arrived at 3 p.m. and took a taxi to the Hotel Bellview. We had a room overlooking the busy river traffic, where the rivers met and canals carried heavy traffic in every direction. We left our bag and coats at the hotel and set out "wandeling." We visited the fine old Grotekerk with its leaning square tower. The sexton let us in and we were free to examine it as much as we wished. From there we went through the old city, crossing canals and several interesting old bridges and seeing two fine city gates as well as many canal boats where people were living. We had a very good dinner at the hotel dining room, eating very leisurely while watching the boat traffic in the water. Pauline and Katherine left soon afterward to take the train back to Rotterdam and Amsterdam. We all agreed we had spent an interesting two days together.

The next morning we went by train to Goes, where our friend Nellie DeWeerd had asked us to call on her relative, Marie Schipper. Marie's father and mother were at home and they contacted Marie at her father's business and she soon came home. Apparently she worked in her father's office as a secretary. They were all friendly and pleasant and were very much interested and excited when they found we were friends of Nellie's. We had coffee and were invited for lunch, and when we said we only had an hour they immediately offered to drive us around in their handsome Chrysler. Marie's grandfather came in while we were there. He was a Goes farmer, 77 years old and still active enough to cycle 50 kilometers in one day. As it was market day he was dressed in the Zeeland costume. They drove us to Schippers' establishment, which was a large new building housing Allis-Chalmers products which he sold. They then left us at the station where the two women stayed with us until our train came. They were extremely friendly people, and we were happy that we could contact them.

We got to Middleburg about 1 o'clock and after lunch at the hotel we walked around for about an hour. Much of Middleburg had been destroyed during the war so most of it was new. We could not get into the church, which was being rebuilt as it was badly damaged. Scaffolding covered the beautiful steeple. It could be seen from every point on Walchren Island. The beautiful Stadhuis was also practically surrounded by scaffolding. It was claimed to be the finest townhall in the Netherlands, with a very impressive facade which was decorated with many statues. Later we found and bought a fine etching of it in Amsterdam.

After Middleburg we went on to Flushing, going into town quite a distance by taxi. It gave one a rather strange feeling to stand on the dike and look out over the North Sea, and then look down 25 feet below to the streets and see the people moving about in their regular traffic. Flushing of course was the English name for it as it has had historically very close relations with England, being the nearest Dutch city. About 5:30 we took a train back to Amsterdam, arriving there about 9:30. The distance was quite great for the Netherlands and there were some delays because we were not on a main line until we reached Dordrecht. We were glad to get home and, all in all, it was one of the most pleasant trips we had experienced.

The Dutch school tradition provides for a long holiday at Easter. Before Christmas I had been asked by the American Seminar in Salzburg, Austria, if I would spend that time teaching in the seminar. The seminar was run by a committee of Harvard University. As the topic was going to be Recent and Contemporary United States, I was happy to accept. While there was no salary, your food and lodging were furnished.

Amsterdam's Easter holiday began a few days before classes started at Salzburg. Sometime before we had been asked by Rodney Loehr, a historian from the University of Minnesota who was stationed at Bonn, with the U. S. embassy, to spend a weekend with him and his wife, Nancy, and our old Missouri friends, the Conrad Hammers. Conrad was also in the embassy as an economic advisor. The train transportation was rather poor as we had locals all the way to Bad Godesburg, where the Loehrs met us. Soon after we arrived at their apartment, the Hammers came over and we spent the evening visiting until after midnight.

The next morning we got up late, had a big American breakfast, and then Rodney gave us a tour of Bonn and its surroundings. While it had suffered considerably from the bombing during the war, reconstruction was much further along than at Cologne. We went over near Cologne to a tremendous castle that we had not seen when we were there before. It was a storybook piece of architecture and showed little war damage. We returned late in the afternoon. Nancy had not gone with us but had spent the day preparing a dinner party for us, the Hammers and four historians who were working with Rodney, two of them with wives. It was a pleasant group, and I was well impressed by the history people who seemed to know their profession. We had a very interesting evening.

The next morning the Loehrs and the Hammers had planned a trip up the Rhine by car, taking the two cars, I riding with the two men and Ruth with the two women and Hammers' daughter, Ruth. It was another pleasant day and we enjoyed the scenery up the Rhine through Koblenz and on to a beautiful spot on the Rhine about which the Lorelei fable is centered. Here we spent some time enjoying the views both up and down the Rhine, then we returned to Koblenz and crossed the Rhine to the south side and went up the Mosel with beautiful scenery here, too. We went to an area where there was a restaurant built in an old mill, which was developed and run by a Swedish woman who served Swedish-type meals. We had lunch there, a very good smorgasbord. When returning to Bonn, we went through the Eiffel, an area that reminded us a great deal of the Ozarks as far as its topography was concerned. We and the Loehrs were invited to dinner with the Hammers, where we spent the evening looking at the treasures they had collected, especially when they were in West Berlin where they had bought things on the black market. Genevieve had a magnificent collection of Meissen china, and Conrad's prize was two beautifully carved sets of ivory chessmen. The next morning Rodney took us to Bonn where we got a fine new train and went back up the Rhine past the Lorelei and on to Munich where we were to change trains. We had about two hours' time in Munich to walk around the much-bombed city. We tried to get into the cathedral although the restoration was such that it was impossible to see much that was worth visiting, but we did see a large part of the central city.

When we reached Salzburg, Shepherd Brooks, the director of the Seminar, was there to meet us and took us to the Schloss Leopoldskron, the famous house of Max Reinhardt. Brooks led us to our room which was up four flights of stairs. Later I counted 102 steps, the last stair being a circular one. In theory the castle had steam heat but at no time during our stay was our radiator really hot. In the morning Ruth had developed a cold that kept her confined to the room for a few days during which we had a local doctor from Salzburg, a young German who did not impress me as knowing his profession very well.

The faculty for the Seminar was made up of Ralph Gabriel of Yale, Glen Van Duesen of Rochester and myself. I knew Ralph Gabriel, and at one time we had considered writing a high school history textbook together. Van Duesen was on his way home from New Zealand, where he had been on a Fulbright grant. His wife and two children were with him. There were about 30 students attending the Seminar and they came from Germany, Norway, Italy, Netherlands, Belgium, and Britain. I should add there was one Finn whose name was so difficult to pronounce that the students began to call him an approximation of it: "Coca-Cola." Most of them were graduate students or young instructors in universities. One of the young Norwegians was from the foreign office, as was one of the Belgians. One was technically from London University, but was a member of the faculty of the University of Sidney and was at London working on a doctorate. The Seminar had a dean named Connors whose wife and two children were a part of our establishment. Virtually all of the employees of the Seminar were refugees from eastern Europe. Many of them were not very efficient at their jobs although they were all agreeable people to work with. We ate in a large ornate dining room at round tables, each seating eight persons. There were no assigned tables and the students, faculty and wives sat at any vacant place when they arrived. The food was rather poor, primarily I think because it was poorly prepared.

I had been asked to offer Recent American Foreign Policy, and I organized a lecture course covering chiefly our post-war history. I also had a seminar where eight students participated on the same subject. The library at the Schloss had been built up by the Seminar and while small was rather good, considering its newness. Ruth and Mrs. Van Duesen helped in the library. As soon as Ruth had recovered enough we began to make trips over to Salzburg which was about a mile and a half away. Occasionally we caught rides but we usually walked back. We went over there for dinner two or three times a week, as it was a relief from the rather tasteless food in our dining room. We took several trips into the surrounding mountain area, which was an interesting experience. We visited a number of picturesque villages in the Salzkammergut area, as well as Berchtesgaden near where Hitler, Goebbels and Goering had their "Eagles' Nest." Salzburg also had many interesting things to see. The Festung, the large fortress on the hill, was the main feature one saw from anywhere nearby. The cathedral and the Mozart museum were also outstanding. On the east side of Schloss Leopoldskron was a lake that added a great deal to its setting, and across the lake was a bistro where many of our students went late afternoons to relax and to supplement their diet with Austrian beer. The administration staff that had good quarters in the castle gave receptions for the students and the faculty nearly every weekend. These consisted of the local Salzburg wine and conversation. Most of these apartments were equipped with beautiful tile stoves.

In most respects I enjoyed my teaching more than I did in Amsterdam because I became very well-acquainted with my students and enjoyed many of them very much. One student from the Netherlands visited us when we returned to Amsterdam, and I helped her secure a grant at Oberlin to get a masters degree in economics. The German group was largely from Hamburg, and they invited me there to address their history group after we got back to Amsterdam. One of them, Wolfgang Reiger, came to visit us in Columbia one summer when he was on a tour of the U.S. He later sent me a copy of a book he wrote, a good book incidentally.

Salzburg was the headquarters of the American government in Austria, and the commanding officer lived on the Schloss grounds. It interested me that we were all instructed to keep our cars filled with gas so that if any problems developed with the nearby Russian zone we could get to Switzerland in a hurry. After I heard these instructions, it occurred to Ruth that we were the only Americans at the Seminar who did not have a car, but it did not bother us as there were many other cars. The Seminar ended before the classes at Amsterdam resumed, which gave us a free week. We decided to go with a number of the students to Vienna, and we went by train which had to go through the Russian zone. Ruth and I were in the dining car with the Belgian diplomatic officer when two Russian soldiers came through to check our passports. Ruth, who carried our passports, put them at the vacant place by her. A young soldier who appeared to be 18 or 19 became quite angry when he picked up our passports, exploded in angry Russian and handed them back wrong side up. It was obvious he could not read them. I asked the Belgian what made him angry and he said, "You didn't hand him the passports. He didn't think you showed proper respect."

We spent our allotted time in Vienna. We usually did our sightseeing with two or three of the students and went to all the magnificent public monuments, including the national museum where about the only thing on exhibit was their fine collection of Breugel paintings. One of the standing jokes was about the American tourist asking the way to the opera house and the Austrian saying, "You mean you can't find it? You had no trouble during the war." It was our planes that had destroyed the building. The wreckage was being removed and the restoration was beginning. We attended an opera in another building which was of course far smaller. One day we, accompanied by several students, took a hike out to Grinzing, a suburb, and then up a high hill overlooking Vienna and the Danube. On the way up the grade, a soldier was standing at attention at a small guardhouse. I stopped and asked him why he was on guard there and he very guardedly, without chance of expression, said, "This is the Austrian White House." On our way back down to Vienna we passed several inns with bundles of evergreen branches hanging over the door, indicating that the spring wine was being served there. It was too early in the day for much patronage, but we stopped at one and had wine and some cakes out under a tree where tables were set up. It was a very pleasant day and the scenery was magnificent.

Ruth and I had planned to go back by way of Venice, as we could see that otherwise we would not get there before returning home. The difficulty was that the station from where the train left for Venice was in the Russian zone, and one had to have permission from the Russians to take the train. I talked to the American headquarters, and I was told that the Russians would give you permission but that they would hold you up a week before you would get the permission, which was their way of discouraging you. We asked for the permission but by the time we were ready to go, it had not arrived. So instead we took the train to Zurich, where we spent a day and two nights. It rained all of the time but in spite of that we did visit the university and art museum, but it was far too unpleasant to enjoy the city. The trip down the Rhine from Basel with a far-advanced spring was even more beautiful than it had been when we were on our way to Salzburg. The vineyards on the north slope which was across the Rhine were all being worked and I found myself wishing that I could see it at harvest time.

The one part of the Netherlands we had not seen was Maastricht. It was late in the spring, and we did have a desire to go back to Paris to see it in the spring, as we had been there at Christmastime which we were told was the poorest time to see Paris. We took the train down to Maastricht which seemed quite different in dialect and architecture than the other parts of the Netherlands that we knew. A museum was being set up which we found interesting as far as it went, but it was not ready to be a good educational experience. We did have a good hotel there and planned on a trip to visit the American cemetery, as the American troops in World War II were heavily engaged in this area and took some large losses. I was informed that it was the largest American military cemetery in Europe. But on the morning we were to go, a driving rain turned us back and we took the train to Leige, Belgium, instead. In many ways except for the change in language to French the areas were very much alike.

From Leige we went by train to Paris, getting in there early in the evening and going back to the hotel where we had stayed before, but we were told to go to the "annex" which proved to be another hotel down the block. There was a great deal of excitement when we reached Paris that you could even feel in the station. Taxis were hard to get, and when we found one it took some determination on the driver's part to get through the police lines and the gathering crowd to get to our hotel. The police were out in force, because a communist group had been organized to try to discredit General Matthew Ridgeway's arrival to take command of the NATO troops. At times during the evening we heard a great deal of noise but none of it was near our hotel. There was a good account of it in the New York *Herald Tribune* the next morning.

As soon as we were settled in the hotel we went back to the restaurant that the Raymond Pecks had told us about and which we had used many times during our earlier visit. We had a fine dinner which made up for the fact that we had no lunch on the train that day. We went back to the hotel and called John Wolf and made an appointment for dinner the following evening with him, Theta and their son, Franz.

Our time in Paris was spent largely in seeing a few of the interesting things we had missed earlier but also visiting places we had already seen. We wasted a good deal of time quarreling with American Express over our return transportation. We took some guided tours of the city and of Notre Dame and certain other buildings in which we were interested. The purpose of the guided tours was to see if the guide could give us further information on what we had acquired by reading and visiting these places ourselves. On the whole we found the guides very poor. Although we took an English speaking guide, his English was poor and usually his information was scant and one got little from his answers to questions.

The most notable thing that I recall was the Cluny Museum which we had not seen before and which was marvelous on medieval life. The Museum of Monuments, a collection of miniature reproductions of the great French monuments mostly cathedrals or parts of them, proved most interesting. Then we went up to Montmartre with Pauline White and Henrietta Kuizinga, who had come to Paris the day after we did as there was a school holiday in the Netherlands. We went into the church which was a magnificent exterior but I thought a quite ordinary interior. The view of Paris from the Mount was excellent. I also recall our going to the Arc de Triomphe where we had been many times before, but this time we took the elevator to the top to get the view of Paris. It was not perfect because it was not sunny all the time but it was a beautiful sight anyway.

We spent our three evenings with the Wolfs. They reported a good year in Paris and were staying on to complete some work on Louis XIV that John was involved in. When we went to the station to take our train to Amsterdam, we found our friends at the American Express office had put us on the Brussels section instead of the one to Amsterdam which was probably their revenge for our complaining about the mistakes they had made on our tickets. We had a pleasant trip to Brussels with a Belgian couple who had been visiting Paris, and who spoke good English although French was their regular language, not Flemish. Before we got to Brussels, Ruth and I went to the Amsterdam section and located some vacant seats, which she held while I went back to our assigned seats in the Brussels section, got our bags and found the train did not let anyone carry luggage from one car to another. I had to get off with the luggage and sprint down the platform and locate the car where we had our seats. Eventually I made it but it did not leave me with any pleasant feeling about the crew in the American Express office in Paris. We had a pleasant trip from Brussels, but reached home tired and happy to be there.

The prediction that I would lose part of my students at Easter holiday proved correct, as it did at the Christmas holiday, although I kept the solid group of non-students who were very faithful. I continued to visit high schools and, in fact, sat in on an oral high school history exam. A representative of the Ministry of Education was present at these, and he with the teacher conducted the examination. I only did this once as I found it led to difficulties. The teacher and the representative of the Ministry were quite at odds on various students. They graded them on a 10-point scale and after a student had been examined, if the teacher would suggest a numerical grade of 5, he would almost invariably say 4 or if it would be 6, he would say 5. I am sure the teacher was trying to make her students look as good as she could. Her questions were purely factual and she was going through the course chronologically dealing with a later section with each student. The representative of the Ministry tried to get away from the purely factual and made the students make comparisons and contrasts and other applications. One thing was easy to observe as the students were waiting together in the halls, a student coming out would report how far his questions had gone chronologically. While it did not help the next student, the second one would be able to give a quick review of what would probably be his period. This was not all of the test, however, as there was a written part that had already been taken. My difficulty came after the test was over and the outside examiner had left. The teacher then asked me what I thought about it, and I told her I thought it was quite difficult as the outsider's questions were quite hard for high school seniors. She immediately told all of the other teachers. It went all around the school and came back to the examiner that I had criticized his students. Thereafter I stayed out of oral examinations.

I had now acquired many things to take home, such as a set of history textbooks and a fine large map of Holland, unmounted, that I had mounted later and gave to the geography department at Missouri. Ruth had also done shopping for fine china and pieces of old silver and pewter.

As we came close to the end, unfortunately Ruth became quite ill, and the very good doctors attending her decided she had to have minor surgery. The Weatherlys were coming to Europe by ship and we had invited them to visit us. When time came for their ship, the *New Amster-*

dam, to arrive at North Rotterdam, I went down alone and saw it come in with the Weatherlys at the rail. After they went through customs, we took the train to Amsterdam and went out to our apartment. We had made reservations for them at the Central Hotel which was only about a block away. We had two days together before Ruth entered the hospital and we enjoyed the time thoroughly. We took the canal trip, walked up interesting Kalverstraat and around the Dam, visited the Rijksmuseum, and had some wonderful steaks at Kaiser Bodega, our favorite restaurant, which we had been telling Ed about for the past ten months.

In the meantime we were entering Ruth in the hospital. The surgeon had directed me as to exactly what to sign up for. Ruth was placed in a Second Class A room, which was a one bed room. One difference between a Second Class A and a Second Class B room was that I was served tea or coffee if I happened to be there when it was served to Ruth. She was cared for by a student nurse who seemed to know her business well. She had charge of Ruth's room and the one across the hall as her only duty. That duty, however, included cleaning the room each day as well as caring for the patient. She spoke English rather well but of course had some peculiar expressions. For instance, when Ruth was getting ready for bed the first night, she was asked if she wanted to "sweep" her teeth. It was a very successful operation and she was out in three or four days with the price for her hospitalization and physicians amazingly low by our standards.

The Weatherlys left after a few days on their trip which they had planned. Really it was a trip to show Europe to their children, and they were going to many places. We had set our leaving Amsterdam as soon as Ruth was able to travel. Through correspondence with some of my students at Salzburg, I had agreed to give a lecture at the University of Hamburg. We went to Hamburg by plane, put up at a hotel, and took a city tour. Hamburg was really a beautiful city although the destruction around the port was extensive. The first evening was the evening of my lecture and the student who had arranged it, Wolf Malinowski, took us to a university building where we found a gathering of about 35 students and faculty. I spoke on political parties in the U.S. and their methods, contrasting them with European parties. I could see that the boys had felt responsible for me because they had invited faculty members to come and were immensely pleased that I seemed to do well. We had some refreshments in the Dutch way after the lecture and before the questioning period. The next day Wolf took us around the university to see some of its operations. We went into two large lecture halls in the law school where lectures were being given to large groups of students, a thing that I had not seen in Holland. The lecturing too seemed different as I had heard stories of poor lecturing in Europe, but what I heard in the law school in Hamburg was excellent.

Later that afternoon we flew to Copenhagen, and as we were having dinner in our hotel to our great surprise Rodney and Nancy Loehr walked in. We then had dinner together, and when it was over we knew something unusual was up because the hotel next door had a rope fence up around the entire front as if some kind of trouble was expected. We were not long in finding out that General Ridgeway, who was taking command of the NATO Forces, was in Copenhagen and the communists were organized to put on "demonstrations" apparently to create the impression that the European public was very much against him. In Paris we had seen little slips of paper with the words "Pest Generale" on one side and a fly on the other, making the communist claim that he had introduced germ warfare in Korea. There were also a few wall posters glued on places where they would be hard to remove. We watched for a while and then went up to our rooms. A big crowd gathered in the square, most of them having nothing to do with the demonstrations. In fact, they were sailors for the most part, among them U.S. and Dutch, on shore leave. Finally, Rodney, Ruth and I went down to get a close view of what was going on. There was a large group of police who seemed well organized, and about every fifth or sixth one had a police dog on a chain. The troublemakers seemed to be organized in groups of eight or nine with an older person in charge and the rest of them youngsters who took orders from him. They did some yelling and exploded torpedoes that sounded like shots, but except for making nuisances of themselves, they destroyed no property. The police were too good for that. It was interesting to watch the police work with their dogs. If one of the communists made a move or threw anything, such as a rock, police would not chase him themselves. They would release a dog and point at the person. The dog would catch him and hang on to his coattail until the police walked up. A few instances like this took most of the starch out of the demonstrators as they were tremendously afraid of those dogs.

I talked to one policeman that we met in wandering around. He said, "These are not all from Copenhagen. They have come in from all over Denmark just for this demonstration. They have been coming in all day." To illustrate the mixture of things, I talked to some U.S. Navy boys and also some Dutch sailors. One Dutchman thought I was a Dane, and he brought over a girl he was trying to make a date with, who could speak only Danish, and wanted me to make a date for him. I had to disappoint him but I think she could understand that much. We could not go directly to our hotel because the police lines had spread out and we had to go around the back way. As the normal crowd disappeared and as the time grew later, so did the organized group and soon the square was quiet, and we heard nothing more.

The next day the Loehrs had their car ferried across to Sweden but we did not want to go with them as we had come to see Copenhagen. We spent the day going about the city. Really the most striking thing was the Tivoli Gardens, I suppose at that time the finest amusement park in Europe, if not the world. We did some shopping as the porcelain was exceptionally fine and reasonably priced. The museum was interesting without any particularly good paintings, but we regretted not being able to get out of the city to some of the old castles which were reputed to be very interesting.

The next day was the Fourth of July. We got up and took a SAS plane to Hamburg and there changed to a British plane to go to Berlin. We landed at the big airport and never had we seen such signs of desolation from the bombing. We had reservations at the Saxonhof Hotel which we found was one that had come through the bombing with less damage than most and had been rather well restored. We were given a good room and then went by underground to the American headquarters where we thought we would do the planning of our visit, forgetting that the American office would be closed on the Fourth. We did get to the American Express, however, and received some advice. We were told that we could cross into East Berlin by taxi even though the American army had stopped running its bus there. We rode back on the subway, but we were very cautious to get off before we crossed the line into East Berlin, not knowing what might develop. The newspapers reported a few days before that five American priests near the border had been seized and taken in East Berlin. Later we walked through downtown Berlin, saw the remains of the old church which was not to be restored but was to be left as a memorial. The next morning a taxi with a German driver arrived from the American Express. We had a good visit with him. He had been in the army, had been captured by the Russians, and had been in a prison camp where he had learned to speak Russian. His Russian seemed good as well as his English. We went to the checkpoint where we were stopped by soldiers. We all, including the driver, got out of the car and he opened the trunk which was empty. The guards were Russian, and they spoke in Russian. He took us through East Berlin, and its difference from West Berlin was that no real restoration had taken place. We were amazed to see women wielding shovels, picking up rubble, and loading it into various kinds of carts and trucks. We went around the university and the government buildings which had been restored to some extent, and then by some recently built apartment houses that were showplaces made for tourists to look at from the outside. The driver told us he had been in some of them and there were no bathrooms in them or any modern conveniences as you would assume from looking at the exterior. Then he took us to the Russian war memorial, which he said was not interesting in itself but which he had to include in his tours. Russians have a talent for outdoor memorials, and this was beautifully designed architecture, sculpture, and landscaping. We walked into it, and when we were leaving we met a German selling pictures, postcard size, of the different scenes in the memorial. I told the driver I was going to buy some, and he remarked very quickly, "You would make him very happy if you would pay him in west marks." He thanked us warmly, making sure no Russian guard was watching. We got back to the hotel without incident and bade our driver good-by. It had been a most interesting experience and our first contact in Russian-occupied territory, except for Vienna, where the atmosphere was much more relaxed. A real effort had been made by the Germans to restore the art museum, and they had an interesting collection on exhibit. I presume that it had been buried during the bombing or shipped somewhere else. Other sections were in various stages of construction and reconstruction, and in spite of great piles of rubble still visible, it would give the impression that they were making real progress and were living far better than the people in East Berlin.

One incident that occurred developed out of the fact that on Sunday Ruth got an intestinal pain that worried me so much that I asked the man at the desk if a doctor were available. He answered he would get one and did. The doctor was an older man and started to speak English, but when I said a few words in German, he did not speak English again and insisted on speaking German. He was under the opinion that there was nothing serious about Ruth's difficulty, which was a result of the recent operation. He prescribed some medicine, and said that in Berlin there was a system whereby drugstores rotated on keeping open on Sunday. He named the closest one that would be open that day, took me to it and helped me get the medicine. Then he said, "Now I want to show you something else," and he took me back to a place where there was a small inconspicuous monument put up by the Germans. The inscription on it was extremely anti-Russian. It was a monument to the German heroes of the Russian-occupied Berlin. The following morning, as Ruth was able to travel, we took an American plane to Frankfurt.

Frankfurt was the center of the American army in Germany and was also a showplace. We took in the usual sights including the restored Goethe House. It is tragic that this building had to be destroyed by bombs, and it is amazing that they could restore it so completely and with great accuracy. Most, if not all, of the furnishings had been saved. One day we took the train to the old university town of Heidelberg and spent the day looking at the university and the Necker River. Among the things I recall is the largest cask for wine that I had ever seen, bigger than I had ever imagined one could be made. The story was that the man who owned the larger part of the area took his rent in grapes and had the wine stored in this enormous cask.

We enjoyed Frankfurt immensely. While there we tried to find our colleague, Herman Barnstorff, who was with his daughter Alberta and her husband, Dr. John Logue. Logue was stationed in an army camp outside of Frankfurt. We found that Herman had gone to his old home in Bremen. The Logues came in one evening and took us out to their officers quarters where we had a most pleasant visit. We had used all our time that we had allocated for Frankfurt, and our plan was to go to England for the latter part of the summer. We took the train to Mainz and there boarded a Rhine steamer that was filled with German people going down the Rhine. Groups got on and off at every stop. When we arrived at Cologne late in the afternoon, we got off with our luggage expecting to find the Loehrs there to meet us. It was only with some difficulty that I finally located Nancy as they had trouble getting through to the landing place, and Rodney had trouble finding a place to park the car. After we found each other, we were soon in the car and on our way to Aachen where we had reservations and planned to spend the night. We went through many villages and had quite vivid descriptions from the Loehrs about how trying it was to drive through these villages during the period of Fasching. According to their observations, everyone they saw in the village had drunk too much and would wander into the road, making driving very hazardous. We reached Aachen in a slight drizzle, got established in our hotel, had dinner, and were tired and happy to get to bed. The next morning when we picked up the morning paper, the headline read "Eisenhower Schlugt Taft," which of course was the first news we had of the outcome of the Republican convention.

We took the highway in the morning going west through Louvain where we stopped to look at the library and some monuments, and then on to Brussels where we had another look at the beautiful facades around the city center. From there we went on to Bruges where we had the pleasure of showing the Loehrs its many interesting pieces of architecture, especially the cathedral and the facades around the square. We arrived at Ostend where a cold, raw wind was blowing off the Channel. The following morning the Loehrs left very early in order to get back to Bonn that night. The wind was quite high and so were the waves. It did not look promising as we with many others went down to the cross channel craft. As it pulled out, it went straight down the Belgian coast so as to make the shortest trip possible out in the channel. Its roughness was the worst we had ever experienced. We went below which as it turned out was a very good move, as we were two of a very few people who did not succumb to sea sickness. The boat was a mess when we arrived at Dover. Customs was, as always, easy in England, and we were soon on the train to London and in a hotel just off Piccadilly Circus. The next morning the papers commented on the "worst crossing of the summer."

We had planned that before we went home in '52 we would spend a share of our time in England, particularly in South England. We reserved an American Express tour similar in type to the one the year before and selected one that ended the day before our ship, the *Veendam*, sailed. We took the free time we had to see more of London, to go to the theater, and to visit the many public monuments again. It was very different living near Piccadilly than Living in South Kensington the year before. Our tour of South England took us through the main cathedral towns. We had an especially interesting evening in Bath and one on the Channel Coast which was sometimes referred to as the English Riviera because of its milder climate. South England was rather surprising to us in the amount of land that seemed to be what we would call rangeland, which the English called moors, inhabited only sparsely. Many of the towns were very old and some of the stone bridges just wide enough for the bus, having been built many years before. The King Arthur legend country had some points of interest as did the Lorna Doone country. The cathedrals, while not as imposing as St. Paul's or York's, were extremely beautiful with striking special features. We had lunch one day at Exeter but failed to get into the town hall as our timing was wrong for the rules. The end of our tour saw us back in London for the night. The next day after lunch we took the boat-train to Southhampton and there we were told that a lighter would take us out to meet the *Veendam*. Our luggage was all piled in the center where it was less likely to be splashed, and we sat around the hull of the boat on seats that had been built for that purpose.

It was dusk when we pulled up alongside the *Veendam*, where a stair was rigged for us to climb up. We found the Weatherlys waiting for us on the deck as well as two of our Fulbrighters from Holland, both of Michigan-Dutch descent, Henrietta Kuizinga and Ann Cooperman. We had an uneventful trip home except for one incident. One morning about 9:30 we noticed that the ship took a 180° turn in the water and started back the way we came. No one in authority would say a word about why this had happened, but gossip soon spread the news that a girl traveling with her parents in first-class had disappeared overnight. It was finally decided she had thrown herself overboard. Apparently under the rules of ocean travel the ship was required to turn and go back to where it might have happened to see if there was any sign of the victim. The folly of our not being told was evident because many people believed wilder stories than were true. The girl had spent the year in England in school, and her family had joined her there and there had been a quarrel. At any rate we spent one extra night on board before we could disembark in New York. We had reserved space on the New York Central's new fast aluminum train, in anticipation of having a comfortable trip to St. Louis. But we were wrong, as the trip proved to be very rough and we spent a very bad night. We switched to the Wabash in St. Louis and when we got off at Centralia, Frank and Louise Stephens were there waiting for us, and drove us home to a dinner Louise had prepared. It was certainly pleasant to see them, exactly one year from the time they had taken us to Centralia to begin our trip. The next day I was in my office where everything was in good order, except that Mitchell Tucker who had taken over my work for the year had been found to have cancer of the lung. Mitch was surprisingly cheerful and glad to get from under that responsibility. I was very glad to relieve him of it and he should not have been trying to carry that burden in his serious condition.

Chapter 17

The Office of President

The early 1950's saw the final assurance of a complete four-year medical school re-established at the University. This had been the result of a long struggle, both in the medical profession and in the University. In the 1930's the medical profession as represented by its officials refused to agree that any new facilities for educating physicians in Missouri were needed. This was followed until its fallacy became evident as the scarcity of physicians, especially in rural areas, forced its abandonment. The question in the 1940's became not whether we should have a four-year medical school, but where should we have it. The claims of the establishment in Kansas City were pressed with great vigor and persuasiveness. The University, largely because of Leslie Cowan's timidity, was itself very slow in taking a position. President Middlebush finally stated the University's position, which was for adding the last two years to the basic school on the Columbia campus and building enough clinical facilities to provide sufficient student experience. Cowan's opposition to the medical school seemed to be because of the great problems it would make in the legislature. The set high cost of medical education would tend to force our appropriations to be either less or stabilized for all other divisions of the University.

No doubt Middlebush shared some of these feelings, but I never heard him express them. At any rate, with the support and leadership of two very important Board presidents, Senator Allen McReynolds and later Powell McHaney, the present University's position was solidified as the University's decision, although at all times there was a minority on the Board that was opposed to the medical school going anywhere but Kansas City. The crucial date was 1952, when the legislature committed itself to that program with an appropriation for half of the estimated cost, the other half to come in the next biennium. Actually the two appropriations were together less than half enough for the final medical school that was built, but the commitment was made. During this contest, Middlebush's relations with some of the pro-Kansas City Board members, particularly Dr. Glenn Hendren of Liberty and Lester E. Cox of Springfield, deteriorated greatly.

At this time Middlebush believed his own health was precarious. In spite of the success of his medical program, he made a sudden decision in the spring of 1954 at a Board meeting in St. Louis to retire virtually immediately. It had been assumed that he would stay on for a year or more at least. The Board immediately set up a search committee consisting of one faculty member, one alumnus, and three Board members, a traditional procedure when searching for a new president. The chairman of the committee was Powell McHaney, chairman of the Board. James Finch, a new member from Cape Girardeau, and Lester Cox were the other Board members. Cullen Coil of Jefferson City was the representative selected from the alumni, and Edward Weatherly was selected from the faculty, although he also could have represented the alumni. The committee made several trips to interview and talk to various people, including the great educational organizations, such as The American Council on Education, and several presidents of large universities. By these means and much correspondence the committee gathered the usual documentary support and non-support of the names that had been recommended.

In the past Leslie Cowan would have played a large part in the decision. But members of the Board, both the pro- and the anti-Kansas City medical school, were very little inclined to give Cowan any part in the process. I doubt that he had any influence on the decision that was made. Middlebush had limited his continuation to September 1 and the Curators had to come to some decision by then. I was called into the Curators' meeting in August, and Powell McHaney informed me that a decision on the presidency had not been reached. He then asked me if I would take over as acting president until the decision was made. Later in the day, after talking with Ruth, I accepted the offer with three specifications. One was that I was not to be a stopgap merely answering the mail and calling the meetings of various committees and going through the routine of the president's office. A second requirement was that Leslie Cowan, who was both Vice President for Business and Secretary of the Board of Curators, had to drop one of those positions. The third was that we would be given time for a brief vacation. The Board agreed to these requests, and announcement was made that I would become acting president on Middlebush's retirement. I actually did not take office until September 8.

The weakness of an acting president in dealing with the public, the legislature, the faculty and students is obvious. Probably it is not a wise position in which to put oneself. But it seemed quite a common practice at the University of Missouri, as Middlebush had been acting president and so were, as I recall, Walter Williams and J. Carleton Jones. The Middlebushes had moved out of the President's House and there was no suggestion that an acting president would move into it. The immediate problem for the acting president was the legislative session that was approaching. Presenting and defending this budget would be my big job as acting president. The budget was already rather well set and was one that had been fairly typical of the last ten years. With some help from Cowan, but overwhelmingly from Ray Bezoni, the comptroller, this was finally in the shape in which it went to the governor and later to the legislative committees. In preparing for the legislative struggle, I asked Powell McHaney to see if we could have a conference with Mike Kinney, the old senator from St. Louis, whom I knew but not as well as McHaney did. We had lunch together in St. Louis and I laid out to Mike what I thought the problem was from the standpoint of the University. That was its inability to get adequate appropriations, and I briefly gave him the story of the last several budgets and what had happened to them in the legislature. I asked him what we had been doing wrong when other universities, such as Illinois, were getting about 50 percent more per student in their appropriations than we were. He answered quite directly by saying, "You don't ask for enough." It was clear to all of us we had not been getting what we were asking for. "You are going to be cut anyway. You had better start with a higher figure so that they can make a big cut and still give you more money." This was probably not good government but it was the only immediate solution that was available, and it was too late to do much with the current budget.

Governor Phil Donnelly was an unusual problem here in that he was serving a second term with one term intervening. In most ways you could not find a better statesman for the State of Missouri than Donnelly. He had been a senator, a governor and was a statesman without too much imagination but nevertheless a good one. His problem now was his age and his failing health. He tended to think far too much in terms of his first administration when it came to appropriations but costs had grown enormously in the years between. The University had also grown and new kinds of thinking about public support had to be developed. This was beyond's Donnelly's ability to conceive in adequate terms, well-intentioned as he was. As far as dealing with the legislature was concerned, I found it most interesting. Many of the members I knew and others, at least those on the appropriations committee, I soon became acquainted with and I had no complaints on the friendliness of any of them. There were a few stock enemies, of course, such as the senator whose son had flunked out of law school, and the house member whose company had not been successful in bidding on some University business. But these, of course, were in the nature of the case and had to be expected and dealt with. Fortunately, their colleagues knew them better than I did.

When I came to the University in 1930, I soon found that in many ways the key administrative officer was the business manager, Leslie Cowan. Cowan had graduated from the university in engineering. After graduation he worked in the admissions office and later in the business office, and soon became business manager and secretary of the Board of Curators. His real power rested in holding the two positions. He was in a position to cultivate the Board very assiduously and had a great deal of influence on its action. He was often responsible for important appointments and he was not slow to let people know when he had helped to arrange their appointment. He had gradually built up a political machine within the University itself whereby many, if not most, of the administrators were obligated to him in some way. He was, among others, partly responsible for Middlebush's appointment after Walter Williams' death. Many people both in and out of the University learned that to get action it was more expeditious to go to Cowan than to the President.

It is difficult to understand the exact nature of the relationship of Middlebush and Cowan. During the last years of Walter Williams' administration, he was a sick man, and during that period many activities were necessarily shifted to other offices, with most of them going to Cowan's. These did not all return to the office of the president when Middlebush took over first as acting president and later as president. Middlebush was not a person to make an issue of such matters unless they were presented to him as a question of authority.

Undoubtedly there had been a gradual shifting of activity from the president's office to Cowan's over the years of which Middlebush was only vaguely conscious. All of the powers that were ceremonial or legal were kept in the President's hands, but they were narrowed strikingly in some instances. Each was such a small movement out of the presidential office, and as the depression and war years were times when little progress could be made without extraordinary activity (which was not in Middlebush's nature), he hardly realized what was happening.

Another factor that is generally not realized was that during his long period in the presidency, Middlebush gave to the University a large sum of money for which he held a lifetime interest in the income. It is interesting that these funds that Fred and Catherine Middlebush eventually turned over to the University may have been greater than the entire salary paid to Middlebush as President.

Some of Cowan's ways were devious but most of them were direct and completely proper as far as authority was concerned. Middlebush was a man of somewhat limited energy and, especially during the latter part of his administration, would absent himself from the campus on weekends when many things came up that needed to be settled. As a rule Cowan, who had no outside activities and no recreational interests, was always there to make the decisions. Gradually this put more and more of the decision-making in the University of the normal and routine kind in Cowan's hands and less and less of it in the President's office. I have no doubt that most of these decisions were made in the interest of the University as Cowan saw it, but he did not have a very sharp distinction between the University's interests and his own power. This situation was so evident that he developed a great deal of antagonism from people who did not like the decisions the University made. This included board members, deans, faculty members and alumni. In fact, he was often blamed for things that were not his decisions at all but belonged in some other area of the University. There were incidents, however, and they seemed to increase as time went on, in which Middlebush was made sharply aware of the fact that Cowan was actually usurping some of his powers and responsibilities. Occasionally there were a few public expressions of this as when Trawick Stubbs, Dean of the basic Medical School, had quoted Cowan as saying of Middlebush, "Oh, I let him go through the door first but I make most of the decisions around here," which was a costly remark if Cowan had made it and few doubted that he had.

Among the other jobs that Cowan had assumed was that of chief lobbyist for the University. He had developed a series of alliances and antagonisms, especially the latter, that centered in Jefferson City and were quite bitter.

Middlebush on the contrary was a very knowledgeable person in administrative affairs, and as time went on he had developed a very wide group of friends among other university presidents. He knew almost instinctively what should be done. His difficulty was that as time went on he became dilatory about doing them. I recall particularly in the period after I became arts dean the deanship of the business school had been neglected since Roy Curtis had gone into government war service and never returned to the University. Various members of the faculty had been designated as acting deans. Some of them were efficient and some knew little about that job. This was true also in the School of Education after Irion's resignation, which was brought on in large part by disagreements with Cowan and Middlebush. On one occasion Tom Brady and I had gone to Middlebush, discussed the problem of the School of Business and Public Administration and had urged him to appoint a dean. William Bradshaw was acting dean and when Middlebush asked for suggestions, I named Bradshaw although I knew Middlebush's opinion of him was not especially high and he was not a Cowan man in any sense. But Middlebush did follow our urging which we put on the basis that the school was being damaged by not having a regular dean. Later we also went to him on the problem in the School of Education, where Loren Townsend was acting dean and he was definitely a Cowan-approved selection. We urged again that someone be named dean, and we agreed with him that Townsend was probably as good as he had on the staff for that job. In some way Townsend knew this, and after he was appointed he came to me and told me how much he appreciated my help in his appointment. I do not know how he learned of it unless Middlebush or Cowan told him.

At the end of the second week after I had taken over as acting president, my first incident of order on the campus arose. It happened on a Saturday night and we had gone to bed at our house. The lights were out but I was not yet asleep when I hear a car come up the drive and then the doorbell rang. I went down to the door, opened it, and greeted the Chief of Police. As I recall his conversation, he said, "Dr. Ellis, two fraternities over on College Avenue are fighting. It has that side of the town stirred up. I can't make them stop. I wish you would come over and try." Well, I knew the traditional enmity between the two fraternities but I had not the slightest notion how I could stop this. But I dressed and went back with him. One fraternity was being beseiged by the other at this stage of the trouble. The attack came from the dark shadow behind the first house where rocks were thrown at the other house. Every now and then the rocks would break a window. The activity had gathered a crowd. A large number of male students from the east side of town were there, and for reasons that were not clear to me, urging the attackers on.

I tried my best by means of a speech to get the audience to go home, as I was confident that if it dispersed the battle would stop. But it was a complete failure. The chief was out of ideas, and I was out of patience at the foolishness of it all but thought I saw a chance to change the situation. I marched up to the front door of the house of the attacking group, rang the doorbell and when it was answered, I asked for the president of the house. In a few minutes a rather frightened-looking student appeared wondering, I am sure, what was in store for him. I looked at my watch and said, "I am giving you 10 minutes to get your men inside the house, the door shut and the lights out—just 10 minutes. If your house is not quiet by then, you will all be looking for places to live tomorrow because I will close your house for the rest of the year." Within 10 minutes the house was dark, the rock throwing stopped and the crowd began to disperse. A group came out of the other house and came over to where the Chief and I were standing and wanted to take us to see the damage that had been done to their house. But I said, "You are as much at fault and you know it."

That ended the incident and the Chief took me back home and I went back to bed. Of course I did not realize that I had no authority to close the house, but neither did the house president. That proved to be the only time I had to take part in an incident of this kind.

After I became acting president the search committee continued its activities. It did not seem to give up until after Christmas, but I was not given any information about this by anyone and was judging only by what I saw and rumors I picked up. Board members asked me about various people who had been recommended to the committee. I gave them the best advice I could. Eventually the gossip began to come back to me that they were going to ask me to stay on, although none of them told me this.

The April meeting was held in St. Louis at the Jefferson Hotel and we had the usual quota of business. The night before the major meeting Cox and McHaney and one or two other members whom I do not recall asked me to go to dinner with them. This I did and we went across Twelfth Street to a restaurant. We filled a booth and then the questioning began, both direct and indirect, and more direct as the time went on. It soon became clear to me their problem was Tom Brady. I knew Cowan had criticized Tom repeatedly to many of them. But the basic problem that night seemed to be Tom's Catholicism. Tom had recently become a convert, largely I felt because he thought that while raising a large family in his wife's faith, he could not do a good job if he did not go along. But he more than merely went along as time passed, as that was Tom's nature. The man that seemed most antagonistic to Tom that night was Cox although McHaney had a personal grievance in that area against Tom, as McHaney's own wife was becoming a convert much against his wishes. She was a long-time friend of Tom's and had gone to high school with him in Richmond, Missouri. While in the process of her conversion she had called and talked to Tom several times. McHaney knew about these calls and was quite aggrieved about them. Essentially what they wanted me to do if I were named president was remove Tom from his administrative position.

When I got it all laid out on the table, I told them I had no interest whatever in doing that. As I look back I realize it had been brewing for some time. I recall that Middlebush had had some problems concerning it with members of the Board. He called me in to talk to me about it during this period, as he seemed to look upon me as Tom's promoter. That Tom was becoming a convert had not been told to me before, but certain Board members had heard it from Cowan, who would know such things before most people would.

Nothing more was said that night or the next day at the Board meeting, but I was excused from the meeting for an executive session fairly early in the afternoon. Paul Peterson, the university attorney who was also at the Board meeting, told me what was up, although I could well guess it. Paul waited with me. Finally I was sent for and found that I had been named president. I asked if the decision were unanimous and Jim Finch said there was one dissenting vote. I learned later it came from Maxine Shutz from Kansas City. I expect it was as much directed at the policies the University had followed, which were quite unpopular at the time in Kansas City, as it was to me personally.

I accepted having talked this out with Ruth before and they made the announcement to the press. In midstream so to speak I was changed from acting president to president, and it changed my public image with the people with whom I worked, both in Jefferson City and on the campus. I was pleased especially that Governor Donnelly asked me to come to his office and told me how pleased he was at the action.

My immediate problem was working with the Board. I knew from many expressions of discontent that the members had been quite unhappy with the way Cowan had managed the Board meetings. With the appointment of Mrs. Mary Robnett as secretary, the character of the office changed and she became just that—Secretary of the Board. Among the things Board members were unhappy about: They seldom knew what was coming up in a Board meeting ahead of time. They did not see any copies of the actions taken by the Board until sometime after the meetings when Cowan dictated a statement of the actions which may or may not have corresponded with their memory of the action. A third thing some of the Board were very unhappy about was the fact that problems were brought to the Board with no suggested solutions. There was not a University administration program it wanted the Board to approve. I told Powell McHaney when he talked to me about this that I would not bring things to the Board without making recommendations, and I think that with possibly one exception I carried out that policy for the entire period of my presidency.

My policy was to bring to the Board meetings an agenda of proposed actions for the Board to approve. I drafted the first of these myself but later Paul Peterson took on this task. Then the propositions were debated, passed as written, or modified and passed, or not passed. It was much simpler for Mary Robnett to write the minutes with the manuscript we had acted on covering all of the actions considered. This procedure, which changed somewhat from month to month as we learned more, took on more of a legal phraseology than I preferred because of Paul's tendency in drafting, but as the Board always had at least four lawyers, it probably was just as well it did.

The matter of the early agenda never worked really well. It seemed that at our monthly Board meetings (we had gone to monthly Board meetings at my recommendation instead of meetings of the executive committee and executive board for the two different campuses) a great number of the more or less routine actions that divisions and departments wanted approval of could not get to me before the final week, which was too late for Mary Robnett to get them out to the Board. It frequently happened that the agenda we sent out had only about half of the items we had on the actual agenda that was presented to them at the Board meeting. We discussed this in the Board and the members understood the difficulty but wanted earlier notice on some of these questions. We tried to tighten up the campus end of the procedure by refusing to take to the Board late actions that were not significant or in which time was not a significant factor.

On the whole, I think the most satisfactory aspect of my acting presidency and later presidency was the good relations I was able to maintain with the Board and the many friends I developed among the members. Most of them were a little younger than I was and the greatest good fortune I had as president was to have James Finch as President of the Board during nearly all of the years. He was a very wise counselor, had excellent judgment on what we could do with the legislature and the public and was always helpful. He became President of the Board in an interesting way in that Powell McHaney came to my office before my first meeting of the Board as acting president, reminded me they were electing the officers and pointed out he had canvassed the situation and he could not be re-elected as he could get only four of the nine votes. He said he could elect Jim Finch as he could get one more vote for him. I told him I regretted the situation but I would rather have Jim Finch than any of the others, and he was elected. He served for nine years, the longest term for a Board President at least in this century. He was succeeded by Robert Neill of St. Louis. Neill was an able Board member who had worked closely with Finch and made an excellent successor.

The General Assembly which met in January, 1955, gave me a new experience. Although I had attended hearings relating to the University on several occasions before, these were usually on particular buildings or programs. I made no changes in the usual procedure but was backed up by Ray Bezoni, Talitha Gisler, and Dale Bowling as well as several deans. I attended House hearings and presented the general picture of the budget. Then following these procedures, I called on some of the deans to present their own divisional budgets because while the university budget was not line item in type, it was almost that detailed in some respects. Dean Wilson of the School of Mines and Metallurgy and Dean Longwell of the College of Agriculture had always presented their part of the budget, and, frequently in the past, Cowan had presented large parts of the budget, particularly the buildings and other capital items. We followed these procedures, and I became convinced before the session was over that it was a poor procedure. It was confusing to the members of the committees, and, in some cases, deans would take more time on their section of the budget than the major university items that I presented. The formal presentations were followed by questions. Some of these were good. Some were meant to be helpful. And some were distinctly unfriendly. I did not pretend to know the answers to all the questions and frequently referred to Bezoni, Gisler, or Bowling for answers which were invariably helpful. I think this increased the committee's confidence in the budget-making procedure.

Changes were made after that session, and I presented the entire budget as one package, as one organized budget. The School of Medicine represented a particular problem at this time because we were trying carefully to make the members of the legislature understand the cost of what they had committed themselves to in undertaking a school of medicine and at the same time not taking it from the other programs of the university. This presented some real problems because of the limited number of students that could be admitted there and the consequent dissatisfaction in many areas because local applicants had been refused. As time went on, however, and the medical service furnished by the hospital proved popular, in rural counties particularly, the medical school added strength to our entire budget presentation.

The amount allocated to us in the first and second appropriations was disappointingly small, and there were no appropriations for buildings. However, in my second session Governor Donnelly asked the legislature to approve a referendum for a bond issue of 75 million dollars for buildings for the state enterprises, specifically for the state hospitals, penal establishments, and educational institutions. Fortunately, he did not break it down and try to distribute the amounts before it was to be voted on, because a bond issue that sets up distribution problems before the vote is taken is almost certain to fail. As it was to be a constitutional amendment, it required only a majority vote. Whatever else this postponement did, it at least left some hope that we would not be completely without building funds in the near future.

Shortly after the session was over, Governor Donnelly called me and asked me to serve on a committee to conduct a campaign on behalf of the passage of the bond issue. I was delighted. Later he had a meeting of the committee in his office, and I was elected chairman. I was the youngest member of the committee. Most of the others were put on because of the public standing of the person and, in some cases, because of an expected willingness that he would contribute to the costs of the campaign for which, of course, public funds could not be used. I soon found that I would get little help from the other members of the committee, that I was not only chairman but, to all intents and purposes, I was the committee, although several of the other members gave generous donations toward the campaign.

In canvassing the assets, it quickly became clear that organized labor would be one of my main sources of support, particularly the building trades. Also, it was clear that the farm organizations, particularly the Missouri Farmers Association (and here Fred Heinkel's membership on the Board of Curators was important) would give all the help they could which was substantial. We also received help from the Farm Bureau. I immediately went to work on the State Chamber of Commerce and got commitments to help from the members which they carried out although there was a great deal of opposition in the Chamber to the action. As I remember, they agreed after the campaign that they would not participate in others. The local Chambers of Commerce in Columbia and Rolla were different stories. The Columbia Chamber lent me the half-time services of its secretary, Charles Isley. We arranged an office for him on the first floor of Jesse Hall. He brought to our campaign good understanding of campaign procedures and a wide acquaintance of his own. We, with Guy (Bus) Entsminger, conferred virtually every morning after which we proceeded to move. We quickly saw that our main sources would come from the alumni associations. The Columbia campus association, with Entsminger's leadership as secretary, was the main support. We had at least a paper organization in every county. We quickly tried to firm these up into working groups with considerable success. Unfortunately, in the case of the School of Mines it had little organization in Missouri outside of St. Louis and Kansas City. It seemed that their alumni were stronger out of the state than in the state. I suspect this was also true of the College of Engineering at Columbia. I met with the state college presidents individually on several occasions and tried to get all the help from their alumni associations that I could. Our plan was that in each district there would be a formal coordination of efforts of the University alumni and the alumni of the college that represented that district. I immediately found that the state college alumni did not have county organizations but just one general organization. On my urging several of the colleges did, however, appoint personnel in each county to serve as liaison with our group. The state hospitals and the penal institutions, of course, were not useful except as local interests that could be pointed to in the locality where they were a local asset, although in several cases members of the boards took an active part in promoting the campaign.

We prepared some literature for mailings and put our great effort on money raising to use for advertising, especially newspaper advertising. I was surprised to find how customary it was for a smaller newspaper to demand its share of the advertising budget. A few donors who were large advertisers used some of their regular advertising space on our behalf shortly before the election. With the complete support of Governor Donnelly and at least the benevolent neutrality of the legislature, we built our campaign toward the election date, making use of the alumni and to some extent of the University's extension service.

The election date was a break for us because no other issue was on the ballot. It was a single issue election. Governor Donnelly could assure the public that it would not raise taxes because the present taxes would provide enough to service a debt of 75 million dollars. In fact, that is why he set the amount at 75 million. His elderly budget director had told him that was the amount which the present revenue would service. This was unfortunate because we could just as easily have carried a 125 million dollar bond issue, which would have given the state badly-needed buildings at a time when costs were low. Although the vote was light on election day, we won by a reasonable majority. We carried all the counties in the state except Bollinger and those in the southwest corner, where either our campaign did not work as effectively or the conservative character of the Republican section of the state did not bring out a strong vote for the bonds.

I think its passage mainly resulted from the work first of the University Alumni Association, second of the organized labor and farmers, and third from the lack of any organized opposition. Officially, the Chamber of Commerce was supporting us. With the election won, the Governor called a special session of the legislature with the sole purpose of considering buildings that could be built. This proved to be a most interesting session for me.

The special session promised to be not only interesting but most important. I felt myself in a difficult position because the contest in the legislature was bound to be institution against institution. We were handicapped in our drive as I had led the campaign for all, but that also had some advantages. I tried to play it fair with the eleemosynary institutions and the state colleges so that the 75 million dollars would go as far as was possible in meeting the great backlog of need in Missouri for housing its programs. Even though I was convinced that it would have been as easy to pass a larger bond issue, 75 million at the prices available in the late 50's made possible a tremendous amount of building—the largest program in the state's history and one that is forever a credit to Governor Phil Donnelly.

We took our list of building needs from our former appropriation request list and reorganized it to meet my and the current Board's ideas of the priorities. I think one illustration will show what these expected priorities were. Before I had taken the presidency, Cowan had decided that the old medical school, which had been added to once and was a badly arranged and poorly located building, could be added to again. It was to be made a home for the business school which was very inadequately housed on the Red Campus in what had at one time been the law school. I suspect that Middlebush did not object too much because he felt that as the former dean of that school he would be considered prejudiced. It seemed to me the worst possible kind of planning as the School of Business and Public Administration was one that, because of its poor housing and small faculty in the past, had been given very little public visibility even though among its faculty were some of our most distinguished scholars.

I convinced the Board that a new building to house the School of Business and Public Administration was one of our pressing needs and should be rated high among our priorities. Another high priority was a home for the Fine Arts which were then scattered between Jesse Hall and an old dormitory, Lathrop Hall, a worn-out building suitable only for demolition. This building housed music. The theater part of the speech department was in Jesse Hall and Art was also primarily in overcrowded Jesse Hall. In working with the members of the faculty on this, we agreed that, except for the History of Art and Archaeology, there should be one center for all the Fine Arts.

Another high priority was the enlarging of the library. Even with the west wing, which we had added with the federal money in the late 30's, we were crowded in all parts of the library including the State Historical Society. Moreover, for efficiency's sake, there was need to bring back some branch libraries, such as those in the College of Agriculture and the Geology Department, which had been made branches because of the lack of space in the main library building. The original plan of the library had called for an eastern wing to balance the west wing which we had added in the thirties. Because of the growth in our needs here, we changed the plan and duplicated the entire existing building. Another structure was planned primarily for a classroom building for history, literature and language courses which would house the departments in those areas that were now housed in Jesse Hall. An exception was made for the classics, which stayed with classical art and archaeology. The engineering school decided its greatest need was space for electrical engineering in a completely new building. Then with some remodeling of the space in the older buildings, the other divisions could be reasonably housed. So an electrical engineering building was proposed. In terms of the number of buildings, the College of Agriculture had more buildings than any other division of the University. It may have been true, as Cowan believed and acted on, that it was easier to get buildings for agriculture from the legislature than for any other division. At any rate there was no doubt of its need for expansion, as the School of Forestry was housed completely in temporary army barracks buildings that had been moved in from an army post. In the end we designed an administrative building for the College of Agriculture which would also house forestry and horticulture. Whitten Hall would become a headquarters building for Agriculture Extension, which needed to get its staff in an efficient operation unit. These were certainly not all the buildings which were needed, as the biological sciences, physics and geology were badly in need of more room.

On the Rolla campus our most pressing needs were space for electrical and civil engineering and a general classroom building that would allow us to abandon the old Rolla building. Both campuses were badly in need of dormitories, remodeling and repairing of several of the old buildings to make them more efficient structures, and repairing and modernization of heating plants and other utilities.

I presented the building requests myself with help from only Dale Bowling and an occasional dean, and I took the lead. As I look back at this, the great change in the way we presented our budget was made at that time. We appeared first before the House Committee and then before the Senate Committee, the Governor having set up an executive budget which he recommended to the General Assembly. When the House bill came out of the Senate Committee, it contained roughly the buildings I have outlined for the two campuses, totaling over 22 million dollars in all. The chairman of the Senate Appropriations Committee, John Noble, who had always been classified by Cowan as an enemy of the University, I had found very cooperative and willing to listen. As long as he remained in that position, he was that kind of senator also. However, the night before the Senate report was to come to the floor for passage, Bus Entsminger, who was working full-time on this lobbying, received word from some of our friends that a group was going to try to reduce the Columbia campus appropriation and that it was centered around Senator Ed Keating from Kansas City and Senator Clayton Allen from Liberty. We consulted by phone with several people and as the Senate would not meet until 9:30, we laid plans for a little extra lobbying of our own, getting the help of Henry Andrae who was a former member of the House, a leading lawyer, President of our Cole County Alumni Association, and later a very useful member of the Board. The three of us met in the Senate wing of the

Capitol at 8 o'clock. The senators were coming to their offices gradually so we divided up the different senators. Andrae, being a Republican, took the Republican senators; Bus and I divided the more numerous Democrat senators. In this way we contacted virtually every senator. On one occasion I met Senator Allen in the hall and he shook his finger at me and said, "We've got you beat this time," to which I smiled and made no reply. In fact, I was afraid he had. After the Senate had assembled, all of our people we were sure of were there. We went to the gallery and watched the floor fight. Senator Keating moved the reduction by an amount to take from the committee bill two of the buildings from the Columbia campus that were recommended. The committee chairman Noble in a few words expressed the hope that the Senate would support the committee bill and when the vote was taken, we had about a five vote majority of those present. We had no doubt Governor Donnelly would sign the bill which he did. About 73 million dollars was appropriated at this time, with two million carried over, a fair share of which we secured later. It was the biggest building program ever enacted by a Missouri government and what it did for the educational and eleemosynary institutions at the low prices of the day was a tremendous improvement.

A few years later I had an argument with Governor James Blair about these buildings in which he told me he did not favor bond issues for state buildings. They should be paid out of current revenue. "Well," I told him, "I would not disagree with that in theory but, as a practical matter, Donnelly was absolutely right, because the cost of building was going up faster than the interest cost on the bonds." Moreover, we were going to have the buildings much earlier than if we had waited for the revenue.

The Board felt that our long-time architectural firm, Jamieson and Spearl, which had designed the library and the medical center, worked at such a slow pace that it could not take on such a large job. So with a special Board committee, myself, and Bowling, we interviewed architectural firms in St. Louis, Kansas City, and Springfield that wished to be considered for some of the work. As a result we gave work for these and certain later buildings to ten different firms that had not previously worked for the University maintaining one firm as supervisory architects for University campus plans.

A large part of the construction program that followed the appropriations of the bond issue went into buildings that were unrelated to those appropriations, as dormitories and student service buildings were all built largely with money which we ourselves borrowed under our legal authority. The north half of the student union had been built as our first attempt at this in 1950 when, with only about half enough money raised from gifts to pay for it, we issued bonds for the rest to be redeemed by part of the student fees. By now those bonds had been rather well paid off, as in 1950 we had borrowed money on tax exempt bonds for two percent. We planned a very large program of dormitory building, centering the men's group largely around the pre-war dormitory, Defoe, on Hitt Street. We put another small group of men's dormitories that would house 500 students just north of the Missouri State Teachers' Association headquarters. The big addition for the women was a group named after Ella Victoria Dobbs, which was on the old golf course and was an unusually fine development. Another addition was Wolpers Hall, paralleling Johnston Hall, which helped to supply the much needed women's housing, the lack of which had retarded our enrollment of women. Still later we added the Bingham and the Rollins groups to round out the housing program for my administration.

All of these dormitories were built with a small amount of University money, never, I believe, over one-fourth, and the rest of it by bond issues which were sold at current market prices for tax exempt bonds to be serviced out of dormitory charges. These buildings, which were built at the time as part of the plan of buildings financed by the appropriations, gave us an historic building program. This program had to be managed very carefully by the business office to make sure that in Columbia and in Rolla we did not overload the local labor market so as to raise the costs of the buildings. Later, as the Student Union space was clearly inadequate, we built on the foundation south of the tower that had already been completed in 1930. Then we induced the Green family to allow us to locate the Chapel, which Mr. Green originally wanted to put by the columns, as part of the south wing of the union. Because the south wing gave little space for student activities, we constructed a second building on the mall which we had planned as a continuation of Ninth Street to the medical building. This was called the Student Commons and later was named for Tom Brady.

Probably the most exasperating building project I was related to was a swimming pool for men at Columbia. The women's gym, small and old, had a quite inadequate swimming pool, and I believe the University of Missouri was the only state university whose men students did not have the advantage of a swimming pool for recreation or for exercise.

We put in an application for an appropriation for a swimming building for men after the special session. My recollection is that we got it through one house the first time. The second time I worked on the other house and got it through that house, but the house that had passed it before did not do so on this occasion. Then having some of my disgust and anger aroused, I really worked and I got the bill through both houses. And to my amazement, when it got to Governor Blair's desk, he vetoed it. My relations with Jim Blair were such that I had not thought it necessary to sit with him and explain the problem. And he may have had some other motivation of which I was not aware. Anyway, I went back and got it through both houses in spite of an emotional plea from a senator from St. Joseph, who was a graduate of the University, that we were making a country club of the University, and the bill was signed by Governor John Dalton.

This was only the beginning of the problem. When we had made the original request for a swimming pool for men costs had been much lower, and here we were with the original appropriation, which had not been wise to change in the legislative process, that was hardly adequate for its purpose. Moreover, in discussions with the student affairs people, especially Dean of Students Jack Matthews, Tom Brady and Director of Student Affairs for Women Gladys Koepke, we agreed that a segregated pool was out-of-date and what we needed was a pool that would be useful for both men and women. This of course took still more money. So in the end we added to the appropriation a bond issue to be redeemed out of student fees and built a fine building that was suitable for both. My own contribution was to insist that since we were expanding our ideas there should be a pool both indoors and outdoors, and that is the way it was built.

In the next few years, we also completed dormitories for men and a student union on the Rolla campus that supplied much needed facilities there.

Governor Donnelly was succeeded by James Blair, a younger man and less inclined to follow the old practices of the state government. Another change about this time that resulted in an improvement was the fact that the salaries for members of the legislature were increased. These were large enough now that it became desirable for young lawyers getting started in practice to run for the legislature and make up a fair share of the General Assembly. This was not confined to lawyers, but included young men who had some college experience and who understood better what our needs were, and I found it easier to explain our problems to them. While it was not so true in the two large cities, yet a number of younger men did come into the legislature from there who proved to be quite willing to consider new and different approaches to higher education. It also coincided nationally with the great growth in higher education. The changes in the birth rate immediately after the war was beginning to have its effects upon enrollments. As the veteran enrollments declined, they were rapidly replaced by larger and larger enrollments of new high school graduates. The Columbia campus had never had a reasonable proportion of its students made up of women. This was due in large part to the fact that it had no women's dormitories except little

Read Hall. But as we made these available through the power of issuing bonds, the number and proportion of women students tended to increase. This increased growth in enrollment of both men and women, which was very strong on both the Rolla and Columbia campuses, made it absolutely necessary to get substantial increases in appropriations and the openmindedness of the new legislators made this possible.

Another helpful factor was that Governor Blair had no fondness for the biennial sessions which meant an appropriation for two years. He had been around Jefferson City long enough to know that it was difficult to foretell what the needs would be in terms of finance two years hence. From our standpoint at the university, it had another great advantage. The legislature met each year. While it increased the labor of the budget presentation, it also gave us two chances instead of one to convince members of the General Assembly and the Governor that the needs were as we represented them and were not padded. Moreover, the growth in buildings that came from the bond issue money and the revenue producing buildings that came from our own bonds did not mean the end of requests for building appropriations from the General Assembly. While Donnelly's state bond issue took reasonably good care of the eleemosynary institutions of the state and fair care of the penal institutions, the higher education institutions were still far from adequately housed and the needs rose each year. Moreover, increases in state revenue, the most spectacular of which was the 1963 sales tax increase of Governor Dalton's, enabled the state to provide considerable in the way of building appropriations.

More important than the buildings were the salary levels. The quite uncompetitive salaries that we were paying in the middle fifties were distinctly handicapping our development as a university. The wisdom of keeping the medical school appropriation separate for the first several years was apparent, as the low salary scale that dominated other divisions of the University was not carried over to the medical school. This set a standard that made it somewhat easier to increase the general salary scales until we were competitive at least with the neighboring state universities, if not with all the Big 10. This did not happen, of course, in one legislative appropriation, but it was the trend and the result of campaigning and pressure on the government for funds to make this possible.

Fringe benefits were another item that had to be taken care of. The first meeting I had with the University policy committee after I became Acting President was to lay before it the charge to develop a retirement plan that would take care of people who had not been able to develop a retirement on their own low salaries, and who were already near retirement. The plan should take care of those persons as well as be good enough for the future to make it possible to secure staff of the quality we needed. With help from some of the faculty who were experts in insurance and similar fields, the committee developed a plan that was non-contributory so it did not reduce the faculty members current inadequate salary. Eventually it was also funded, the money for the funding coming from a percentage of the salary budget, but originally it was not to be funded but to be paid from current appropriations. This was not received with great enthusiasm by some members of the Board. Powell McHaney, Chairman of the General American Life Insurance Company, was very suspicious of any plan that did not follow any regular policy such as his company was familiar with. He furnished the committee a consultant to help it work on the plan, but that was soon given up as the consultant's ideas were so different from the committee's that he was of no help. The committee, chaired by Professor Raymond Peck, found a consultant of its own whose main function was really to convince the Board that most of the parts of the plan that had been developed were sound retirement policies although more of the industrial type. Peck was not particularly interested in a funded plan. But I quickly saw in discussing this with the Board that it was one element that I could not get accepted. Moreover, my own experience with the legislature had already taught me that any pay-as-you-go plan out of appropriations was fraught with great danger that in time of emergency the legislature or governor would just cut it off.

Eventually, we developed a plan that the Board found acceptable and put it in operation, our main opposition curiously enough coming not from the Board, but from the local chapter of the American Association of University Professors which objected that it did not follow the national line of the AAUP. Before the faculty adopted the plan of the policy committee, we had the largest faculty meeting I can recall up to that time, where the issue was debated. The AAUP plan was very much more costly on our budget, made no provision for the people nearing retirement who would have nothing from the University for their past services, but we had some party liners who were all for it. They were led by Professor Bower Aly of the Speech Department while the committee case was presented by Raymond Peck. In the end the faculty voted overwhelmingly for the committee's plan although, in the years that followed, the AAUP chapter kept a constant barrage of complaints against the plan. The thing it objected to chiefly, in the end, was that it did not vest immediately. In fact, it was designed purposely not to do so. That was a major factor in keeping its beginning costs low. Personally I took great satisfaction in the plan because it did a great deal for the faculty, young and old, and did it with the least charge on the University's budget of any college or university plan with which we were familiar. It carried a minor penalty in that the AAUP, in publishing its salary lists, refused to include our plan because it did not vest soon enough to satisfy its rules. Besides Raymond Peck, Raymond Schroeder and W. L. Eckhardt were very important in designing the plan.

The non-academic staff also presented a situation much like the academic. The first step there was to adopt a workman's compensation plan that the state had developed. But that contributed nothing toward retirement, and the state retirement plan, for which our people were eligible, was a contributory one of 4 percent. It was a poor plan and except in a few cases was not in line with good policy. When the state decided to make it compulsory on all employees not under any other plan, we acted to put ours under our faculty plan and it has worked out, I believe, very well.

The retirement plan committee had set its goal for a retirement compensation that would give a faculty member with a reasonable length of service half of his highest salary when social security was added to it. While this was only roughly achieved in the formula, it was reasonably so and soon increased further.

The same faculty committee and under similar leadership brought in for a plan for a health and hospitalization insurance, using our own staff and at least one outside consultant. From the start we were agreed we wanted catastrophic insurance rather than general health care, because it seemed that faculty members could take care of normal health needs and it was the catastrophic type against which they needed protection.

After this was planned the question of the non-academic staff's health insurance was brought up and as in our retirement plan, we adopted the same plan but made it more flexible. Under it one could elect a smaller deductible amount if he wished, the cost being assessed in either case against his salary. I think it is a safe generalization that staff on low salaries took the lower deductible and the faculty and many of the staff elected the more purely catastrophic type.

Chapter 18

University Administration

The opportunity presented by the Donnelly referendum made the building program a good point of departure for the history of the administration. But measured by either effort or time other matters were more important.

Equal to or even superior in importance to my relations with the Board were those with the administrative staff and faculty. Except for Cowan, I kept the administrative staff I had inherited intact. But there were changes that were very important that were not necessarily title changes. Unquestionably my principal advisor on the internal affairs of the University was Tom Brady. We had become very close personally during our years in the history department as well as in later administrative assignments and I learned to have great respect and confidence in Tom's judgment. The staff recognized this and frequently went to Tom for things they did not want to bother me with. He had a wider acquaintance among certain parts of the University staff than I had, and frequently had important information that I would not have known had he not told me. He stayed in the same position he had held since I had gone to the arts dean's office. This was the head of the Division of Extra-Divisional Activities and these he administered very well, appointing excellent people to the departments under his administration. One of the things about Tom that I was most grateful for was that you could always lay your cards on the table with him and get a straight answer, unbiased and unselfish. He taught a course in the history department which was useful to both of us, as it was one source of information on teaching and faculty affairs that I would not have had otherwise. He also had excellent relations with the non-academic staff. I have already related one of the problems that came up because of his marriage to Mary Leslie, whom he had met while on a vacation in Colorado.

When I talked to the Board about a retirement age limit for top administrators as a desirable regulation that would also serve as a means of getting Cowan out of my hair, it meant there would be no Vice President for Business Operations although this title could have been given to Ray Bezoni. At this time I chose not to do it. My main reason was that it seemed good administration to me to separate the business and financial functions and have them each report to me instead of one to the other. The Board naturally raised the question about this and pointed out that it would leave me with one Vice President, which would look like he was my second in command. That, in addition to the other antagonism to Tom from some members of the Board, made from their standpoint a problem. After speaking with those whom I could talk to confidentially, I talked to Tom about this and told him the problem. I told him, "I may have to change your appointment from Vice President to Dean," and Tom without batting an eye made no objection but said, "Go ahead and do whatever you need to do to take care of your Cowan problem." Later the office of vice president was abolished and Tom's administrative functions were classified as a dean's which was somewhat more logical than the title of vice president because all of the academic deans reported directly to me as had been intended from the beginning of that office.

Tom's worst handicap was the development of his serious illness, which was finally diagnosed as Hodgkin's Disease. At first it could be cleared up very quickly in appearance with x-ray treatments, but the number of those a human can tolerate is limited. There was at Massachusetts Institute of Technology at the time an x-ray development which did not penetrate deeply into the flesh and, on advice of his doctor, Tom went there for treatment on two or three different occasions. This too lost its effectiveness, and Tom suffered greatly in his latter years.

After Tom's death in 1964, some of his friends and I talked several times about things we might do to memorialize Tom. Jack Matthews had the best suggestion which was to name the University Commons, a student building, for him. Jack, as Dean of Students knew Tom's involvement in all the matters concerned with student affairs. Jack Matthews had been Tom's selection to head the student work and, in this as in many other matters, his judgment was sound and his treatment after appointment of a subordinate was such as to encourage him to do his best work, which indeed Jack did. Another of Tom's selections was John McGowan whom he picked to develop a program for handicapped students, which the federal government was largely financing and which, through Tom's and McGowan's work, designated the University of Missouri as the federal training center for seven states from Missouri and Kansas north to Canada. Tom did a small amount of work in Jefferson City for the University before I became president, particularly with Governor Forrest Smith, a very close family friend. It was largely Tom who convinced Governor Smith to support the building of a new auditorium to replace the old, near-worthless one on the east end of Jesse Hall that had always been called Jesse Auditorium.

By the time I accepted the presidency I had already decided on what to do with my former position in the College of Arts and Science. Francis English had done an outstanding job as assistant and acting dean, in spite of the fact he did not have a long history as a faculty member but came up through the public school administrative route. He did a very acceptable job and seemed to satisfy all of the important elements in the college. In filling his place we had no question about whom we wanted, which was Ed Palmquist from the botany department. Again here we were weakening our teaching force by pulling into the administration a superb teacher. But it was my growing conviction that if you wanted a good administrator the highest recommendation you could start with was that this person was an outstanding teacher.

My other deans presented various kinds of strengths and problems. Huber Croft in engineering, while near retirement as dean, was an excellent administrator and popular with his faculty. Earl English was similarly placed in journalism. As he was younger than I, he would normally carry on through my administration. One of the real big developments on the campus occurred in journalism during this period when we celebrated its 50th anniversary as the first School of Journalism. English managed this with great success and used it as a means of attracting the attention of leading newspapermen the country over. Many of them were on the campus for various of his programs. One development in which I enjoyed participating was a luncheon meeting of the alumni of the School of Journalism in New York City. At the request of the members I had asked President Harry S. Truman to be our speaker. He accepted, and it was made a special feature of the Advertising Club's New York meeting. I introduced him at the meeting, and I recall the chairman of the Advertising Club of New York City remarked to me at the luncheon that he was sure that no other journalism school could bring out the journalists that had come out to our meeting. No doubt our speaker deserved a large share of this credit. For President Truman that event tied in with a money-raising dinner that was raising funds for the Truman Library. It was a dinner which I was happy to attend and take part in, meeting a great many of Truman's associates during his presidency.

The main development out of the 50th anniversary celebration was the founding of the Freedom of Information Center at the School of Journalism to be headed by Paul Fisher, who was exceedingly well-suited for the job and who was of great assistance to Earl English in getting it on its feet. Like most of the professional schools and colleges there always were divisions within the profession and the most acute one we had was that between the broadcast journalism people and the press. I was waited on once by representatives of broadcast journalism who complained bitterly that the School of Journalism did not train for their kind of journalism—

only for the press. I had alerted Dean English that these people were coming and asked him to be available. After a brief discussion I called English and had him come to my office to meet with them. Then I took up these criticisms one by one and Dean English was able to show that they had little merit, were based on misinformation, and that the school was sacrificing a good deal in order to supply them with competent people.

How really superior our school was in its faculty and programs was impressed upon me a few years later when I went with an accrediting committe of schools of journalism to visit another Big 8 school of journalism. I was selected by the North Central Association as a university representative to go with the professional group and protect the main university involved against excessive special demands that would injure other divisions if they were carried out.

The most experienced University administrator on our staff was Dean John H. Longwell of the College of Agriculture. He had come to us, a graduate returned, incidentally, from the presidency of North Dakota State University at Fargo. He had a broader experience than the rest of us and was a man of excellent judgment on university matters. Middlebush had frequently used Longwell as acting president when he was to be out of town. I continued the practice. A replacement for Longwell had to be chosen during my administration and the choice finally fell on Elmer Kiehl. I had discussed this with many of the senior faculty of the college and did not use a college committee, as I feared such a committee might be too inclined to divide into groups favoring certain specialties. Traditionally, deans of agriculture had been animal husbandry specialists as Longwell was. The appointment of Kiehl was in a new trend of using agriculture economists as deans and was, indeed, a very good source but was not the basis of my choice. I frankly had a hard time choosing between Kiehl and Raymond Schroeder, who was my closest friend in the College of Agriculture and for whom I had and still have great respect. Kiehl proved very competent, and the transition in the college was not difficult.

The Law School presented a quite different problem because Dean Glenn McCleary came to me and said he wanted to retire as dean. He had been put in as dean by Middlebush during a fairly messy situation that had been created by an inadequate dean whom Middlebush had chosen. I did not appoint a committee here as the law faculty was sufficiently small that I could talk to each member myself, which I did. They made suggestions and recommendations as did a number of lawyers in the state. In the end I selected Joe Covington, who was dean at Arkansas and who was an excellent dean, although he retired before the end of his term of office. His reasons were personal to him and he never told me the full story. I received no complaints about his work and had none of my own. He was an excellent leader.

The division of the University that I knew best after Arts and Science was Education as I had served on its faculty for some twelve years. Dean Loren Townsend was doing an acceptable job and, except for some vendettas with certain faculty members, had the division working together. But as his time of retirement approached the matter of a successor gave me some problems. I appointed a committee and put a great deal of dependence on Sterl Artley as chairman. He and I talked about several local people who were well-known to the faculty. I told him frankly I did not see any prospects that were better than Herbert Schooling, who was superintendent of schools at Webster Groves. He had been a graduate student of Rufi's in educational administration and I had become reasonably well-acquainted with him during that period. He had gone from here to the University of Chicago where he was on the staff for two years before he was appointed Superintendent of Webster Groves Public Schools, which no doubt was one of the best systems in Missouri. I had seen him from time to time and had been in his school. I think all the members of the committee knew him and, after considerable discussion and some interviewing, Sterl finally brought me the report that the committee agreed that Herbert Schooling was the best prospect it could find and I arranged for his appointment. I was not disappointed in what he did except for one thing. When I brought in a new dean I had a habit of taking him to the next Board meeting dinner and having him talk to the members of the Board. I did that with Schooling, and the speech he made was not very impressive to some members of the Board. I never knew why—perhaps the fact he came from the public schools and not some academic area may have influenced it.

I should mention in this connection when I accepted the presidency, certain members of the Board were very insistent that I get an assistant whom they visualized as someone who could charm money out of the state government. I had no illusions there, and I considered that as one of my major jobs that could not be delegated. I dragged my feet on the appointment and eventually brought in the name of Irvin Coyle from the State Department of Education. I had known Coyle as a graduate student and had visited Flat River Junior College where he was dean. My reasoning in appointing Coyle was largely based on the feeling that the university clientele that I knew best was the public education people, and I could see as I consulted lawyers, journalists, and businessmen that I was now probably neglecting the school people. I wanted someone around my office who would do this, because I considered it very significant that we maintain these connections in a comfortable and mutually respectful way if we were going to make the University play the part it should. I used Coyle somewhat on my speeches also, and he was not an undivided success here. He fit admirably into the background of the public schools and their problems. He was very good on a high school commencement speech for instance. But on the more important speeches that I had to make which concerned a wider public, I reached the point where I was rewriting so much of what he did that it became embarrassing to me and I am sure it was to him. So I changed the procedure here and started to draft those speeches myself and then let him criticize and make suggestions on the draft that I had, which was more satisfactory to both of us. While he was not able to provide all the help I had hoped, he was an exceedingly loyal and discreet person to have in the office, and I never regretted his appointment. In the meantime I think those Board members had retired or had forgotten their expectations that I would get a magician on public relations that would solve all those problems for the University, and most of the Board members never had such an idea. I had kept over from the Middlebush administration his secretary, Maurine Woolf, and her assistant, Edna Holt, who handled all my correspondence. They both were competent and fine people to work with.

The University of Missouri like other land grant universities had operated two extension divisions for a long time. The general extension which was heavily courses in professional education had been before the depression a very large and active organization. But the economics of the depression period had forced it back to where correspondence courses were the chief emphasis and the main program. Agricultural Extension of course had come in with the development of the land grant system as a means of making the results of research on farm problems, including home economics, available to its clientele. Because of its federal support and county agent system, it had weathered the depression without serious damage and seemed to be performing efficiently, but it presented a great problem as I took over my duties as president. Its director James Burch had been an energetic driving personality who had promoted, as its great purpose, a program of what was called Balanced Farming. The biggest part of it was the development of soil conservation. Indeed the College of Agriculture had promoted this well before it became a national program. But growing into the federal government's agriculture program was a separate soil conservation program that began developing after the 30s. Soil conservation was established in most states and counties by voting on whether or not they would accept that service with the added federal aid. This had been met with a great deal of undercover competition from our extension division. One of the principal means of soil conservation promoted by the extension division had been terracing, which overlapped directly with directives of the Soil Conservation Service. It became a matter of considerable controversy in the state, as we were one of the few states that was keeping the Soil Conservation Service from playing any substantial part in its agriculture. The key usually centered about the elections, whereby the county adopted the soil conservation aid or refused it. There was little doubt that in many areas of the state the extension division had secretly opposed the adoption of the service. There were important self interests involved, as many former county agents had left the service and organized terracing contracting services that were particularly strong in the northwest corner of the state but existed everywhere. These former agents had a great deal of influence with the service itself and with the legislature. There was no doubt that this was all in the long run detrimental to Missouri agriculture. Money spent on soil conservation by the extension service was not available for other phases of their work, and soil conservation money was not coming to Missouri farmers in many counties. Before I assumed the presidency, the Board of Curators had gone on record as opposing any participation by county agents in these elections. But it was a different matter to carry it out in the extension service which was difficult, even impossible, to regulate in any detail unless you had a director who was committed to it. I had already learned before I became president it was rather dangerous to let our director appear before an appropriations committee because of antagonism to him in some areas.

The terracing contractors attempted to secure action by the legislature to solidify their control over the terracing work. While the agriculture extension division did not appear in this, it was clear that it was in complete sympathy and unofficially supported the effort. I opposed this with many members of the legislature, and had at one time arranged that the bill would not come to the floor. Late in the session, however, the committee held a hearing on the question, and I appeared against it. I think it is safe to say that the soil contractors had at least some sympathetic support from the Farm Bureau and the soil conservation people had support from the Missouri Farmers Association. There were also others who were convinced either that the extension division would do a better job or it would be better to put it all in one agency—both of which might have been true. As far as I was concerned, I had no choice, and it seemed to me foolish state policy to spend our federal and state funds on programs that the federal government was willing to support outside of our budget. As it was late in the session that hearing was held close to midnight and was quite a bitter affair. I was guilty of the statement that if it were not for the terracing contractors there would be no problem and no opposition.

Shortly before this happened Director Burch had retired on the basis of age, and I had with help from Dean Longwell searched for a successor who would bring in some fresh ideas. Because of its political significance I felt I had to keep the actual selection in my own hands. We brought in two people for interviews after a great deal of preliminary work. One was an associate director from Minnesota and the other was Brice Ratchford from North Carolina State. I tried to touch all bases with these interviews, even sending each person to Jefferson City to be interviewed by the Commissioner of Agriculture. In spite of this there was a large sentiment, most heavily among the terracing contractors and their friends, for some local man who would be loyal to their present programs. I had talked at length with Burch, and he recommended one of his men who did not meet in any way the standards I had set. It seemed to me that we should bring in an outsider who would not be controlled by any local faction. After the interviews it was clear that, of the two men, Ratchford was by far the better prospect. I had some doubt that Ratchford would accept the offer as he had turned down a similar position in Wisconsin even though James Hilton, president of Iowa State and a friend of Ratchford, had assured me Ratchford would take our job. However, President William Friday of the University of North Carolina had assured me that if Ratchford came to us he would find a way to bring him back to North Carolina. At any rate I recommended him to the Board and he was appointed.

It proved to be a very popular appointment. We felt that we had made a real advance, and in the second year of his administration, with Tom Brady's concurrence, I talked with him about heading both extension divisions as a unit. This presented problems mainly in the sense that the general extension service was being directed by a competent man, Amos Snider, and neither of us wanted to alienate him in any way. Snider could not qualify for the agriculture extension, while Ratchford with his Ph.D. in economics was quite suitable and was a man with the kind of energy and intelligence who would make the amalgamation work. We talked to Amos Snider, got his reluctant approval, and the two divisions were united under Ratchford's leadership. It was very interesting to me that four other states followed our example within a year, but it became evident to me that the problem would be different in states such as Iowa, where the state university and the land-grant university were different institutions. Each institution had its extension division which each would want to keep. However, the movement seemed to succeed wherever it was introduced by the land-grant university.

Of all the deans I inherited, I worried most about Henry Bent of the Graduate School. To his credit I must say that shortly after I was confirmed as president he came to the office and offered to resign. I asked him why he was suggesting that and his answer was that he thought I ought to have the opportunity to name my own associates. Although it would have been very distasteful for me to do, it would have been in the long-range interest of the University if I had taken advantage of his offer. Instead I told him if I wanted his resignation I would tell him.

Research was one of my worst problems and I found it was getting no encouragement or stimulation whatever from the graduate office. I had meetings with Dean Bent about this several times. I used as the basis for discussion the fact that we were getting very little of the federal research grants that I was learning about from my meetings with other presidents and organizations of presidents. We were getting the grants where we had a professor who needed no encouragement from the dean's office, and usually had his own connections with the granting agency and did his own "lobbying." After we had built some of our new buildings, Dean Bent came to see me and remarked that he knew now why we were not doing very well in securing federal grants, and I asked him what he had found out. He said we had put our own money in the business school and in home economics and grants were not being made in those areas. I was astounded at this statement, and I pointed out to him that it was not true as far as we were concerned, and it was not true as far as the grants were concerned. But I made little impression.

In 1961 I talked with E. B. Fred of Wisconsin who had retired as president the year before and was very knowledgeable in administrative problems in state universities. We had developed good personal relations and I asked him if he would be willing to spend some time on our campus and analyze how we could improve our program. He made a half commitment and in the end visited here twice. He came at times when there were a number of faculty committees holding meetings which he attended, and he also met with individual deans and in many cases professors. When leaving after his second visit he had very little time to talk with me, as he was rushing to catch his plane. He briefly said, without elaborating on the other problems we had discussed, "I have come to the conclusion that your main problem is Bent." We had talked about the research problem before and it did not need any further discussion. One factor that kept me from replacing Bent as dean at that time was that it would put him back in charge of the beginning chemistry course where he already had too much influence for the good of the University. Consequently, I called him in and told him that I was making Raymond Peck in geology his associate dean. Peck would specialize on research grants, and he would have nothing to do with the present routine of the office. That seemed agreeable to Bent. His conscience seemed to be bothering him after our talks about his failure in this aspect of his office.

After the first year I separated Peck entirely from the Graduate School and made it clear that his obligation was research stimulation, in which he had started very well and in which he continued to improve. Eventually I found him so useful that I made him a multi-campus officer with the title of Vice President for Research, where his work was very productive.

Some of the smaller and more specialized professional schools showed great growth during this period and frequently made substantial improvements in their work. Veterinary Medicine is an example, as after post World War II, Iowa State University ceased admitting Missouri students in that field. A movement developed in the legislature stemming from the livestock industry, which changed our poorly supported department into a school that would graduate doctors of veterinary medicine. When I became president A. H. Groth was dean of the School of Veterinary Medicine and he was a good one. I had less internal knowledge of that division than any other, but I never had reason to feel I had to pay more attention to it, because Groth was competent and thorough. My main problem was in getting buildings and equipment for him and in that I followed Groth's recommendations entirely.

The Department of Home Economics was a division of the College of Agriculture. Its work was expanding greatly and we secured an addition to the building out of the bond issue money. The very competent chairman, Margaret Mangel, was anxious that it be classified as a school and made independent of the College of Agriculture. I was reluctant to move that way simply because when I inquired into it with Dr. Mangel, the only real reason she could give for the change was that it could be departmentalized with a chairman in each field. On searching further, it was clear that there would be less teaching by these individuals and other instructors would have to be employed. I kept calling attention to the fact that schools of journalism and education did not have departments and seemed to work very well. She was following examples of other schools of home economics that were independent of the college. We made it a school, but during my administration, did not make it an independent division. In some work of a consulting nature with Texas Tech after retirement, I worked with several authorities, particularly at the University of Nebraska, and became convinced that it was desirable to make it an independent division. I so informed Chancellor John Schwada when I returned to Columbia.

Another division of the College of Agriculture was the School of Forestry. As forests began to revive in the state following the original cut-over period and the development of national and state parks, the profession of forester became one that offered many opportunities for employment. Missouri had a tremendous acreage given over to tree growth of one kind or another—some of it commercially profitable and some not. At any rate there was obvious need in the state for foresters. While some teaching of forestry had long been a practice of the Department of Horticulture, no professional program had been developed until R. H. Westveld became chairman of the division, after which it soon became a school with Westveld as director.

In 1954 the School of Forestry was housed in an abandoned army building that was quite unsuitable for its needs. Its richest resource was probably the University forest near Poplar Bluff which was made up in a large part from our land-grant lands in the area from the federal legislation of 1862. While the lands could not be marketed profitably, it was a very valuable possession of the University for the forestry school. During the changes that went on we had decided to dispose of all of this remaining land grant, which was Ozark land so scattered that little of it was useful for either commercial or university purposes. In many cases it was freely used by residents in that area. The first time this came to my attention was when the Highway Department offered to buy a piece of it for a road it wanted to build. When Dr. Westveld began to work on this problem, I realized that even our University forest in Butler County was quite inefficient, because it was not solidly unified forest but was interspersed with federally-owned forest lands. There were discussions with the federal forest people, and an agreement was worked out where we would exchange land in Butler County so that the University forest would become a unified whole—much more useful in training our forestry students. It took state and federal legislation to get this accomplished, but it was completed to the satisfaction of the University. We then were able to build up our camp living and teaching facilities to make them better serve their purpose. The main problem was housing on the Columbia campus. We were able to build a College of Agriculture Administration Building from the state bond issue where we decided to put the forestry people in good academic housing, and as there was sufficient room we moved the horticulture people in also. Whitten Hall, which had been assigned to horticulture, was then left open, and as our extension service was scattered over the campus we united it in Whitten to the benefit of efficiency all around.

Westveld was an excellent administrator, and the summer camp that the division developed at the University forest provided an excellent educational program. To anyone who was interested in Missouri industry, this was a matter of pride and satisfaction.

One agricultural crop that the School of Forestry sponsored was the growing of Christmas trees commercially. This was a different type of evergreen than formerly had been used, which proved to be satisfactory and developed a money crop that many hill farmers could grow profitably on a two-year basis. This was only the best known of several programs in commercial and recreational forestry that grew out of its work. It developed a full program of extension and research, as well as teaching, that was a great credit to the University. Closer to the main campus, it made considerable use of the Ashland Wildlife Refuge, another University facility.

One of the most difficult appointments I had was the replacement of Huber Croft when he reached retirement age. While he stayed on in his professorship until age 70, he retired at 65 as Dean of the College of Engineering. He had been a very successful dean.

In Croft's case I appointed a committee consisting largely of chairmen of departments. We went through an elaborate scheme of getting names of prospective deans and files of information about them and had interviews in a few cases. The committee finally recommended a man at Michigan whom we had interviewed and who had many good qualifications, but I thought he had a very colorless personality. After doing some other consulting of my own at Michigan and with Croft, I offered him the deanship, which after considerable delay he refused. The committee had reached agreement on him only after long and difficult discussions that involved many disagreements. I probably was more disgusted with the use of the committee than I should have been, and I called the committee together on a Saturday morning soon after that. We discussed a few people, including some local people, and I expressed my opinion that we were proceeding in a very poor fashion. I said flatly that I thought one of our young men would fill that job better than any of the people we had interviewed. There was some discussion back and forth and finally I entered the name of Joe Hogan, a young professor of electrical engineering. Joe was a graduate of our own but had taken his doctorate at the University of Wisconsin. The chairman on the committee rather indignantly said, "You really want us to vote for him, don't you?" I said, "Yes, I do." The committee did so.

That department chairman was of course quite disappointed that he was not chosen to be dean, and while he was older and not in good health, he would in many ways have made an acceptable dean. He had talked to me about it on his own initiative and played up his long service to the University. I finally said to him, "You probably don't realize it but you never moved to Missouri. You still live back in New England where you spend three or four months out of every year. I don't blame you if that is your choice, but it is not quite the university-minded dean I want over an important division."

I recommended Joe Hogan to the Board, and he was accepted without question. I think the most surprised person on the campus was Joe. I had called him over before I wrote the Board on this, as I wanted to be sure there was nothing to keep him from accepting the position. Most faculty members who are called in when you are looking for a dean are conscious of the fact but Joe certainly was not. Joe Hogan proved to be a popular appointment in the college. He had very good judgment dealing with faculty members and the recruitment of them. He talked to Croft frequently, which was wise to do as Croft had been a very successful dean. Joe had an abundance of energy and a great deal of wisdom about engineering as a whole. The only way he disappointed me was that after a period of time he accepted an offer of a deanship at the University of Notre Dame. I tried to reason with him that he was better off where he was, but Joe admitted he had had a sentimental attachment to Notre Dame since he was a kid and he just could not say no to the offer. I was sorry to see him go.

It was natural I suppose that one of the most difficult administrative problems I had was with the School of Medicine, natural because of its recent expansion to a four-year school. Middlebush had selected Dr. Roscoe Pullen as the first dean for the new school, who was an attractive young administrator from the University of Texas Graduate School of Medicine. Dr. Pullen was recommended to him by the Education Committee of the American Medical Association which was headed by Ward Darley, a former president of the University of Colorado whom I knew and respected. Pullen took over energetically and did a very good job of recruiting the original faculty for the school, but the problem of administering the school seemed to be more than he could carry. Some of these matters were coming back to me indirectly, some more directly. One day the Highway Patrol reported that Dr. Pullen had been arrested near Warrenton for driving while intoxicated and had spent the night in the Warrenton jail sobering up. I called Pullen and told him I wanted to talk to him. He came over immediately as if he had been expecting a call. I repeated to him what I had heard, and he said it was all true. Then amazingly he produced receipts for four martinis he had drunk in a restaurant in Wentzville. I talked to him very seriously about what had happened and told him the possible consequences of it. Fortunately the metropolitan press protected the University by not reporting the news and it was only published in the Warrenton newspaper. His alibi was that his job gave him so much to do he could not stand the strain without some release. I had heard alibis like this before from him, so I picked it up immediately and asked why he had to be in St. Louis at that time. The explanation was pretty lame, as it was with many other problems he had. As I look back at it from a longer perspective, he was a great hand, when he had executive decisions to make that required hard thinking, to go into the hospital and busy himself doing routine work that belonged to other people. So he was up to his ears in busy work while the important decisions went unmade.

The medical school was so complicated and diverse that it took a man of more than average judgment to know what had to be done first. I left the whole question up in the air with a promise volunteered by Pullen that he would lay off the liquor. A short time later when I was present at a medical professor's home to meet some visiting dignitary, Roscoe was there and when the drinks were served he very pointedly came around and told me he was drinking ginger ale. A short time later Dale Bowling reported that when passing a liquor store early that morning he had seen Pullen leaving the store, quite obviously on his way to his office to begin the day. I admit that I was completely non-plussed as to what to do. He had a semi-invalid wife who seemed to have little influence concerning his problem, and he obviously was of little help to her.

In the meantime I was going over Pullen's work and finding instances that I had not known and which were not in the interests of the school in any sense. I reported to the Board at the next meeting what I knew and what the situation was as far as I could tell. The president of the Board, James Finch, had passed on some information which he had secured. The Board was of one mind that we had to replace Pullen as soon as possible. This led to a situation that was the most disagreeable to me of all in my term as president. I asked him to come to my office sometime during the afternoon, and I had to tell him he was through. He seemed amazed and felt mistreated. I told him that he could give me a resignation by morning or I would have to announce his dismissal. I had no one to replace him of course, but I took four faculty members of the School of Medicine who knew the school well and put the deanship in trust with them temporarily. I looked for a dean and appointed another committee of the faculty who consulted with me. A number of names came up from our faculty. Eventually, to find my way in this scattered situation, I restored to the same system Middlebush had used for Pullen. That is, I went up to Chicago and met with Ward Darley, Chairman of the Committee on Education of the American Medical Association, and his right hand man. Darley was the man who had recommended Pullen, and he took complete responsibility for that fiasco.

We went over the list that I had and a list from the Association. We finally came up with recommendations for two persons. One was an

Assistant Dean at Northwestern and the other was the Associate Dean at Kansas University. I went home, met with my committee and we invited both of these men to come to the campus. They both were extremely attractive personalities and either one of them looked like he would make a responsible administrator. I became aware of the fact during the interview, however, that since the Northwestern dean was very ignorant about state universities he would have real problems. The other man impressed me immediately as a person who would fit our position. While I had written evaluations of both of them, it did not take long to make up my mind as to which I preferred. Before I met with the committee I was relieved of the necessity of making the choice by a letter from the Northwestern man saying that he had decided he did not want to leave Chicago. The committee voted unanimously in favor of my recommendation of Vernon Wilson.

I really had a great load taken off my shoulders when Wilson arrived. He was an ideal administrator for the School of Medicine. One of my evidences was that no problems of any merit came to my desk from there. He frequently came to the office with things he intended to do, all of which were desirable and all of which I approved. There is no question that the school made great progress under Wilson and its reputation began to reflect it.

The School of Business and Public Administration was an unusual school in that it and Washington University alone had that particular orientation—business and public administration. With the exception of Roy Curtis I think that all of its deans had been political scientists and William L. Bradshaw was no exception. Bradshaw's death created a problem, as I was told that it was difficult to get staff in the field of business management under a political scientist dean. I never believed this, but I did have in mind a business management replacement as a change that might be worth trying. We worked hard with the faculty here and finally came up with a man from Texas who had an excellent reputation; the only thing about his papers I did not like was he had done so many things outside the university. William Baughn came, his leadership of the school was encouraging, and I congratulated myself that we had solved a problem as the old alibis did not come back to me. Unfortunately he suffered very greatly from hay fever in Missouri, and at the end of the second year he told me he had been offered a position at Colorado where he had previously lived. There he had been free from hay fever, which made him decide he must accept the offer. I very much regretted his leaving, and again I found this problem was now back on my desk. I was able to fill in the intervening period by bringing John Schwada home from Jefferson City where he had been on loan to the governor as budget director.

Schwada returned as acting dean of the School of Business and Public Administration for one year. We were agreed he would then become Chancellor, a sort of assistant to the President as we saw it then.

With Schwada on the job the two of us were deeply concerned with a replacement in the business school, and Schwada was in a good position to know what we needed. Pinkney Walker was a man on the faculty who was exceedingly well thought of everywhere but whose attitude toward administration left something to be desired. Schwada and I talked several times over the possibility of making him the dean, and finally we called him in and told him our problem. With little hesitation, Walker said if we were offering him the job he would take it, and I was happy to say I would recommend him to the Board. He was an excellent dean and the school prospered under his guidance. Any antagonism that he had toward administration seemed to disappear when he actually had the problems himself. At a later period he unfortunately had to resign, due to the illness of his wife.

The School of Social Work has been a distinct contribution to the state over its history. Courses in social work were taught in the Department of Sociology quite early and our first school was established in St. Louis early in the century. This was later taken over by Washington University and given a basis that we could not duplicate, since we were limited to working out of Columbia. When I returned from the Army in 1945, Arthur Nebel was the senior member and chairman of the Department of Social Work. It was a division of the College of Arts and Science and remained that until it became a school. Our off campus beginning was continued in a different way in Kansas City with a federal grant to attempt to develop a professional school off campus. This was carried through to the completion of a group of students for the length of the grant and proved quite successful in raising the level of social work in the western part of the state. Nebel had very close relations with the state social work agencies, and in one sense our first work was primarily the upgrading of their personnel to competent social workers. In some years this exceeded the work of training new people who wanted to get into that profession. It made little problem for me in the dean's office or in the president's office later, as Nebel was an administrator who got things done and done well. The growth and development of the school was indeed a tribute to his sound work. Nebel combined the deanship with the chairmanship of the University Committee on Athletics and the work in both places was exceptionally fine.

While courses in library science had been taught from time to time in the University and we had a small department in the College of Arts and Science, I had resisted along with many others the introduction of a full graduate level library science program, feeling that it was one thing we could leave to the University of Oklahoma which had a fully accredited school. I tried to get Oklahoma to agree to a mutual exchange of cancellation of our out-of-state fees with some of our programs, but I could not interest President George Cross. I met a great deal of pressure from some quarters to establish the school. I had talked to the Missouri State Library people about the problem several times and to its secretary, Paxton Price, who transferred to the Health, Education and Welfare Department in Washington after considerable experience in Missouri. On one of my trips to Washington attending educational meetings, I had dinner with him and talked about the problems at length. The thing that moved me, however, was the fact that he said unequivocally that the federal grants for library assistance which were coming into the picture in an important way were going to be limited to those public libraries which were staffed largely with people who were graduated from accredited library schools and that graduates from the Kansas state colleges would not qualify. It was clear to me we had to do something to remedy that situation. I talked the matter over with Ralph Parker, our librarian, and Virginia Young who was on the state board. As a result I asked the Board to approve the introduction of a graduate program that could be accredited for this purpose, and I set up a committee consisting of our current teaching staff which included Francis Flood, who devoted some time to the library, Ralph Parker, and Homer Thomas, chairman of the Library Committee. Their primary purpose was to get someone to head the program that would not only build a sound program but one that could be accredited. I could see nothing wrong with Flood's work but he was not well enough trained for the kind of program we had in mind. We had some difficulty locating eligible people who were available, as many other universities were busy in this same direction. Then the suggestion came to me, originating with some of the other library science people who had talked to the committee, that we should make Ralph Parker head of our school. He had an ideal background with a Ph.D. in history in addition to his library expertise. Eventually that was what we did, which brought the problem of finding a new librarian. That proved to be difficult and resulted in several mistakes in the library. The School of Library Science was soon functioning and taking care of Missouri's need for trained librarians to the expressed satisfaction of the State Library Board as well as many other sources of information. The Library itself profited very much by the leadership of Homer Thomas, Professor of Art History and Archaeology, who served as chairman of the Library Committee during these years.

Chapter 19

Enriching a State System of Higher Education

From my first experiences in Missouri I was pushed into the problems of state-wide higher education. The biggest factor here was the work with the University's Committee on Accredited Schools and Colleges which dealt with the private high schools and all of the junior colleges. The high schools were inspected by the high school visitor, who reported to the Committee, and the junior colleges by annual reports and visits by members of the Committee. The private four-year institutions that started after 1900 had worked in the beginning with the Committee and had in their early stages been accredited as junior colleges. This accreditation had continued until the college had graduated at least one class with bachelor's degrees and was entitled to ask the North Central Association for accreditation as a senior college. These were chiefly Catholic and Baptist related schools since these were the new ones being established, the others having been established earlier. The University of Kansas City was the outstanding exception.

The public junior colleges group had started in Missouri about 1908 with institutions at Kansas City and St. Joseph. These junior colleges were parts of the local school systems and financed by local taxes. Consequently, some high school people thought of them as using tax money that rightfully belonged in the high schools and grade schools. The public junior colleges, handicapped as they were by the fact that their support was limited to the local school district, were overwhelmingly senior college preparatory schools in curriculum and, except for the one program of secretarial training, offered virtually no vocational programs. The costs of most vocational programs were too great for their budgets. There were in addition older junior colleges that were private schools, most of them schools for girls. Many, if not all of these, had started as private academies. Two junior colleges for men were military schools that still maintained their high schools as well. The arts colleges of the state had an organization, of which the arts college of the university was a member. It was probably the strongest organization of institutions of higher education. It included the universities and the private four-year colleges, but not the teachers colleges. The five state teachers colleges were also organized and acted together on common problems.

St. Louis was perhaps the worst example in the state of the lack of public colleges of all kinds. Kansas City was almost as unfortunate as far as vocational training was concerned. St. Louis did have two teacher training institutions supported by the local school district, Harris and Stowe, two because of the laws that forebade the education of the two races in integrated institutions. These institutions gave four years of work, but they gave no work that did not correspond to their teachers training program, which was the schools' vocational interest in maintaining them. Several other states had set up systems with state aid for junior colleges to help support them, particularly in their vocational work. St. Louis showed its lack of public higher education in the fact that, as I recall the statistics now, among the 34 largest industrial cities, St. Louis ranked 31st in the percentage of college graduates in its population.

Shortly after I became president of the University, the White House organized a Conference on Education Beyond the High School, and its main effect was to stimulate the states to organize similar conferences or commissions. President Paul Reinert, S. J., of St. Louis University represented Missouri in the National Conference. In his report to Governor James Blair he recommended that a state committee be appointed to study the problems and report back to the state government. Governor Blair decided to do so, and after discussing the problem with me asked that I share the chairmanship with President Reinert. There were some 36 members in this committee; about 10 were college and university presidents, both public and private, and the remaining members were laymen, a few of whom were professional educators. They were able people, among whom was James Finch, President of the Board of Curators. This Missouri Committee on Education Beyond the High School had several important results. Its recommendations included one that the state start a program of state aid to junior colleges, and another that a permanent state-wide commission on higher education be established, which would make recommendations to the state government. It also set up a special commission for St. Louis to study its particular problems, which employed an educator from the University of Pennsylvania to study the problem and make a report. The man chosen was Professor Edward B. Shils, who made a report that I thought was biased against public higher education.

In 1960 I worked with a group of junior college people to have a bill introduced in the legislature to bring state aid for public junior colleges, and I did some lobbying in favor of it. I was asked by the AFL-CIO organization to meet with its executive committee to discuss the problem, with the result that the organization supported the bill effectively in the legislature and it was passed, changing the nature of our public junior colleges and increasing the number somewhat. The change in nature was primarily the stimulation of vocational work. St. Louis acquired a junior college system of three branches in different parts of the district and an expansion occurred in Kansas City to the same end. They were supplied with more vocational programs than the state had offered before. Some years later the Junior College Association presented a plaque to me, naming me a friend of Missouri Junior Colleges.

For the next session of the legislature the Committee on Education drafted legislation for a state commission on higher education that would, in the minds of almost everyone, be heavily concerned only with the public institutions. As we drafted this legislation we included on the commission the president of the University of Missouri, a president from the group of state colleges and Lincoln University, one from a public junior college, and one from a private college or university. All of these would be appointed by the governor, except for the University of Missouri president who served by virtue of his office. In addition the governor would appoint six non-educators who had superior voting powers on appropriation recommendations to the state groups it reported to.

Another recommendation that the Committee on Education made was one for a system of state scholarships. I exercised a great deal of care here because it was being supported mostly by the private schools, and I had it phrased so that it would be based on needs of the students as well as their ability; it would apply to both public and private colleges. Moreover, it was limited to a modest amount. In our discussion I agreed with the private school people that I would support permitting tuition to be counted as part of the test of need, so that the private schools would find real use of the scholarships. This is one recommendation that never was enacted and I am not sure exactly how it was changed, but all the bills introduced that supported it turned out to be restricted to students at private colleges. On the understanding that it was carrying out our recommendation I attended a hearing of the House Appropriations Committee, being asked to testify for it. When I arrived at the meeting I found that the bill drafted applied only to private and not to public institutions. I therefore objected to it and urged that it be defeated unless changed, which it was. Although it was reintroduced at later periods it never was accepted. I am still convinced that the original proposal that we made could have been passed had it not been restricted completely to private colleges. I regret that my relations with some of the private colleges were not improved by the controversy. But I can think of no reason why I should have taken another position. I realize now that I should have drafted a bill that met these specifications, but I was more interested in the problems of the junior colleges and the state Committee on Education and placed my effort on those.

Governor Blair's successor, Governor John Dalton, appointed an excellent group to work on the Commission. At our first meeting we elected Lang Rogers chairman. Rogers was publisher of the *Joplin Globe,* a former president of the State School Boards Association, and knowledgeable about education. For secretary we chose Earl Dawson, the President of Lincoln University, who had been selected by Governor Dalton from the five state colleges and Lincoln University from whom one president was to be selected. These were both excellent selections. We offered the directorship to Dr. Ben Morton who was director of a Kansas City regional committee on higher education at the time. We met regularly, usually in Jefferson City or Columbia, and the recommendations that the Commission made were at least listened to by the state government, if not followed. The presence of Dawson and myself together with the other college presidents seemed, however, to make the legislature and some of the public suspicious that we had too much influence in the Commission. I would dispute this, although there is not any doubt that the lay members did all agree our presence on the Commission made the necessity of much staff work unnecessary. Rogers continued to be chairman as long as the Commission lasted, although Governor Warren Hearnes replaced Dawson with President Mark Scully of Southeast Missouri State College at Cape Girardeau. I enjoyed working with the group very much, and I am sure it was a force for substantial good in the state as long as it existed. But some years after I retired the Commission was changed to a "coordinating board" that had no representation from the institutions and lacked that familiarity that they brought with the problems that existed. Our main problem, of course, was making recommendations regarding appropriations, in fact, passing on the appropriations requests that came from the institutions. I can say without any hesitation or regret that as a group we pushed for better appropriations than had been allocated, and perhaps that characteristic was what led to the feeling that the college presidents had too much influence in the Commission. After the Commission's life was over the lay members and I held a meeting of our original group in St. Louis with a dinner which I found very pleasant. It was a delightful group to work with and a group that had the interests of education very much at heart.

The main cultural resource of a university is of course its library. But in addition to the library are the art and scientific collections. Nearly all of our science departments, including the agriculture college, had reasonably well-equipped collections of specimens, most of which were enhanced by the collecting activities of members of the staff. We had an uneven history in the field of art and related archaeology. Some fine exhibit material had been acquired as long ago as the World's Fair of 1904 in St. Louis. The best of the permanent museum material was a fine collection of casts of ancient statuary. By the time I became dean of Arts and Science this collection had deteriorated badly, and was in a very poor type of storage as its one time museum was needed for more pressing instructional use. There was no museum of casts in the forties.

One of the more interesting features of the presidency at the University of Missouri involved the membership in the Board of Presidents of the Nelson Art Gallery in Kansas City. In his will, William Rockhill Nelson had left his fortune for an art museum, and he had specified that the presidents of the Universities of Missouri, Kansas, and Oklahoma should serve as a committee to select members of the Trustees who would more directly oversee the museum. This involved each of the three presidents in the basic management problems of the museum, especially with the expenditures of the income from the Nelson estate to buy objects of art for the museum. While it involved only one meeting a year, that was always a very pleasant and interesting affair. In addition contacts with the professional staff and the program of the museum went on through the year. President George Cross of Oklahoma served all the years I did on that committee, and Chancellor Franklin Murphy of Kansas was on when I came and stayed until he left for UCLA in 1960, when he was replaced by President Clarke Wescoe. It was a fine learning experience for me and helped me in my university administration.

An interesting collection of paintings had come to the University when the State Capitol was built. The original models of the murals in the Capitol had become property of the University as a sort of payment for the assistance John Pickard, Professor of Classical Art and Archaeology, had given the Capitol Decoration Commission. Pickard had served as chairman of the commission to oversee the artistic design of the Capitol. Unfortunately, these were not much valued by a succession of later members of the department. Apparently, after having been shown in the original section of the library, built about the same time as the Capitol, they were placed in storage in the library and for all intents and purposes lost. I remember my embarrassment as Dean of Arts and Sciences when Mitchell White of the *Mexico Ledger* told me that he had made a search at the University and could not locate these models. I set up an organized search under Librarian Ralph Parker, and they were found in a storeroom of the library, undamaged but completely out of sight and had been unused for a number of years. They were soon hung in the library where they would be seen.

In the middle forties the Associated American Artists induced the Scruggs-Vandervoort-Barney Department Store of St. Louis to commission a number of paintings of the state that would be on exhibit at the store and on loan in other cities from time to time. Similar arrangements were made for Pennsylvania with Wanamakers in Philadelphia, and for Michigan with Hudson's in Detroit. The announcement of the collection, consisting of, as I recall, around 50 to 60 paintings done by several artists with national reputations set off some excitement among Missouri artists. Thomas Hart Benton, more famous than any of the painters represented, denounced the project because of its "boycott" of Missouri artists in a collection of pictures to represent the state. Frank Mayfield, the president of Vandervoort's was, I am sure, completely taken by surprise at this reaction, realizing that the store's investment might not only be lost but be a detriment to the store's reputation. Consequently, he publicly invited Benton to confer with him in St. Louis and advise him, which Benton did. As a result several Missouri artists were employed to add other pictures to the collection. In the end almost 100 pictures were in the collection with several Missouri artists represented, including Fred Shane of our own faculty, one of whose paintings we had bought for our home. The large collection made a very favorable impression in St. Louis and in Kansas City, where the company had become the owner of the Emery Bird Thayer store. It was exhibited in most cities in Missouri, many in Illinois and twice at the University. After conferring several times with President Middlebush about the matter, we decided that, as eventually the store would have to give the collection to some public institution, we would try to make it clear that the University of Missouri was the proper site for it to be permanently placed. With considerable help from Fred Shane and still more from Mrs. Mary Gamble, one of our graduates who was in charge of advertising at Vandervoort's, we succeeded. Mrs. Gamble not only had a great desire to help out the University on this matter, but, as the collection and cost of its maintenance and management was on her budget for advertising, she realized its value for that purpose had greatly declined since the original interest had worn off. In 1952 Mr. Mayfield on behalf of Vandervoort's presented the collection to the University of Missouri. We, for want of a better place to show it, hung it on the first two floors of Jesse Hall, chiefly in the halls but also in the outer offices of several of the administrators who were housed there, especially the president's office. We took over the supply of the beautifully illustrated catalogs Vandervoort's had, and while they were limited we were able to make good use of them for people who came to see the collection.

It was about this time that under Tom Brady's counsel we added Saul

Weinberg to our classical art and archaeology staff. He was an archaeologist with a substantial reputation and a very great interest in all kinds of art. He had been at the American School in Athens the year Tom was there on a Fulbright Scholarship. Saul's wife, Gladys, was also a trained archaeologist and museum expert. Without any particular encouragement from the administration, the Weinbergs began to rebuild the old museum. First they restored the cast museum, doing a beautiful job of restoration of what many people were ready to junk. Actually the collection had grown considerably in value as the making of casts from the originals of famous statues had been stopped as a practice, as it was decided that it was not conducive to the permanent health of the original.

The Weinbergs, whose reputations were so good that they could secure grants from foundations, decided that they would take some interested students and do some excavating in Cypress. Saul had located a site there that looked productive and they spent one year on this project, bringing back to the University that part of their find that the government of Cypress was willing to share with us. After the eastern addition to the library was built in 1960, they were able to find a space on the fourth floor which they could develop into a small museum of the most valuable articles.

In the meantime, Saul had succeeded in getting some very useful gifts. He urged me to secure at least a small purchase fund with which we could go annually to selected dealers, and purchase some items that we needed that were in the less expensive category. This would cultivate the dealers in such a way that they would be willing to tip us off as to possible donors who had tax problems they were solving by making gifts of art that they owned. We were able to do this on a small scale, and the purchases themselves were directly useful. But more important, this developed a clientele of donors that Saul cultivated, and we were the recipient of some very interesting gifts every year.

Our largest gift was a part of the distribution which the Kress Foundation made from its collection of paintings that were in the custody of the National Gallery. The Foundation had found itself in possession of this very large collection, as the purchase orders had continued for a long time, and the National Gallery had more of this type than it could use. After making gifts to some regional museums, it adopted the policy of making "study collections" to universities that were showing promising development in the field of art. This came to our attention and we applied in the name of the University for a study collection, consulting before we did with Mrs. John Shapley, who was Curator of Painting in the National Gallery and served as the advisor to the Foundation on the make-up of these collections. In time I was invited to a meeting of the Foundation

Board in New York where the entire matter was discussed. Franklin Murphy, the Chancellor of Kansas University, was one of the trustees and was a source of support for us in our application. I had met with some of the trustees in Kansas City earlier at an opening of a Kress collection gift to the Nelson Gallery, and I already knew the key people of the Foundation. I recall that Mr. Guy Emerson, the chairman, expressed considerable interest in a painting of Fred Shane's that he saw on exhibit at the Gallery, particularly Fred's El Greco-like sky which was a hallmark of much of Fred's painting. The substance of the New York meeting was that I came away assured that we would receive a collection, and I had confidence that Mrs. Shapley would make a fine selection from what was available for that purpose. All this worked out even better than I had expected, and I was greatly pleased with it. It was the only real addition to our art collection after Saul Weinberg came to us in which he did not play the major part. The fact that he was actively building our museum and developing our teaching program was the major factor in our receiving the gift.

Mrs. Shapley was the only person who had received a Ph.D. in art history at the University of Missouri. Her husband, a brother of the famous astronomer, Harlow Shapley, was an art historian who taught at various times at Johns Hopkins and at Catholic University while she went into museum work. I called on her several times at the National Gallery and enjoyed immensely the association and informal education I received from her. I had first met her when we had conferred an honorary degree on her sometime before.

During the time after Saul came to the University, and under his prodding, I made continuous efforts on my own part to find a gift that would give us an adequate museum. Saul had convinced me that if we had a large, fine, safe display area, our number of gifts of valuable art and archaeology would increase enormously. I spent most of my time working on William Kemper, an alumnus, who not only had the adequate wealth but also was an art patron. I had the benefit of the advice of his nephew, Crosby Kemper, Jr., and also some active solicitation by Bus Entsminger. In the end I failed to secure anything from William Kemper. I did not limit myself to him but tried to interest two other wealthy persons in the state who also had interests in art and archaeology.

The first of these was Morton D. May. I had met May in several connections, and one time in particular on a trip to New York we happened to ride together on the plane. He was probably the leading merchant of the state and managed the Famous-Barr Company in St. Louis. He had made a contribution of his collection of German modern paintings to Washington University. I knew he had probably the best collection in the world of figures of the deities of Indians of northern South America. I made an appointment with him and made my case for a museum building, explaining that it was impossible for us to secure appropriated funds for such purposes, and gave Saul's argument about how our gifts could be tremendously increased if we had more proper display space. He was very generous with his time but was not convinced by my argument. He then saw little obligation to do anything for the State of Missouri outside of St. Louis and, like so many of our wealthy city people, saw no connection between a state-wide institution that included the city, even though a great deal of his business was done outside the city. But it was an honest belief, and I could not convince him otherwise. I was pleased that he later made some fine gifts to our museum.

The second person whom I approached was Joseph Pulitzer II of the *St. Louis Post-Dispatch*. His reception of my idea was far less favorable than that of May. Pulitzer then showed no interest even in St. Louis, let alone Missouri, and saw no purpose in donations to any institution but those with his Ivy League background. It was a very disappointing and unpleasant experience with a man whose money had been made by his parents, largely in Missouri, and which was the source of his present wealth and privileged position.

Surprisingly enough, however, what I could not get as a gift was developed internally by Saul himself. Before I retired I had secured appropriations for a large addition to the chemistry building on the White Campus, which was intended among other things to replace the organic chemistry building which was on the Red Campus and, contrary to most of its neighboring buildings, was very well-designed and built. Norman Rabjohn, our chief organic chemist, called Saul's attention to the fact that this building could be made into a good museum. Saul immediately saw its possibilities and, when the chemistry department moved out, he secured from Chancellor Schwada the assignment of the building for a museum. A fine rebuilding job was done that made it not only designed to hold the museum and the history of art department, but to make it virtually fireproof and theftproof. Thus the University acquired a fine museum. It was a great achievement on Saul's part and he was responsible for naming it for John Pickard, who had started the work many years before.

A separate and distinct museum collection that was developing at the same time was that in American archaeology, and here the major figure was Carl Chapman. He did not start the collection, as the University owned several stored and mostly unclassified museum items that had been given at various times. About the same time that I came to the University a new sociologist, Brewton Berry, began to introduce work in

American archaeology and to develop some interests in excavations. He found an enthusiastic cooperator in my colleague and old officemate Jesse Wrench who, while his archaeology experience and training had been Near Eastern and Ancient, was an energetic driver who was a promoter by nature. The approach here was somewhat different in that they organized a society of the many amateurs, some of whom were quite knowledgeable and, while mostly self-trained, several were well-trained. The Missouri Archaeological Society was founded by Berry and Wrench, and it became a strong organization somewhat like the State Historical Society, but more closely related to the University. I believe Wrench put me down as one of the founding members, although I did not attend the meetings after the first one. One of Berry's students was Carl Chapman, who immediately found his major interest in collecting and classifying research and teaching materials of the pre-European residents of Missouri and related areas. After he graduated here, he went to New Mexico University where the work in the area was well-advanced. While at New Mexico University he met and married another young archaeologist. As Carl's dean I was well enough acquainted with his research and scholarship that I had told him he need not become concerned about qualifying for a doctorate. The American archaeologist in the Smithsonian Institution, Waldo Wedel, had assured me that Carl knew American archaeology better than most Ph.D.s in the field who had worked many more years. However, I did advise him to get the degree as a professional protection. He did this at the University of Michigan, chiefly by a series of short period attendance and part-time work. We brought Carl back to Missouri to take over Berry's work when he went to Ohio State. Carl and his wife, Eleanor, worked hard in building the archaeological society and exploring the archaeological remains of the state. Federal funds were generally available for archaeological excavation work in areas that were to be flooded at various dam projects, which were becoming numerous in the state. Carl with his group of excavators, not all of whom were students, had their summers fully occupied in exploring these areas and exploiting them for their remains. In fact, some summers he had more than one "dig" going and in different parts of the state. Eventually with help, particularly that of Henry and Jean Hamilton of Marshall, he developed an outdoor laboratory and museum, which for administrative purposes was placed under the Missouri Park Service. The more valuable materials were brought to the basement of Switzler Hall, which was our museum and laboratory, and provided students and faculty with laboratory work of an exceedingly useful kind. After the geology department had moved out of Swallow Hall and into its new building, and the archaeological department had become a full-fledged Department of

Anthropology, it was moved to Swallow Hall where it had better quarters, especially for exhibit. In the meantime the Missouri Archaeological Society raised funds from its members and sponsored publications, including the *Missouri Archaeologist.* This was heavily Carl Chapman's work, and he served as secretary with the constant assistance of his wife Eleanor. Jesse Wrench served for several years as president of the society and after his death was succeeded by Henry Hamilton.

It had been obvious to me for a long time that one of the most effective ways of reducing costs in state educational programs was a practice of state exchanges. These were extremely difficult to arrange, as institutions in each state were naturally jealous of students who had to leave for educational programs which they did not offer and which they would like to offer had they the resources to do so. In many cases the fact that these programs were not offered meant that demand was limited and consequently had not built up enough pressure to gain attention.

One of my problems as President arose over architecture. I was approached fairly often by architects, the state organization of architects and cooperative legislators to establish a School of Architecture. Superficially, this would seem easy on a campus where you already had a college of engineering, landscape architecture and substantial work in most other aspects of art. But it was not. My own examination, including the cost of schools of architecture at other universities, convinced me that the main effect of establishing such a school would be to decrease the support of the programs we were already offering.

Architecture was offered at Washington University in a substantial school, but it was expensive and many Missourians could not afford the costs. My inquiries indicated that a great bulk of the Washington University students were not Missourians although many stayed in the state to practice. Our neighboring states—Nebraska, Kansas and Arkansas—had schools or at least departments. These were not popular with Missouri students as the out-of-state fees made them costly, although not as costly as Washington University. I tried to work this out on an interchange program and made some agreements, first with Nebraska and with Arkansas, in which we agreed that we would not charge students from those states out-of-state fees in certain fields that they did not offer if they would not charge Missouri students out-of-state fees in their programs of architecture. The best trading stock we had with those two states was our schools of veterinary medicine and forestry. This did not prove very successful. Nebraska seemed a long way off to many Missouri students, and Arkansas had to limit its total enrollment so severely that virtually no Missouri students could be admitted. We solved this problem, however, when the University of Kansas City became a part of the University of

Missouri, as its School of Dentistry made generous trading stock with Kansas, whose School of Architecture was easily available. Unfortunately, the plan did not work in the case of Iowa or Illinois since the adequacy with which these states supported public higher education was sufficient to cover all fields, and there was no need for additional programs. And we had nothing to trade.

As I look back, it was unfortunate we could not make more progress here than we did. I feel in certain fields of limited demand that far better arrangements could have been worked out had we started earlier than we did, and we would have improved institutions in several states by not duplicating facilities in the neighboring state.

Among the regional organizations that I was active in for a time was the North Central Association of Schools and Colleges. I served in its research section and later became a member of its executive committee. Few of the state university presidents were active in it, usually permitting their people concerned with secondary education to be the sole representative in its work. When I was reaching the end of my term on the executive committee and questions had been raised about undertaking service as association president, I objected saying that the executive committee was all the time I could give to the organization. I was put on the program my last year and made an address to the group in which among the questions that I discussed was the matter of state cooperation in specialized professional education, calling attention to the fact that the New England states had a mutual agreement whereby students from one of the states that did not offer a certain professional program were entitled to be admitted, without an out-of-state fee, to a program in those states that did offer it. I urged consideration of this by the North Central Association. But the problem was really too big in the North Central Association, as too many of our states were like Iowa and Illinois and had no lack of professional schools where they were able to take care of their own students.

Chapter 20

National Organizations

While they did not take up as much time as the state organizations, the national organizations that became available provided me with a very useful education. I had already worked with the National Council for the Social Studies, the Mississippi Valley Historical Association, and the American Historical Association so I was familiar with such groups, in specialized fields at least.

As a sort of ending to my army history work, I was asked to become a member of the advisory committee on army history which was made up of civilian historians and advised on the army programs. The appointment made me chairman of the committee. I was the only member who had served in the army history program.

Robert Greenfield was the director of the Army program and was nearing retirement at the time I became chairman of the advisory committee. I do not now recall all of the members of the committee, although S.F. Bemis of Yale was one of them. We later purchased his personal library as a basis for the Truman Library collection. These commitments consisted of a meeting once a year in Washington, a review of the year's work with comments from the committee and from time to time recommendations by the committee.

It seemed to me from the beginning that the size of the planned history was so great that it would break down from its own weight. But from my early experience I realized that it had already been greatly cut and there were many disgruntled historians who had found their work was not to be published. The only thing that I recall of any importance that I did for the Army History Program in these years when I served was in connection with selecting Greenfield's successor. The staff was firmly convinced that a particular political general was using his connections to be appointed to this position. He was known to the staff, and I agreed that it would be a most unfortunate selection. I made an appointment with the Secretary of the Army whom I had never met and conferred with him about it, telling him what the situation was and urged him by all means to select a trained historian for that position. I made no recommendations of anyone. He followed this policy and named an historian, although I do not know that I influenced him significantly.

I had attended a few meetings of the National Association of State Universities and Land Grant Colleges before I became University president; once I believe as a substitute for Middlebush. I became well acquainted with its secretary, Russell Thackrey. Afterward I found it the most useful school that I attended while president. All state universities, and those which were land grant colleges in particular, were tied in with important federal legislation in such a way that it was necessary to keep one's self familiar in that area. There was no better source of information than Russell Thackrey and his staff.

I served on the executive committee for some time, was asked if I would accept the presidency on one occasion, and I had to answer no, as I was already scheduled to go to India to survey our program there. Shortly before I retired, I was approached again, did accept and served a regular term in which I made appearances before the committees of Congress on behalf of our organization as well as others, as I usually represented more than one group. The staff of the university organizations in Washington worked together very closely and briefed one very thoroughly before an appearance before a committee. The staff also drafted a presidential address for me, which was the only speech I ever had completely drafted for me. I was so unhappy about it that I rewrote the main message almost completely and sent it back. When it was returned to me, there were no suggestions for changes in my draft.

I was asked to serve on two federal boards. One was the Board of Foreign Scholarships, from 1958–1961, which was no doubt a follow-up of my Fulbright to Amsterdam, and again it was educational and interesting. One sidelight was twice we made trips to the White House, once to confer with President Eisenhower and once with President John Kennedy.

A very interesting assignment was in the Department of Agriculture's Advisory Committee on Civil Rights on which I served from 1965–1968. I was appointed to this by Secretary Orville Freeman. The Committee usually met in Washington but there were other meetings: one at Jackson, Mississippi, and one at Houston, Texas, that were more in the nature of public hearings. The meeting at Houston primarily concerned Hispanics rather than Blacks.

The American Association of Universities was in some ways a more interesting national meeting since it was limited to the presidents of about 25 large universities and the number increased slightly during the period. Substitutes for the university presidents were not permitted; consequently, I got acquainted with a group of private school presidents that I did not see at my other meetings.

The greatest satisfaction that came to me from this group was that I was designated as one of ten American observers to represent the American universities at the meetings of the British Commonwealth Universities, which met every five years in Great Britain. My selection was made by President James L. Morrill of the University of Minnesota, then President of the American Association of Universities. Ruth and I attended by combining this meeting with our summer vacation. We went to the meetings as guests of the University of London, Ruth going with me as did most wives of the American representatives. We were entertained at a reception where the Queen Mother, Chancellor of the University of London under the British system, was our hostess. She was an interesting personality, and when we returned five years later we were received by almost the same group. The Queen Mother was then in a wheelchair with a sprained ankle but amazingly enough she not only recognized us but resumed the conversation we engaged in five years before. I often wondered whether there was some system of recording these things or if she had that kind of memory.

We had a dinner meeting at the first reception and afterward went to a popular musical. The second time we had the Prime Minister, Anthony Eden, as speaker, and I found that he had a sense of humor that I had never realized from the news reports. Our official sessions of the first meetings of the Association were at the University of Birmingham. We went by way of Exeter, as the University there was being accepted as a full university, after having served for a time as a sort of extension center of London University. The ceremony included the inauguration of the Dutchess of Devonshire as its first Chancellor. It was here we met Sir James Duff for the first time, a man we came to like very much. We first saw him at the speakers table and he spoke briefly in some capacity, and because of his appearance and speech, I always referred to him to Ruth as Sir John Bull.

From Exeter we went to Birmingham where we had two days of sessions on academic problems while the wives were entertained in other ways. One of Ruth's most impressive visits was in a factory for making fine porcelain. Our organization meetings included not only British and Irish university people but also representatives from South Africa, Canada, Pakistan, and other parts of the Commonwealth. While I had a small formal contribution to make that I had been assigned ahead of time by our chairman, President Morrill, at the end of the first day, he came to me and asked me to make another one. He said he wanted someone from our American group to discuss our methods, procedure and theory of admitting students to the universities. I agreed to do it and I centered my presentation partly on a contrast between the British and our systems on the basis of national needs, theirs being a society adequately supplied with professional people and ours being one which needed not only replacements but a larger supply of physicians, engineers, and other professional people. This as well as educational theory had influenced our different procedures in selection, as ours was aimed at getting as many of the capable as possible, while theirs at keeping out the incapable.

At the end of the Birmingham meeting, a small group of us Americans went as guests of the University of Manchester where we visited not only the university but the great telescope which the British were developing just outside the city. We also visited an interesting library with many old manuscripts and books with the most outstanding illuminated manuscripts I had ever seen. From there some of us went up to Glasgow. I primarily went to see the university, but some of my colleagues were really bound farther north to play golf at the famous course at St. Andrews. I had an interesting day at Glasgow particularly in the museum, as the university was not in session, and the museum had many historic scientific instruments that were intriguing. From Glasgow we flew home, well satisfied with our trip.

Between the two meetings in Great Britain there was a special Commonwealth session in Montreal, Canada. I attended this as a representative of the AAU, and a great many other members of our presidents were there as visitors. While it was not elaborate in its formalities and ceremonies, it was a most interesting session in which the British were well represented and virtually all the Canadian administrators were present. We spent one day of the meeting in Toronto, where we visited the Canadian Parliament and heard a debate on a problem of general interest.

I had agreed to spend two days in Washington during the time that the British Commonwealth representatives were visiting there. The AAU provided guides to show them the high points of the city, and we gave them a brief, but I believe impressive, picture of the American government. One important thing that I remember happened when I went with a two-busload group to the Supreme Court. We were welcomed by Justice Felix Frankfurter, who gave us a most interesting lecture contrasting the American legal system with the new Indian system which the Justice had been studying. On the way to the Court a police escort stopped a parade to let us pass through. It proved to be a Shriner's parade. They were in full regalia, and much more colorful than one customarily saw in an American city. I recall a Vice Chancellor from one of the Muslim universities coming to me in some excitement and saying, "Why, they wear tarbooshes. We quit wearing them several years ago." I had to explain to him that it was not customary for that fraternity to keep abreast of changes in costumes or ceremony for they went back to the Crusades for their inspiration.

The American side of the visit had been arranged so that groups could visit selected universities, and the University of Missouri was on the list for one group. Our group was in charge of Sir James Duff, and it had a mixture of academics from Britain and Commonwealth countries. There were slightly over 30 in the group including some wives. This group went first to Illinois, Champaign-Urbana; then I met them with a Greyhound bus at the St. Louis airport. I had first planned to take them to Washington University, but as time was short I made arrangements with President McClure at Lindenwood to show them an American women's college. McClure arranged luncheon for us and afterward he spoke to the group on "Women's Colleges in America." We then came on to Columbia where I placed our guests in our newest dormitory, as the visit occurred just before the fall semester opened. That evening we had a cocktail party at the President's House and a dinner at the Union Ballroom, with the deans and other administrative officers of the University as hosts. After the dinner, we showed a film which the Extension Division had just made on the university and its work. The next day was spent in seeing the University campus and in discussions of our programs by certain divisional deans where I thought their interests would be engaged. That evening we again had a cocktail party for them at the President's House and afterward each couple or individual was taken by a dean or faculty member to his home for dinner. This had two purposes. They were very tired, and I also wanted them to see something of how faculty and administrators in an American university lived.

After breakfast the next morning, we loaded our bus again and drove to Lincoln University which was already in session. Segregation had just been abolished and almost half the students on the campus were white. Our visitors had been prepared for this. We had lunch, and President Earl Dawson made an interesting speech on the problems of integrating a black university. Two of our visitors were vice chancellors from South Africa. They had some interesting comments on the new stricter segregation being forced on them by their government. Afterward we resumed our bus ride going through Westphalia, as the only side trip, and stopping on a few occasions for views of the Ozarks. At Rolla we looked over the campus, had tea for them at their suggestion, which we had forgotten in Columbia. We had dinner, where Dean Curtis Wilson talked on engineering education in the United States. Ruth and I bade them goodby as they boarded the train at Rolla, and after visiting the University of Texas and Vanderbilt University they began their trip homeward.

Our attendance at the second meeting of the Commonwealth Chancellors in Britain was quite different in the sense that Ruth and I now were well-acquainted with a great many of the people. When we went to

England for the meeting, we had accepted a personal invitation to the University of Nottingham from the Vice Chancellor Bartrand Hallward, who had been in the party that had visited the University of Missouri. We also had agreed to visit the University of Durham under the guidance of Sir James Duff after the sessions were over.

We had a pleasant visit in London before the meeting and we also visited Nottingham during that time. We took the train to Nottingham, and just before we left the station three gentlemen entered the train, opened our compartment door and very courteously asked if we "minded" if they joined us. Of course we did not and the three entered. One was a handsome fellow, at least 6'4" and must have weighed close to 300 pounds. The day, by London standards, had been hot and when taking off his coat he turned to Ruth and asked, "Do you mind if I let down my braces?" Ruth was not sure what braces were but, being polite, she said she did not mind. He let his suspenders down which seemed to be unnecessary anyway. They introduced themselves and we introduced ourselves. The large man turned out to be the Sheriff of Nottingham and his colleagues were associates of his in that city. They had been at a meeting of the association governing the playing of rugby football in Britain. Obviously they were all old rugby players. They knew Vice Chancellor Hallward, and we had a pleasant trip to the famous old city. We were met at the station by our host and taken to the very old home where the Vice Chancellor and Mrs. Hallward lived. It had beautiful grounds and the building had been a beautiful building, but it had passed its prime some years before. The plumbing and the electrical wiring were particularly fragile. I could not use my electric shaver even though I had an adapter.

We had a delicious dinner and a pleasant short tour of the campus while it was still daylight. The next day we spent going over the campus, visiting several of the buildings and absorbing the atmosphere of the old but still provincial university. I was surprised at the amount of space given for playing fields. I believe it exceeded most American universities in this respect. We spent our second evening very pleasantly with the Hallwards and the next morning we took the train back to London. During our visit we had learned the Hallward's son-in-law was a master of one of the colleges at Cambridge and while we were there, he entertained his relatives and us. He presented me with a copy of a historical work he had written that was an interesting history of a long local controversy between the gentry and the church over dominance in the community in which the gentry eventually won. The visit was an exceedingly pleasant experience.

The meeting was at Cambridge which Ruth and I had visited briefly in

1951. We were housed, held our discussions, and were served meals in the university buildings. The university was not in session but many of the college faculty were there and joined us at meals. The most memorable day that I had at the meeting is the additional day we took off to visit the parts of the university in which we were especially interested. I designated the library and the University Press, the latter primarily because we were in the midst of organizing ours at Missouri. I was the lone visitor to both, and the librarian gave me a guided tour and talked a great deal about the library and its history. I then went to the Press and found they were engaged in cooperating with the Oxford University Press in publishing a new translation of the New Testament and these pages were stacked all over the place. While the director told me this, I saw a different sort of paper and I asked him what this was—pulling out a racing form. He smiled and said, "When our presses are idle we are doing all kinds of printing jobs and these people have a pretty steady account with us." It was good management but somehow it amused me that the racing forms would be published alongside of the New Testament.

Our visit to Durham followed the meeting at Cambridge. It was a little awkward because Sir James had retired as Vice Chancellor and was now either Director or the Associate Director of the British Broadcasting Company. But he lived near Durham and urged us to come to Durham where he would meet us. At the end of our meeting in Cambridge, David Henry of the University of Illinois and I rented cars to try our luck at driving on the wrong side of the road. It was on a Saturday that we started our separate trips north. I have to confess that Saturday was a miserable day for me as I had great trouble remembering to stay on the left hand side of the road. On one occasion when I had to make a U turn to change directions, I wound up driving on the right and when I saw a car coming I took to the ditch which was a safe place to be for my state of driving.

We began to worry about hotels and decided to stop early to be assured we had a place. We stopped at a city named Godmanchester, where we contacted the hotel and found no vacancies. The manager courteously offered to call ahead for me which he did, with the same negative results. I recalled that we had passed a large pub on the other side of town that had a sign which indicated that it rented rooms and served meals, so we returned there to find a colorful wedding in progress. We eventually were assigned a fairly good room with the usual facilities down the hall. The main part of our evening was a walk along a small river to a church that had an old churchyard filled with interesting gravestones. The next day we went on to Newcastle which was according to plan; actually part of the University of Durham is located in Newcastle. We had reservations at a faculty facility where we had good meals and an excellent room. I spent my afternoon with members of the physics department, going through the new physics building which had many interesting innovations in its design. Newcastle, however, was very much an industrial center and all was dark and gloomy. I regretted seeing that the fine physics building had been built in a very dark colored stone that looked almost black in the misty weather. Newcastle had been an important site on the old Roman wall and we spent some time looking over the ruins of this, as well as the local museum concerning it.

The next day we drove back about 15 miles to Durham, and found a most congested little city where the main streets seemed to be all one-way. We found the suggested hotel and in a short time Sir James arrived. He immediately took us on a stroll over to the castle and we went over it from top to bottom. He took great pleasure in describing all its features, its history and incidentally how much it was costing the university to maintain this historic structure. It clearly was his pride and joy.

After a fine dinner and pleasant evening he left for his home, a few miles away. The next morning we examined the university with a guide and after lunch drove back to Cambridge, turned our car in and took the train to London. After the difficult Saturday I seemed to have become completely adjusted to driving on the wrong side of the road. Maybe that is the way human character is—with a little practice you can go the wrong way as easily as the right.

Chapter 21

The Need of More Land

One of the developments that most land-grant schools had, which included the Columbia campus of the University of Missouri, was the gradual absorption of agriculture experiment areas adjoining the campus for the central university development. Generally speaking, these had been acquired when the Land-Grant Act of 1862 had been accepted by the state, and at that time were not only on the edge of the campus but outside of the urban development proper. Thus the White Campus at Columbia is the former university orchard. When the medical school was built, another large section of university experimental land was absorbed into the campus and, like many universities and colleges, some of the athletic fields such as the old Rollins Field were also absorbed into the academic campus.

Our problem at Rolla was simpler since there it was largely one of taking over the athletic facilities for academic building sites, and moving the athletic facilities to other land which the university owned. The connecting link between the two campuses at Rolla was the large dormitory block which we built by a self-liquidating bond issue. In the case of Columbia, though, the acute problem was that of agriculture, which was greatly in need of expansion rather than contraction, and both had to go on at the same time. In 1948 the federal government gave the university a large acreage near Weldon Springs, which was bordered by Highway 40 and the Missouri River. It had been used as a safety area for a large TNT plant that was desperately needed early in the war but, after a change in technology, was no longer needed. This was not particularly well located for our purposes, as research for northeast Missouri could easily be managed at the Columbia fields, and duplicating research in more than one area where it was not required by different soils was wasteful. Weldon Springs was a large area and could have maintained a large development; but there was little way to use it. Consequently, the college established a group of breeding and feeding experiments for beef cattle, which did little to solve our major problems.

Another problem was the need for experimental areas in different parts of the state where soils, crops, and climate were enough different that experiments had to be carried on to service its needs adequately. We were renting areas in southwest and southeast Missouri, and had recently been given a farm near Spickard in northwest Missouri, which with buildings and other improvements was quite adequate for our purpose. The southeast Missouri problem presented some difficulties, as we had a prospect of a gift to which there were serious legal complications. This was near Portageville. We already had rights to land near Kennett that was to become University property eventually. The experimental people in the college were convinced that for their purposes there was no comparison between the two sites. The Portageville site was by far the more desirable. One advantage was it included a piece of land that was inside the levee in the flood plain of the Mississippi River. It was owned by two women, Mrs. Margaret M. Marsh and her daughter, Mrs. Matilda Cavanaugh, whose title was good provided the daughter outlived the mother. Otherwise it went to distant relatives whom they did not know. The husband of the mother had willed it that way in case of the sequence of the deaths of his wife and daughter. We took this on what was virtually a rental basis, with their rights to the land pledged to the University. They were very well disposed toward the University, largely because of professors T. J. Talbert and Raymond Schroeder, who had given them a great deal of help in making their farm a paying enterprise. Talbert was gone, but Ray Schroeder was primarily responsible for this contingent gift. We were able by condemnation to buy title to a part of the land where we placed the buildings for our center, and proceeded to make it into our Southeast Missouri Experimental Farm. Fortunately for the University, the daughter outlived the mother which solved our legal problem. It was not without some political controversy, however, as there were groups in Kennett that wanted the experimental farm located there, and they had more political clout than the much smaller town of Portageville.

In southwest Missouri, on the other had, we did not find a donor and had to buy a suitable area of land which we did near Mount Vernon. These three places, without Weldon Springs, gave us all the geographic distribution we needed, but the problem became one of the main research centers close to the campus. This was now centered in what we designated the South Farm, an area of land about six miles south of Columbia, one corner of which was used for the television station, KOMU-TV, which began operating in 1953. In addition we had a new horticulture farm near New Franklin and the Penney Dairy Farm north of Columbia.

This problem was only one of the more pressing needs for additional land that were coming to my attention immediately after I became president. All drove home to me the need for acquiring land as near the campus as possible in a substantial quantity. I recall spending one Sunday driving around the campus trying to locate possibilities. There were obviously several residential areas, some of which had been owned by the University 100 years before, that were now occupied by houses that were mostly large, some quite old, and some quite attractive. It was clear that these would have to be purchased, and I had already learned that when you bought a residence the site received was very small indeed, but you paid for the residence as if it were going to continue in that use. This would cause bad public relations as well as be exceedingly expensive, leaving only one possibility that I could see, and that was the remains of the old Rollins farm that lay south of Stadium Road, which the Highway Department was building for access to the new medical center. With considerable help from our general counsel, Paul Peterson, I began to talk to its owner, James Sidney Rollins. The part of the farm which was north of Stadium Road was being sold by him and his son, James Sidney, as lots to make a residential section known as Grasslands. The selling of any large part of this was bothersome taxwise for the elder Rollins. Consequently, he had been limiting his sales to a very small number per year. My approach to him was the advantages, tax and otherwise, in selling to the university the farm south of the highway, an area of about 450 acres. Since we had acquired the E. W. Stephens property west of Providence Road earlier, it was the only open land adjoining the campus. I made my appeal to Rollins, not only on the basis of his own tax situation which I thought we could manage to his benefit, but also to keep the historic Rollins name in the center of the university development. I pointed out that the old Rollins Field was being used as a track for only minor meets and it would soon be a thing of the past. I offered to move the Rollins Field gate that was on the corner of Rollins and Maryland to the new Rollins Field, which would be primarily devoted for the time being to athletics and to some agricultural research. We worked this out with Peterson doing most of the details, negotiating on the basis of $500 per acre to be paid over a 13-year period to suit Rollins' tax situation. At the time we made the agreement it was a reasonably good price for the land. Three and four years later it was obvious that the university had acquired a bargain. The baseball diamond, several football practice fields, and a large area of agriculture experimental plots were moved to the area immediately, and I began to look for a possible donor for a golf course on an area of the farm that seemed to lend itself to that development. A. L. Gustin, Jr., of Kansas City, virtually retired and a graduate of the University, became interested in this and, with help from Dutton Brookfield and Bus Entsminger, we induced him to give the university $75,000 for designing and building an eighteen hole course. After it was completed he followed through with a gift of $25,000 to build a clubhouse. The A. L. Gustin Golf Course was a great improvement over the nine hole course we lost when it was absorbed by campus buildings.

This did not itself solve all the College of Agriculture's need for research areas in its main center at Columbia. We were willed the Sinclair Farm, but it was too far west to operate economically with the South Farm. Another possibility was the Middlebush Farm on Highway 63, which was closer to the South Farm than the Sinclair Farm was. President and Mrs. Middlebush had developed this farm as a vacation-weekend home. Among its attractions were two lakes, well stocked with fish. We had every reason to believe this would come to the University eventually, but Dean Longwell was quite sure it was not close enough to the South Farm to make a good unit for efficiency in their research work. We looked further and found the Bradford Farm, a mile east of the South Farm, as the best prospect possible. This farm had been in the Bradford family for many years although the present family had not lived on it. Alex Bradford was a banker in Columbia where he, his wife, Mary, and their daughter, Estelle, lived. Mrs. Bradford was an invalid and her husband was quite elderly, ill and hospitalized most of the time. Through Peterson, who knew him well, I raised the question of the eventual disposition of the farm. We knew it would make a real tax problem for him, whether he sold it, gave it to Estelle now, or by will. I made one trip to the hospital to talk to him, and Peterson worked out an arrangement whereby we would pay rent for the farm for the duration of Estelle's life. Estelle was agreeable to this, as she did not welcome the prospect of managing the farm. It was a generous move on Bradford's part and he was delighted to benefit the University. This really saved the experimental unit of the College of Agriculture and, with the South Farm, gave an admirable center for its main research. As the University paid the rent, it was in a way compensation to the College of Agriculture for the land which the University had used for other purposes. The Sinclair Farm then was taken over by a group for research on the process of aging, working on animals, primarily by veterinary college faculty, but with people from several different divisions of the University. Raymond Peck from my office and Carl Marienfeld from Medicine were both active in its development. It was not entirely confined to domestic animals, as we took some wild species from zoos which had adequate records on their history before their old age. Before Fred Middlebush died in 1971, he and Catherine Middlebush gave their farm to the University. It was assigned to the School of Veterinary Medicine for experimentation purposes.

One of the more interesting additions to the University's responsibilities was the acceptance of the Tucker Prairie as a gift for the use primarily of our Department of Botany in its research activities. This was bought from the J. R. Tucker family at Fulton with funds raised by people in the state who were concerned primarily with the preservation of the last pieces of the long grass prairie land in Missouri, grass that is over head high when it has its full growth if it is not cut or pastured.

A difficult and unexpected problem quickly developed. The Federal Bureau of Highways and the Missouri Highway Department had designed what later became Interstate 70 in such a way that the eastbound south lane cut across the boundary of the paririe and made a substantial dent along the north side. As the interstate highway had been long planned and the road east and west of Tucker Prairie was completely designed and partly built to use this route, it was difficult, or perhaps one should say, far too expensive, to change. The actual problem was not great since it did not make much difference whether the area was 145 or 160 acres for research purposes or nature preservation. Many of the people who had given money had been led to believe that every foot of the land was sacred and should not be touched for any purpose. We eventually worked out a compromise with the Highway Department, whereby the least possible amount of Prairie would be disrupted, and that serious attempts would be made to use the native grass as a cover for the grade that would protect it against erosion. This quieted most of the criticism that we were subject to except from some of the local farmers. There was no service road paralleling the south slab so it was awkward and inconvenient to get around in the locality without going long distances to get on the highway or the north service road. I was waited on by a group of the farmers with the demand that we let a service road be built south of the highway, which would use up as much of the prairie as the highway itself. To their great astonishment I refused to consider it or even to take it to the Board. They had to build their service road on the south side of the prairie which was inconvenient and used their own land. In the meantime, good use was being made of the prairie for various research purposes and we erected a metal building there to take care of our research equipment.

There were certain uses of land where we had to offer and give land we owned to federal agencies, which could be induced to establish some of their research laboratories where they would be useful to the research work of the University. The U.S. Fish Pesticide Laboratory, for instance, which had been located in Colorado, was moved here and located on the South Farm in a spot that it found very desirable and the College of Agriculture felt it could live without.

Of great importance to us was the Veterans Administration Hospital. The possibility of locating it here had been communicated to me fairly early in my administration by my friend Al Monk, who had been the University business manager before going into military service during World War II. Instead of returning to the University, he went into work in the Veterans Administration where he rose rapidly in the administration, eventually becoming Assistant Administrator. Monk was the person who was largely responsible for locating the hospital in our medical complex, although I ran some errands and pestered him when I went to Washington to find out how we were progressing. Later Dean Vernon Wilson did likewise. The building of the hospital took 16 acres badly needed for parking area, but it was worth it many times over to acquire this important affiliation to our medical center facilities.

A somewhat similar development was that of our atomic reactors. The availability of federal funds for training and research became a reality, and the Rolla faculty decided that a training reactor would add greatly to the facilities needed for the development of the school. We could be more certain of getting the training reactor and we could get it almost immediately. It was approved and became the first reactor in the state to go critical.

The College of Engineering under the direction of Huber Croft decided to apply for a large research reactor. He put in an application and followed up with vigorous representations. We were successful here as at Rolla but it was a longer process. The reactor was designed by its eventual director, Ardath Emmons, who had been Assistant Director of the University of Michigan reactor. The College of Engineering was assisted in this by the chairman of the Department of Physics, Newell Gingrich.

This, along with certain other buildings which included a space science center, partly state and partly federally financed, utilized the rest of the research area which the College of Agriculture had in the Rollins Farm area. But, with the Bradford Farm, this was no longer significant. The availability of good sites had been the key to our ability to attract these unusual facilities.

Chapter 22

Expanding the University

The relation of the University of Missouri to the higher educational institutions in Kansas City had been a relatively close one before I joined the University staff. I began to understand it fairly well through my work with the Committee of Accrediting Schools and Colleges. The Kansas City Junior College was one of the two oldest public junior colleges in the state and was part of the city school system. During my second year at the University I began visiting it at least every other year with a faculty committee, and became well-acquainted with its administration and its social science staff. It was a highly academic institution designed to give two years of freshman and sophomore college work, so as to fit its graduates directly into the junior year at four-year colleges and universities. Except for the secretarial training program, this was its sole objective, and in this it was like all the other public junior colleges in the state in that the local school funds permitted nothing more. It was housed in rather inadequate quarters even for purely academic work. But in spite of this, it did the job for which it was designed in an excellent manner. As time went on, the lack of more specifically vocational work at the post-high school stage became more and more evident as the great need in the city. But this situation was not to be improved in any real sense until after the state aid to junior colleges became a reality in the Dalton administration.

The accrediting structure in most parts of the United States, certainly in our North Central area, had one serious handicap when it came to establishing new four-year colleges. For instance, Rockhurst College, a Jesuit institution for men only, had been in existence for some time, but there was no way for it to become accredited except to graduate a class with degrees and then apply for accreditation; the students, in the meantime, taking the risk involved in not having the school accredited. As a means of lessening this problem with Rockhurst, the Committee on Accrediting Schools and Colleges had been accrediting it as a junior college covering only its first two years of work. Although the University of Missouri unofficially did recognize its junior and senior years of work when it began offering it, the committee had no authority for accrediting senior college work. Rockhurst was handicapped by not having full accreditation for several years. This process was underway when I became acquainted with the college and its determination to make itself a thoroughly accreditable four-year college. St. Theresa, a high school for girls, not far from Rockhurst, had established a junior college in addition to its high school and was making progress toward its full accreditation. Eventually it became a four-year institution, even though we on the committee thought its resources were meager indeed. At present the high school is known as St. Theresa, and the college has become Avila College.

The largest development in Kansas City, however, and of greatest importance to the University of Missouri, was the combination in 1933 of several earlier movements toward the establishment of a "University of Kansas City" that would unite several existing professional schools with a strong arts college. A gift of 10 million dollars came from William Volker which, under its terms, could be used at the rate of one-half million dollars a year in getting the institution underway, with the expectation that in the period it would have raised enough endowment to be self-sustaining. It had the usual problem of accreditation and, as in the case of Rockhurst College, it worked closely with the Accrediting Committee. After securing accreditation as a Junior College, with our coordination and assistance it could reach accrediting in the North Central Association. There was no problem with the first two years, but the second two years gave the new university considerable trouble as the costs were high and enrollments low. Fortunately, it began at a period of high academic unemployment and it was able to secure an excellent faculty. We informed it that we could no longer accredit it as a junior college the year it was up for accrediting by the North Central Association as a four-year college. Unfortunately, the North Central Association turned down the request the first time, and the graduates and juniors were left with credits from a non-recognized institution. After considerable struggle with this problem, we agreed to re-accredit it as a junior college and publicly announce that the graduates would be admitted to our graduate school and the fourth-year students would be admitted to our senior class. This was going beyond our own rules, but it seemed the only reasonable position to take. The next year the North Central did accredit it, and it came off our junior college list as Rockhurst had before.

The history of the University of Kansas City was one of some real achievement and some general failure. I believe that before its beginning, Kansas City was the only city of its size in the United States without a university. It started too late, as it proved, to raise the kind of money for endowments that a private institution had to have. In spite of several substantial gifts of property about the university campus, and an ideal location for a university, it was becoming clear that it would never make it by that route. Possibly different leadership in the early days would have saved it, but the leadership in general was poor until Earl McGrath was appointed president. While he was responsible for some excellent academic programs there was no successful financial planning. When this was not forthcoming, he resigned. Then Richard Drake became president, until he gave it up as hopeless. His successor Carleton Scofield, first as acting president and then president, continued to labor hard and long at the task. Its great success in these years was in getting the amalgamation of the old independent professional schools—law, pharmacy, dentistry, and music—merged into the university structure. These had all been in existence since sometime in the 1880s, and were the strongest elements of the university after they joined it.

In the meantime, the University of Missouri was having trouble in serving the needs of Kansas City, especially the needs of government, business and industry in training employees at what was roughly the masters level at the University of Missouri, tasks that the University of Kansas City was unable to perform with its weak structure. We, consequently, were under pressure and under the necessity of establishing masters level work in business administration, in engineering, in education, in social work, and in some other fields. This was taught usually at night at rented quarters in downtown Kansas City, or often at Rockhurst College or the Junior College. In our budget request for 1963–65 we asked for funds for a building in Kansas City to house our programs there, as more of them were outgrowing the evening-Saturday class category. Some friends of Kansas City University looked on this as a threat that we would start a complete university if we had a building. There had been many discussions at various times about the possibility of some collaboration of the University of Kansas City with the University of Missouri to strengthen it and to solve the University's problem. The first suggestion for amalgamation that came to me was from James Kemper, Sr., the leading banker in Kansas City, who at one time in his rather direct and rough way, had asked me, "Why don't you take it over? They are never going to be able to make a go of it out there when the Volker money is gone." Chancellor Drake once mentioned informally to me that he saw no future for the University of Kansas City, except as a part of the University of Missouri. After several other similar suggestions and later some discussions with Chancellor Scofield who was convinced that, since the Volker money was gone, there was no possibility of their maintaining the university, and that something should be worked out whereby we could at least help each other. It also should be mentioned that the Kansas City Association of Trusts and Foundations had financed a study of the university's future, which was done by Dean McHenry of the University of California at Los Angeles during Drake's administration. Among his suggestions was that it become part of the University of Missouri.

The first serious discussion that I had concerning this with an outsider was with Homer Wadsworth, the director of Kansas City Association of Trusts and Foundations. After clearing it with James Finch, our Board president, and testing informally the political sentiment in Jefferson City, I had taken up the subject with Wadsworth and he had immediately seen its potential. In fact, I had a feeling that he had been expecting it. He made an immediate appointment with Arthur Mag and we walked over to his office nearby. Mag was advisor to several people who were involved in some support of the University of Kansas City, particularly Elmer Pierson, who had just made a heavy donation to build a multipurpose center on the campus. We had our discussion and talked with several others including John Morgan, who was president of the Board and a very statesman-like businessman.

In the meantime, I had kept our Board informed, particularly President Finch, of these discussions and we arranged a meeting on the University of Kansas City campus with Scofield and five or six members of its board: Arthur Mag, John Morgan, Charles Kimball, and Henry Haskell among them. Finch and I participated. I do not now recall that we took any other Board member. I took with me John Schwada, who had become Chancellor of the Columbia campus.

There was opposition in the University of Kansas City Board, and there were soon some resignations of persons who were not interested in the University if it became a public institution. But those who had worked closely with the financial situation all seemed convinced that a merger was the only way to save the University of Kansas City.

While there was considerable personal discussion and negotiation going on, the formal meeting was held by a committee of their Board of Trustees. Primarily their lawyers met with Paul Peterson, Bob Neill, Jim Finch, and others of our Board of Curators here in Columbia on one Sunday, and spent most of the day threshing out the legal details. Frankly, there were many details here that I thought Scofield and I could have settled more quickly and amicably than the lawyers, as some of the legal aspects became very sticky. In the end it was settled, proving that the state government would go along. One thing that had come out in the discussion that I had not been informed of before, but that I had suspected, was that the University of Kansas City was close to one and one-half million dollars in debt, a debt acquired since the using up of the Volker money. It seemed to be running a deficit of about $500,000 a year since the Volker money had been exhausted or about the amount of that annual addition.

One of the members of the Kansas City Board, Charles Kimball of the Midwest Research Insititute, had asked me at the Kansas City meeting if I had planned to put Schwada in charge if the merger went through and I told him no. I expected to leave Scofield in charge until he reached retirement age which was two years away. I think that reassured Kimball and enabled him to assure some of the reluctant members of the Board to go along with the plan. We had agreed we would use the word "merger" of the University of Kansas City campus with the University of Missouri. We would use the same terminology that California was using—University of Missouri at Kansas City.

This being decided, I made an appointment with Governor John Dalton and talked to him about it. I had mentioned it to him several times before and had not been rebuffed. I also brought up the situation in St. Louis where a different process had been going on and found him, as I expected, completely in accord with what we planned. Our situation in St. Louis was entirely different from Kansas City. The new junior college law had solved the worst of St. Louis' problem of education, especially for the low-income groups in the city. But it had not promised to do anything beyond that.

In the meantime, the University of Missouri had developed an extension at the old Bellerive Golf Club in Normandy. This was at the urging of the public school there and its superintendent, Ward Barnes. They were looking toward a branch of the University of Missouri, but at this time we committed ourselves only to developing a junior college on our usual plan. There was little difference in our development here than in helping a school district start a junior college, but at the end of two years we did not insist on an application to the North Central Association for accreditation as a junior college. Its great advantage lay in the possession of a fine campus site for an educational institution, the former Bellerive Golf Course.

The program was poorly housed in the old clubhouse of the golf club. Its administration was by the dean of the College of Arts and Science and the principal of Normandy High School. This was satisfactory for the time being. We rendered such assistance through the arts dean's office and his staff as we could and, except for a very inadequate library, the center got off to a good start. But immediately its connection with the University of Missouri led to great interest in St. Louis in the university starting a campus there. The real pressure on the University was still for post-baccalaureate work in the many educational programs in the city designed for teachers, engineers, and other special groups. We were even teaching the academic courses in some hospital schools of nursing in the city as they were not accredited for that work. We were under great pressure from other groups for more programs that we could not satisfy.

Some engineering was offered from the Columbia campus and one engineering program from the Rolla campus was on an evening school, Saturday-type schedule which varied from semester to semester. The education was all post-baccalaureate except that with the nursing schools.

Mayor Raymond Tucker of St. Louis had interviewed me one time and suggested that if we moved to St. Louis, he could secure a site in the city for us, rather than the one in Normandy. I answered that I considered Forest Park the only site in the city that was superior to the one in Normandy, and I knew we could not secure that. The school superintendent of St. Louis City, Phil Hickey, had also talked to me about the University taking over the city's Harris Teachers College, which was a fully-accredited school devoted to training teachers for their elementary school system. As I recall, I answered that if we should develop a campus we would be glad to include it as the teachers' college of the new institution, keeping the name Harris, but that I would not want to guarantee taking over all the faculty.

The Normandy group had done an excellent job in making their case for becoming part of the state university well-known, and had a great deal of support in both the city and the county, although there was no organized movement of any kind and at no time had we promoted that idea.

Now their situation was that some additional buildings had to be built if they were going to continue as our extension center or become a junior college. This made an ideal time for the University of Missouri to take over the property and place on it an institution closely related to the University that could carry the junior college on to a four- and five-year college, and meet such other needs of the city as developed that were not being cared for by the institutions already there. We were anxious to relieve our faculty at Columbia of the need to offer a great variety of masters level work to which we were committed. The St. Louis Junior College was now moving ahead very effectively with the state aid that had been approved beginning in 1961, and a large number of young people were attending the junior college that would not have attended any school had it not existed.

With complete understanding that the School District of Normandy would turn over all its rights in the golf club site if the University of Missouri would develop an institution there, I carried these details to Governor Dalton after having already cleared them with the University Board of Curators. After the Governor's approval, legislation was drafted which provided appropriations and authority for the University to merge with the Kansas City University and develop our extension center in Normandy School District into a campus of the University. In each case we asked for appropriations, and in the case of the Kansas City campus we asked for an appropriation that could be used either for capital expenditures or operating funds, as we were not sure how the needs would work out since it was hard to predict enrollments and costs. Our plan provided that we would not lower the tuition Kansas City University had been charging for the first year, in order to cushion the shock of the entire cost coming on the budget. This would end with the next biennium when the fees on all campuses would be made uniform.

I was surprised at the ease with which we, meaning primarily Bus Entsminger with Brice Ratchford who had begun to help with some of the lobbying, were able to carry this through. I had always had little difficulty getting support from St. Louis County but had great difficulty getting as good support from Kansas City as I thought the University deserved. In this case we worked directly with the political factions, the organized labor groups, particularly with James H. Davis, lobbyist for the AFL-CIO, and with our usual farm organization support. It went through in the spring of 1963. Without both Kansas City and St. Louis involved this would have been impossible. The next fall we had four campuses.

We had been using as administrative head at St. Louis the high school principal, Edward Driscoll. He was able and handled the two jobs well. We kept him the first year while we looked for a permanent staff. After considerable discussion with various members of this staff, I selected James L. Bugg, Jr., of the History Department at the Columbia campus to be dean of the center at Normandy. The next year we changed his title to chancellor, as we did that of Dean Merl Baker at Rolla, corresponding with Chancellor Scofield at Kansas City and Chancellor Schwada at Columbia.

The good fortune of getting our appropriation for Kansas City in such general terms became apparent immediately, as we were faced with many costly problems that we had not anticipated. Kansas City University was a good example of how uneconomical it is to operate an institution with inadequate funds. Its utilities as one result had been put in on such a cheap basis that we had to redo the greater part of them before the year was out in order to operate.

The creation of the four-campus system was really more difficult in Columbia than on any other campus because this was where the central direction would remain. How the central direction would be separated from the governance of the big university at Columbia itself proved to be the toughest problem. I never was satisfied that we had reached any final solutions of any of the problems, but I felt my way using largely North Carolina and California as guides. North Carolina seemed to be the more relevant to our situation because of its size and its budget. It was not relevant in other respects such as the size of the cities involved and the geographic distribution of the institutions as they were in 1963. The great danger in moving into this was to overelaborate administrative structure in a way that it would be highly uneconomical and inefficient.

In addition to the general problem there was another problem of working out the exact relationship between John Schwada's chancellorship and the president's office. When John and I had originally discussed this, it had presented no great problem. He was to be my administrative assistant. Having four campuses, each of them having a chancellor, and in the three campuses outside the Columbia, the chancellors necessarily having a quite high degree of independence, changed many of the assumptions we had made in our earlier discussions. John found it very uncomfortable at times. In the beginning there were some very substantial differences. The most important I think to John was his office, because the change in structure did not create any more office room, and we had to go through the procedure of including in our capital budget an appropriation for a central university building. I wanted at first to put it on the northwest corner of the Red Campus, north of McAlester Hall. While it would be separate from the Columbia administrative structure, it would still keep it conveniently tied in with many of our basic services that I assumed we would use in common. This was important, too, to the other campuses who were inclined very strongly to believe that they were administered by the Columbia campus. In the end the Board would not go along with my location, and insisted on a larger geographical separation from Jesse Hall which would be the administrative headquarters of the Columbia campus. My objection to the Board's location was chiefly that it separated the central administration from all faculty and students and made it far more of a government bureau than I approved myself. In fact, I told the Board that I saw little difference in putting it on the golf course and moving it to Jefferson City, a fate that I dreaded beyond all else.

I took with me to the central administration many of the key people in the structure that had existed when there were only two campuses and one, Rolla, was administered as another college on the Columbia campus. In place of people like Bezoni, Bowling, Peck, Wilson, and Ratchford, new selections were made from within to administer the more purely campus matters, but these were approached very gradually. Many of the people, such as Bowling and Peck, were spending a great deal of time on other campuses. Superficially things did not change very fast or as fast as many expected they would. While this kept us from making mistakes of a serious nature, it also gave an outwardly appearance that there was as yet little difference between the Columbia campus administration and the central administration. But each year we moved toward more definite organizational structure with lines of authority becoming clearer as we experimented with all the campus structure in relation to the central.

During the last year of my presidency a very disagreeable situation developed, which increased in John Weaver's administration. This was the situation as near as I can analyze it:

John Schwada was the heir apparent to the presidency if the Board chose from the campus. I had recommended him to the Board along with Vernon Wilson and Brice Ratchford as possibilities on our own campus. Schwada was well aware of his key position with the Board of Curators if they chose someone from the campus, and I suspect was counting on it. His experience in the state budget office was a strong factor in his favor. At the same time I recommended him, I had also recommended six outsiders, all but one presidents of smaller universities, much younger than I, and to whom Missouri would be quite an advancement. They were people I knew well and any one of them I was confident would make a good administrative head. The one of the group who was not a president was John Weaver, Vice President at Ohio State, who had similar experience at the University of Iowa, and had been Graduate Dean at Nebraska and Dean at Kansas State.

Schwada knew Weaver and when I showed him that list he said almost immediately, "They'll take Weaver." Schwada was also dissatisfied with his situation in Jesse Hall. I had originally arranged with him to take over the quarters that Raymond Peck had occupied on the second floor which were directly above the office occupied by Bezoni and to a lesser extent by Mary Robnett, the Secretary of the Board. He soon moved from there to a first floor office in Jesse Hall near mine, far less desirable than what he left, except that he seemed to equate first floor office with administrative authority. He came to me one day and virtually demanded that he be given Bezoni's office which was across the hall from me and had the same amount of space although differently arranged. I discussed it with him, and I was surprised at how determined he was. Finally I recall telling him something to this effect, "John, one of the few things about administration that I have learned is never move a good man that you want to keep working at top speed out of his office without his initiative." I had authorized Bezoni to take over those offices when Cowan retired. Schwada remained very unhappy about that situation, and he also might have felt discriminated against since, unlike the Kansas City and Rolla chancellors, he was not furnished a house. I had assured him that the presidential house would certainly become the Chancellor's residence as soon as I retired.

After Weaver came, this conflict over position did not lessen but actually increased and was mutual. It led to wasteful duplications as Schwada insisted on setting up an office subordinate to him whenever Weaver added one in the central administration. I was personally most disappointed by their setting up two public relations offices.

I had secured an appropriation for a central university office building, which I thought was adequate in a minimal way. When Weaver studied what I had done he decided the appropriation was too small to build an adequate central office, and he put an additional appropriation request in the University budget. He got no support from Jefferson City and carried this on a second time, and in the end, with rising prices, he had to accept a smaller structure than he could have built with the appropriation that we already had. Until that building was built, Weaver officed in what had been traditionally the president's office in Jesse Hall. Naturally the other central administration officers, such as Bezoni and Bowling, also stayed in Jesse Hall. This of course aggravated the situation while the new building was under construction, and I found myself on several occasions defending one of the opponents to the other over particular issues and problems. Fortunately it was settled by Schwada getting an offer of the presidency of Arizona State which he accepted and which was good for both him and the Columbia campus. But the backstairs conspiracy on the campus had damaged considerably the early structure of the central administration and the campus administrations as well.

Interestingly Schwada made an excellent record as President of Arizona State. I have no doubt in my own mind that he would have had similar success if naming him President at Missouri had gone through as it seemed at one time it would.

While the situation at Rolla was quite different from that in Columbia it also required adjustments. Rolla had unquestionably been an unwanted child of the University which was the price it paid for the locating of the College of Agriculture at Columbia rather than placing it elsewhere. Rolla was started as a school of mines and metallurgy in the beginning which was its divisional name within the University. It had developed by one means or another into a general school of engineering, offering the basic fields that were offered at Columbia as well as mining engineering and some additional fields. Mining was a declining curriculum the country over, as the mining industry seemed to want engineers trained in specialties rather than general mining engineers, and the curriculum had been given up in several universities. Had it not become a general engineering school it would have undoubtedly been a very small division indeed.

Middlebush had found a very good administrator in Curtis Wilson, who was doing an excellent job managing a very difficult situation. The campus was lacking in buildings, using some that should have been condemned officially, and the first real break we succeeded in making in this was the use of the funds of the Donnelly bond issue. Rolla had a large enrollment increase after World War II, but a serious decline came afterward with the enrollment dropping to about 1,000 students. The school had a good outside reputation and had some strong science departments, particularly geology. The two geology departments at Rolla and Columbia while competitive had worked together a great deal better than most other parallel departments at Missouri or any other multi-campus university. We floated a bond issue to build a small student union, and also built some dormitories. At the same time we were getting, during the sixties, a steady increase in enrollment especially in the basic fields. I made an effort to get the two engineering schools to coordinate their entrace requirements both from the high school and the junior college, but finally had to give it up as only a partial success.

The immediate future of Rolla was going to depend a great deal on the replacement for Curtis Wilson who was nearing retirement age. In contrast to previous procedures I set up a faculty committee of three senior faculty members, and had them gather names of possible successors and the information about those that looked probable. The only local possibility seemed to be Dudley Thompson of chemical engineering, who had many strong qualities but failed to impress the Board. The trend of the faculty group also was to go outside. I met with the committee, discussed the leading possibilities at several times and made my own inquiries, unknown to the committee. My inquiries, of course, were through administrative circles in universities where the men were known. The first question the members of the committee asked me was one which they feared would be answered "yes." All previous deans had been in mining engineering, and the question was, "Did they have to confine their search to mining engineers?" and I answered "no." I stated that I hoped their choice would be an engineer, but it could be in any field where we had a department on the Rolla campus. This seemed to please them very much as they had felt handicapped by the identification as a mining school.

The man we finally selected was Merl Baker who was on the staff at the University of Kentucky and had a doctorate from Purdue. Baker was a very acceptable administrative head. He worked well with people, perhaps too well. He began some innovative procedures and programs that were needed on the campus. His wife Emily was an attractive person and worked at the job of being an institution head's wife in a very useful way. Merl's great weakness as a dean was his inability to say no to the faculty.

I soon found I was making his decisions for him as all the propositions which came to him from a department or faculty reached my desk with his approval. In the beginning I went along on some that I probably should not have, calling his attention to the fact that it diluted our resources to offer new programs, when the new programs for the most part had no proven demand and would replace the ones that we were doing now and doing well. He was a person that took this all in good grace, but he continued to send me these decisions. I believe the last communication I had with him before I left the presidency in the summer of '66 was through a letter to him, repeating many of the things I had been telling him since he had been dean and later chancellor of the school. I chiefly emphasized the fact that his expansion was diluting the resources so greatly that the quality could do nothing but decline. In spite of that I felt he was a better than average administrator. The spirit on the campus seemed to be excellent, in large part because of the better salaries we were able to pay. Of the new buildings we were able to build I took the greatest pride in the new library, even though we had to tear down the old gymnasium to put it in a proper location on the campus.

The two older campuses were not all of the problem. There was a tremendous amount of work to be done in organizing the details of relationships on the four campuses. There were many choices that had to be decided one way or another. We used at first the awkward title of University of Missouri System to describe the four campuses, extension, and all the other bits and pieces that did not belong on any particular campus but on all or several of them. I think I put more time in on Kansas City the first two years than any other campus, simply because Scofield was going to retire at the end of that time and we had to find a successor. Scofield did a good job of administering the campus under the new order, except for a few contacts with Jefferson City with which he had had no previous experience. But the main problem there fell upon Dale Bowling and Ray Bezoni in straightening out the unbelievable business and financial mess. It seemed that any faculty members had been able to buy anything they felt they needed and charge it to the university. We quickly brought this under centralized control, but not without considerable complaining.

One interesting little item that shows what some of the problems were occurred about January 1, 1964, when the vending machines in Pierson Hall had to be let by competitive bids. As Elmer Pierson was the Vendo Company, one of the two large manufacturers in the United States, Vendo machines were already in use there and had been since the building had opened. Pierson had contributed quite heavily to the general student building. Under our procedures we let our contracts by competitive bids;

and Vendo was not the low bidder. Consequently, we took the low bidder. Pierson, who was a gentleman in every sense of the word and a very generous person for causes he believed in, made no complaint whatever but I felt guilty about it for months. It illustrates one of the problems that private institutions have to fight which is the tendency of donors to have a privileged position in getting the university's business.

The greatest weakness in Kansas City was its library situation. The original general library that had been built would hold about one-third of the library the Kansas City campus owned in 1963, as it had been the recipient of some very generous gifts. The remainder was stored in space in the Kansas City Public Library, but these books needed to be made available to the University. The only thing that saved the situation was the Linda Hall Library, which was surrounded by the campus and was a library specializing in science and technology, and in its field it was magnificent. The librarian, Joseph C. Shipman, and his board were most generous in letting our students and faculty use it. It was, however, unreasonable to ask them to provide service to undergradute students that we should be providing ourselves. The purchase of the St. Paul Theological School, which was on the edge of the campus, enabled us to use it for a business school and to take over its library space as a library for our business school. That solved a small part of the problem, but it was two years before we had any general improvement. Some use was made of the Rockhurst College library whose cooperation agreement was very useful to us.

The weakest of the professional schools was the Business School, and finding a dean who could strengthen an almost hopeless situation required considerable effort. It was an appointment in which I took a leading part. I got a line on the dean at Wichita University whose school there had very poor support and who might be interested in a move. Jack Heysinger had taught at the University of Kansas before he had gone to Wichita and was, as I recall, trained at Wisconsin. The first year I decided he was our best choice, as he had good relations with business in Kansas City and an excellent record as a teacher and administrator. Even with Scofield's approval and cooperation, we were unable to convince him that he should accept the offer, and frankly we had a poor staff on which to build. But the second year we renewed the offer and he accepted. I was convinced that we would be well off in that school, giving him time and money.

As I studied the priorities that had been made on the campus for new buildings, it seemed to me they were based almost entirely on the strength and determination of the deans of the schools involved. Before I prepared my first budget for capital items, I reworked these completely, putting the library and dental school at the top. But the greatest problem was the one of finding a successor to Scofield.

Through Homer Wadsworth I learned that Mrs. James A. McCain, wife of the President at Kansas State University at Manhattan, was rather unhappy not living in a city. Jim had been there for some time and had done excellent work, and I thought he would make our University of Kansas City campus a good chancellor. His acquaintances in Kansas City were extensive and were ones that had great potential for university support. I had a good opportunity to talk to him about this when I had him as our summer commencement speaker at Columbia in 1964. He brought with him a Kansas City banker whom I did not know but who was a close friend of Jim's and a graduate of the University of Minnesota. I talked at length with Jim about the job and he promised to give it every consideration. It was clear that he was intrigued by it. In the end, however, the answer was no. He said, "If the university were in the East or somewhere except near Manhattan, I would be glad to do it. But I have canvassed the situation and I simply can't leave Manhattan and take a job like that at the University of Missouri at Kansas City. It would be too much like going over to the enemy." I understood his problem and appreciated it, but I still wish he had taken the job.

I had an odd experience in connection with the problem afterward because McCain's banker friend was also a friend of Bud Wilkinson, the famous football coach at Oklahoma, who had retired and had a job in Washington. Soon after McCain said no, I was asked to meet with this gentleman, Charles Kimball, Dutton Brookfield, who was the former president of the Columbia campus alumni association, and one or two others whose names I do not recall. The banker wanted to suggest to me that we ask Bud Wilkinson to accept the chancellorship and he gave me a long song about how influential he was in Washington, how we could get our research contracts approved, and so forth. I listened and in the end simply said no. Their belief about his influence in the area of research contracts was pure moonshine among other things. It surprised me that Kimball would lend his support to this idea because I knew his orientation in this field was good and he must have known better, on the research idea anyway. But my memory is he said nothing, but merely lent the idea of his presence.

One of the strong deans on the Kansas City campus was Hamilton Robinson, Dean of the School of Dentistry. He was operating what seemed to be an excellent program. One of the immediate needs of the Kansas City campus, of course, was a building for the dental school that would actually be built to serve its purpose and function that way. This whole matter was complicated by medical planning for the future of

Kansas City. Many people who were interested in medicine and its practice involved in developing Hospital Hill as a large medical development to meet the future needs. Among them was Homer Wadsworth of the Kansas City Association of Trusts and Foundations and several other people who were important in the future of the University. I spent considerable time discussing this with various people, visited and studied the plans for Hospital Hill, and consulted with Dean Vernon Wilson on the Columbia campus who was exceedingly well informed on it. In the end I supported it and told the Board the provision in the plans for our School of Dentistry and a location for a future medical school, although certainly this was not emphasized at this time. It was in the plan designed to coordinate with the dental school and the future medical school with a common library. It was difficult for me to come to the conclusion that these schools at some future date would be located off the main campus, but the geography made it inescapable. The Volker campus did not lend itself to an expansion large enough to house a medical center even though Menorah Hospital bordered the campus. My experience at Columbia had convinced me we needed far more space than we could find anywhere in our Volker campus area. Moreover, the hospitals to be used for a future medical school would be on Hospital Hill. It was simply common sense to put a medical campus there, realizing there were substantial losses in the separation of the science and other departments of a university and the medical school itself. As for the medical school, we did not have any plan with a date, even an approximate date. That would have to depend on opportunities and availability of funds and to a large extent state politics. But that it had to happen was beyond question.

The other professional school that was in good standing and had good leadership lost its dean the year after the merger. This was the law school. Dean Frederick Lewis wanted to move to Florida and take a position there in one of the law schools. Temporarily, Scofield recommended to me Patrick Kelly as acting dean while he, with the members of the law faculty, would search for a dean. I kept in close touch with this procedure through Scofield because it seemed to me a key appointment as the Bar in Kansas City had recently devoted a great deal of attention to raising the standards at the school. The search for an outside dean by Scofield and the committee was not very productive, and in the meantime I had grown to know Kelly and to appreciate his good qualities as an administrator. By discreet inquiries among some of the leading members of the Bar in Kansas City, I found that he was well-thought-of. Most of them would welcome him in such a position. Finally in conference with Scofield we agreed that rather than continue the fruitless search that had been underway we would simply select Kelly as dean which proved to be a very wise choice.

These were the things as I recall them that occupied my time in Kansas City. However, the major problem continued to be finding a successor for Scofield who reached his retirement age of 65. I found this a rather difficult public relations job because I wanted the Kansas City campus to feel involved. I set up a committee to recommend names to me for a possible successor, and I also received many nominations from other members of the faculty. Here I made what I think was the biggest mistake in my administration, at least in that part of the University. Several of the persons that we brought in for interviews on the campus were not too happily received by some key faculty and some of the old Kansas City University Board, which we had continued for legal reasons as some of the Kansas City University assets were not transferrable directly.

Eventually it boiled down to two men who on paper were tops. One of them, who with his wife seemed to charm everyone at Kansas City, was Randall Whaley, Vice President of Wayne State University. There was no question the enthusiasm was based partly on the idea that he was urban university experienced and therefore fit the Kansas City situation exceedingly well. I checked with the presidents of Wayne University and of Purdue University where he had taught and was well-known and received enthusiastic recommendations. I also went to a dean on the Wayne campus who was a personal friend and asked for his more careful judgment, and he was enthusiastic. I still had a hunch that he was not what we wanted. But with this kind of information, I laid it all before the Board with my own qualifications, and they appointed him chancellor on my recommendation. From the start he was a great disappointment. He had no sense of order of state government or how you had to deal with it, or of a large university with several campuses. When I called meetings of the chancellors, he almost invariably begged off, pleading a meeting somewhere else in the country that he had promised to attend. As a result he largely escaped this form of education if indeed he was susceptible to it. In fact, it seemed to me he went to every outside meeting for which he had any excuse to go, as if to get away from his job. He reminded me of Roscoe Pullen, the medical school dean I had inherited when I became president. I suppose the crowning climax occurred in the spring when I had tried to induce the general assembly to appropriate money for purchasing the structure that had been erected for the Federal Aviation Authority a few years before which was on the edge of the campus. It was a flexible building and very useful for many purposes, which would make a very desirable addition to the campus area. Bowling and his staff had negotiated a very good proposition, and we wanted the building first to serve as a temporary library where we could house all our materials that were not already well-housed. It got lost in a controversy between the Senate and the House with the House supporting and the Senate opposing it. It was a rather nasty situation with a lot of hard feelings on both sides but I think in the end it lost in the Senate committee by one vote. I then proceeded, as we told the general assembly we would have to do, to rent the building on a plan that would give the legislature a chance to reconsider the following year, and if it agreed to buy, the rental paid would be part of the price of the building. There had been no problem until our Kansas City chancellor called me one Sunday morning and read a statement he wanted to make to the press, the substance of which was how we had succeeded in getting the building in spite of the legislature. I told him he could not say that; that he had no business issuing a statement of that kind except through our public information office; and that he should be consulting with them and not with me. He claimed that the *Star* was on his trail and I answered, "You don't have to say anything." In the end, he issued a statement not as strong as he had read to me but one that carried the same implications and the fat was in the fire with the general assembly.

The Chairman of the Board, Robert Neill, Whaley and I were ordered to appear before the interim committee to justify our actions in renting this building. Whaley immediately called me and said he had a meeting somewhere and wanted to get out of appearing before the committee. Nothing could have pleased me more than to keep him out of the meeting. I called the chairman, Senator J. F. Patterson, and said I thought that all they needed to see was the President of the Board and me. He agreed. So Robert Neill, President of the Board, one other member of the Board, and I appeared before the committee in the Capitol in Jefferson City. Neill, who was a lawyer, had the floor first before the committee with an excellent legal defense of the Board's constitutional right to do as we had done. He was queried by various lawyers on the committee, and I thought we had not improved our position very much. Fortunately, Senator Patterson had done his homework and had listened to the tapes of both my appearances before the House appropriations committee as well as his Senate appropriations committee. He heard me say again that if we could not get the funds from the state to purchase the building we would have to rent it in order to operate with any efficiency. He called the committee's attention to this before I began our defense of the position and after that it was rather simple. I put our defense on the grounds that I had laid my cards on the table and they had failed to appropriate the money by one vote, knowing if they had listened to the testimony that we would then rent it. The House half of the interim committee was already for our action as they had voted for the purchase, and after my presentation the committee voted unanimously to approve our action.

The last few conferences I had with Whaley before I retired in August of 1966, I tried to make it clear to him that he was not doing his job and that my successor would undoubtedly want to reassess the whole situation. But I made no impression upon him at all. He seemed to feel he had nothing to learn about administration and that as long as he cultivated socially the Kansas City University Board of Trustees that he was making good progress, and that all the troubles he was causing us in Jefferson City were no fault of his but ours.

Academically I had laid down some general guidelines that I insisted be followed and they were as far as I know. Before Whaley, a physicist, came I warned him there would be no engineering school in Kansas City in the near future and that he should not expect that. At the same time I assigned to the engineering school at Columbia the problem of developing a masters level program in engineering for employed engineers in industry who needed further training, which I had been assured by Charles Kimball among others was the only need they had in Kansas City for engineering education.

After talking to several Kansas City people involved in manufacturing, I had concluded definitely that the general engineering curriculum which was a course in engineering science was unimportant to them, and they never used its graduates as a source of employees. At the same time I had urged them to develop what they were strong in and what Kansas City needed—education, the performing arts, business and law—in addition to dentistry.

The St. Louis campus presented a different problem and in some ways a much simpler one. One of its difficulties was inheriting a junior college qualified faculty. It had problems of upgrading it to full collegiate quality, and on this chancellor Bugg and his staff did a very good job although we had some trouble with some of the people he had inherited. The main difficulty I think rested in the fact that we were a university in name and the status was hard to upgrade, especially if you needed funds for large numbers of undergraduates who began to enroll as soon as junior, senior work was offered. There was little real pressure for professional schools, as the private universities supplied adequate professional education although at a higher cost. The St. Louis campus took over the masters level education as soon as it became qualified. This had been operating out of the Columbia campus at considerable difficulty.

Engineering presented a problem somewhat similar to Kansas City. I assigned that responsibility to the Rolla campus to expand its post-baccalaureate work in engineering to service St. Louis industry. At the same time I assigned Kansas City to the Columbia school. The large extension program that we had developed in the St. Louis area through the extension division was not residential and centered on the campus. It provided St. Louis with better service than we had been able to give previously.

The J. C. Penney Company owned a warehouse in downtown St. Louis that had been built to be a distribution center for shoes. Because the company took advantage of a strike and changed its method of distribution, the warehouse had been empty for some time. The company saw it to their advantage to use it as a tax-deductible gift, and after consultations and inspections, we eventually asked for it and accepted it. This was not from Mr. Penney himself, as his gifts to the Columbia campus were, but was from the company and it was to the University as such, not to any one campus. Dale Bowling and I wasted a good deal of time in trying to market this facility in a way that would provide funds for some useful purpose, as we could see no practical use of it in an educational way. Eventually the best we could do was capitalize its value at an amount of one million dollars, and under such circumstances sold it to the Edison Brothers Shoe Company. This money was devoted to the construction of a building on the St. Louis campus to be a center for extension work there.

I found nothing to complain about in Jim Bugg's administration of the school. He had to be restrained somewhat from his natural ambitions to expand. I fear he felt somewhat unhappy about his relations with Washington University. That is, the unofficial relations. For reasons I never completely understood he felt very keenly that Washington University was demeaning his program in various ways that touched his pride very seriously. In spite of the fine growth he was showing there and the beautiful campus we were developing, he was far from satisfied.

At an academic meeting at Williamsburg, a gentleman introduced himself as a member of the Board of Old Dominion and asked me about Jim as an administrator. I gave Jim a very good recommendation and told him I did not think he could move him, as I believed our St. Louis campus had better prospects in the near future at least than had Old Dominion, which had also developed from a junior college. Eventually Jim received an offer, and I think he thoroughly agreed with me that the St. Louis job was the better of the two for him. We talked about it several times. He had agreed that he would not take it, which relieved me a great deal because he was a native Virginian with his degrees from Virginia institutions and had many ties there. However, he called me one morning and told me he had changed his mind overnight and he was accepting the Old Dominion position. His reasons he chose to believe were primarily his feeling that in St. Louis he would always be subject to barbs from Washington University. He felt this more keenly than I had realized. I was exceedingly sorry to see him go as he had meant a lot to the beginning of the University of Missouri at St. Louis.

Chapter 23

Emeritus

As I approached my 65th birthday in July of 1966, I was looking forward
to retirement with many regrets. There were suggestions that I stay on a
few years, the most insistent coming from the Board of Curators. They
officially offered me a two-year extension and Robert Neill, the President,
sat with me until after midnight one night trying to talk me into accepting
it. I cannot say I was not tempted but the retirement rule I had sponsored
for 65 year old administrators and the colleagues to whom it had been
applied was too great an obstacle to overcome. The retirement was
announced and the Board appointed a committee to find a successor. I
supplied it with the names of five state university presidents whom I
thought should be considered and to whom the selection would have
been an advancement professionally. I also talked to the Board of the local
possibilities, and as we left that discussion John Schwada seemed definitely to be the leading local candidate.

The summer before I retired we had a fine vacation as the International
Association of Universities had its five-year meeting in Tokyo, and I was
asked to go as the representative of the Association of State Universities
and Land-Grant Colleges. I had been president of this organization the
preceding year. Ruth and I decided to make the trip our vacation as we
had pleasant memories of December 1959, when we spent a week in Japan
on our way to India. When we arrived in Tokyo we went immediately to
a resort with the view of Mt. Fuji where, after the first day, a heavy rain
kept us inside almost all the time we were there. We had arranged to join
a tour which stopped there its first night out of Tokyo. All in the group
were Americans and many were connected with university education.
We wound up back in Tokyo at the headquarters hotel, and I attended the
sessions which proved to be most interesting. The attendance was interesting itself, as only two Russian universities were represented while in
contrast every East German university was represented. One of the
Russian presidents made himself obnoxious in the discussions. At one
time he insisted that Russian should be one of the official languages of the
meeting which was now limited to Japanese, English, and French. The
President of the University of the Philippines answered him, pointing
out that while there were only two Russian universities represented,

there were over 30 Spanish-speaking universities here and, if there was an additional language, it should be Spanish.

The American official delegates were numerous but many American university presidents attended who were not delegates, and we found we knew a great many of them.

We returned home to prepare for retirement. In many ways I felt pleased at the University's situation. The cause of this was the changed situation between 1953 and 1966. The faculty situation was clearly improved, especially in morale. Our long commitment to good teaching had shown distinct results and research was much more evident. The facilities for the faculty were greatly improved. Probably the largest factor in morale was the improved salary situation along with a generous retirement benefit. While housing, libraries, museums, and other facilities all showed major improvements, we were not yet outstanding but at least we had become much more respectable.

The Department of History invited me to undertake a program of teaching and research for the years until I reached 70, which was the retirement age for faculty. I declined this as I had already considered it and realized that I had not taught a class since my Fulbright at Amsterdam in 1951–52, and to return to teaching would take at least a full year's preparation. Recent American History, my principal field, changes very fast when you are not actively teaching it. We decided that it would help my successor if I would get out of the way for a few months so Ruth and I left for Europe after a short delay to honor Margaret Brady's wedding. We returned in late October, and I was soon busy with the program of consulting. The number of invitations was surprising. The most attractive one was from the Rockefeller Foundation, asking me to go to Colombia, South America, for a minimum of two years. I replied that I would not agree to go abroad for that long an assignment. I was then asked how long a foreign assignment I would consider, and I answered six months. Then I was offered an assignment to consult with the Universidad del Valle in Cali, Colombia. I agreed to this after making a trip to Cali, looking it over and no doubt being looked over myself. We returned to Cali the following fall for a five-month stay. The university had been built around a medical school largely with Rockefeller money and had many administrative oddities because of its history. I hope I helped it and made it somewhat more efficient. It interested us enough that we went back on our own the following year and stayed a week on the campus to see what changes had been made. We then went to Bogota, where we joined a tour. We went by plane around South America, visiting all the countries except Venezuela and Bolivia. Perhaps the most interesting to us was the Inca world in Peru.

Requests came from various universities for spot consulting on specific problems, sometimes from the administration and sometimes from a state government agency. I made trips to Kentucky, North Carolina, Tennessee, Virginia, Arkansas, and repeated visits to Texas Technological University. A new organization, the Education Commission of the States, offered me a position in the higher education section but I compromised by doing spot consulting for it instead. In the meantime I had accepted membership on the Stephens College Board of Curators and the Boone National Savings & Loan Association Board. I carried over several appointments, such as the chairmanship of the Truman Library Board and the State Historical Society Executive Committee. Later Dean Elmer Kiehl of the College of Agriculture asked me to make a trip to India to look over the agriculture university we were assisting the state of Orissa in developing at Bhubaneswar. I flew there in the spring of 1970, stopping a day each in Paris, Beruit, Tehran, and London on my way to and from India.

Our retirement was marked by receptions at Rolla and Columbia and with portraits of me being presented at each place. The Fortnightly Club of the University of Missouri-Columbia had a luncheon for Ruth that was similar in character. The Columbia Chamber of Commerce also had a dinner with an outside speaker that was very pleasant. In the meantime we purchased a recently built house in the Grasslands section of Columbia, very close to the University, and we left the President's House in June 1966.

Probably the most important function I carried on after retiring was the presidency, as it was called, of the Truman Library Board. It was formed by the late President Truman after we laid the cornerstone of the library at Independence. He asked me to be the president, and I enjoyed the work. I think he was pleased by the speech I made at the cornerstone ceremonies. I carried this on until my 20th year in the position, and refused the re-election because my hearing problem made presiding difficult. During that time I became acquainted with almost all the men who had been members of the Truman Cabinet who were now members of the Board. They were all interesting, but the one who left the greatest impression on me was Averell Harriman.

I ceased consulting with my Orissa experience. While it had some interesting features, too often the local administration knew what was needed and only wanted your support to convince higher ups that it was realistic. Moreover, my hearing had forced me to use hearing aids which handicapped me in working with groups, such as the Stephens Board. A committee of six was about as large a group with which I could function well so I stayed on the Savings and Loan Board but resigned from the Stephens College Board. The group that kept my services the longest was the State Historical Society of Missouri whose executive committee was one where I could be useful. My name was carried on several university committees but my work consisted largely of special consultations.

The major difficulty in building Missouri into a great university lay in its financial situation. While the University of Missouri was one of the oldest of the state universities, being the third oldest west of the Alleghenies, it had not been able to increase its state financial support as had most others. As I studied this problem before I became president I placed the main reason on its location in the state. Missouri developed as a state with two large cities, on opposite sides of the state, and the University was centered some 120 miles from each of them. Consequently as a political force, its leadership was never able to capitalize on either city's consideration politically as a local interest. As a contrast, Minnesota was also a two-city state but the cities are adjacent to each other; the state university was located between them and it has strong political support from both of them. While there are few examples quite as sharp as this, the one-city states such as Michigan and Illinois were never subject to the same neglect as the University of Missouri suffered from St. Louis and Kansas City. While not a major factor in our planning, I had the hope that in supplying a more adequate university system for the state, it might break down this handicap. But in that I was disappointed, as neither I nor my successors have been able to overcome it. Consequently, we continue to have to operate where the tax support for the state university is one of the lowest per capita in the nation.

On the other hand, measured on the basis of the more fundamental factor of enrollment, the evidence is clear that we have built an institution that is meeting the needs of its young people in a reputable way. The following enrollment statistics illustrate this:

	1953	1963	1966	1986	1988
UMC	7,379	14,265	18,332	22,727	23,568
UMKC		4,394	7,891	11,583	11,628
UMR	1,189	3,655	4,938	6,318	5,724
UMSL		673	6,347	12,328	13,932
Total	8,568	22,987	37,508	52,956	54,852

These show that this achievement is possible but only by an unusually devoted faculty and staff.

Index